Praise for Cooler

"Clear, readable, and genuinely smart, *Cooler Smarter* answers the question concerned citizens everywhere are asking: What can we do to make a difference?"

—**ELIZABETH KOLBERT,** *author of* Field Notes from a Catastrophe: Man, Nature, and Climate Change

"Finally, an excellent, short, and readable book that is replete with examples of what each of us can do to improve our lives and, at the same time, reduce our carbon footprint by using energy more efficiently. Whatever your view may be about climate change projections, there are no good arguments that favor wasting energy and launching the world's climate into an uncertain future."

—**NEAL LANE,** *Malcolm Gillis University Professor, Rice University, former White House Science Advisor and former Director of the National Science Foundation*

"*Cooler Smarter* provides great advice backed by data, analysis, and examples. I was surprised how only a few simple steps can cut your environmental footprint by 20 percent—and most of those steps don't involve sacrifice, but rather pay for themselves and help you lead a healthier life. I plan on implementing several of these strategies and hope others do, too!"

—**RICK NEEDHAM,** *Director, Energy and Sustainability, Google*

"We *can* break our addiction to fossil fuels, stave off the worst of global warming, and generate quality jobs that allow us to support our families and build for the future—but only if we work together and each of us does our part. This smart, sensible, and easy-to-use book lays out the most effective steps each of us can take right now."

—**VAN JONES,** *President, Rebuild the Dream, and author of* The Green Collar Economy

"Global warming affects all of us, no matter what our ethnicity, politics or religious affiliation. This book offers the latest scientific thinking about the most effective steps each of us can take to lower our emissions. It is a valuable tool for congregations and others who care for God's creation."

—THE REV. CANON SALLY G. BINGHAM, *President,*
The Regeneration Project, Interfaith Power & Light

"It's doubly important now for each of us to act to reduce our carbon footprints because Washington is doing so little. I love this book—a smart, accessible, clear-headed guide that we can all follow."

—JAMES GUSTAVE SPETH, *author of* The Bridge at the Edge of the World:
Capitalism, the Environment, and Crossing
from Crisis to Sustainability

"This accessible, science-based book gives each of us the information we need to do our part to reduce our carbon emissions. This is the smart tool for action many of us have been waiting for."

—TIMOTHY E. WIRTH, *President, United Nations Foundation*
and former U.S. Senator from Colorado

"A wonderful guide to smarter energy use and a cooler planet that shows how each and every one of us can contribute part of the solution for a better future. Splendidly written, accessible, and essential for any citizen—both virtually and metaphorically cool."

—THOMAS E. LOVEJOY, *Biodiversity Chair, The Heinz Center*
and University Professor, George Mason University

Cooler Smarter

Expert Advice from the Union of Concerned Scientists

Cooler Smarter

PRACTICAL STEPS FOR LOW-CARBON LIVING

SETH SHULMAN

JEFF DEYETTE

BRENDA EKWURZEL

DAVID FRIEDMAN

MARGARET MELLON

JOHN ROGERS

SUZANNE SHAW

 **ISLAND**PRESS

Washington | Covelo | London

ISLAND PRESS is a trademark of the Center for Resource Economics.

Library of Congress Cataloging-in-Publication Data

Cooler smarter : practical steps for low-carbon living : expert advice from
the Union of Concerned Scientists / Seth Shulman ... [et al.].
    p. cm.
  ISBN 978-1-61091-192-4 (pbk.) — ISBN 1-61091-192-X (paper)
1. Sustainable living—United States. 2. Environmental protection—United
States—Citizen participation. I. Shulman, Seth. II. Union of Concerned
Scientists.
  GE195.C74 2012
  363.7'0525—dc23   2012008656

Printed on recycled, acid-free paper

Manufactured in the United States of America
10 9 8

Keywords: climate change, global warming, carbon footprint, greenhouse
gas emissions, eco-friendly, energy efficient, sustainability, greening your
home, organic food, LEED certified

CONTENTS

This book is a powerful tool for action. It cuts through the politicized rhetoric that too often clouds public discussion regarding climate change by offering practical and manageable advice as to how each of us can take steps that, collectively, can effect meaningful change. I believe it is exactly the kind of synthesis we need, with accessible, up-to-date scientific knowledge that we all will find useful.

My scientific research has delved into many aspects of climate science for more than three decades. When I began my career, most ocean scientists expected to see little change in the world's oceans over the course of their lives. After all, the oceans are vast, with an average depth of more than 12,000 feet. Moreover, it takes about a thousand years for ocean currents to fully mix the oceans and, because of strong density gradients, most of the deep ocean is influenced only very slowly by what happens near the ocean surface. I simply could never have imagined that I would see the dramatic changes in our oceans that have been documented over the past few decades.

I still vividly remember an eye-opening experience in 1986, while I was at the National Center for Atmospheric Research in Boulder, Colorado. I had taken a sabbatical leave from my position at Harvard to start a new scientific journal and launch a new international research program. One day, a colleague walked into my office with new data showing surface ocean temperature over the previous several decades and said, "Jim, it looks like the oceans are warming." That same year, Antarctic ice core data were first published showing a clear link between atmospheric concentrations of carbon dioxide and temperature over the last 100,000-year glacial-interglacial cycle.

Compelling evidence for human-caused climate change arises from observations of deep ocean warming, recent melting of land ice and ice shelves that had been in place for many thousands of years, an acceleration in sea level rise, ice cores that show how Earth's temperature fluctuated with atmospheric greenhouse gas content in the past, and ocean-wide data documenting unusually rapid changes in ocean chemistry (aka ocean acidification). All of these recent changes are consistent with the unusual rate at which heat-trapping gases, primarily carbon dioxide, are being released into and retained within the lower atmosphere.

Developments in climate science have progressed swiftly over the past several decades. We now know that climate change is happening 100 to 1,000 times faster than at any time since humans first inhabited Earth. Textbooks are being rewritten. We now see that climate and the ocean carbon cycle are inextricably linked, and each is highly sensitive to perturbations in the other. We now know with ever-increasing precision that significant change in atmospheric greenhouse gas concentrations can cause reverberations throughout the entire climate system.

As a scientist, I am acutely aware of the implications of the changes now underway in our climate system and the peril they portend. Sea level rise, for instance, poses a grave danger to the disproportionate number of people who live near coastlines. Analyses demonstrate linkages between global warming trends and an increase in the number and severity of heat waves as well as the severity of intense precipitation events, both of which pose dangers to human health and well-being. As a parent and grandparent, I think often about the consequences of these changes for my children and grandchildren.

Much of my work over the past several decades has involved the science-policy interface, and I am dismayed by the current politicization of the debate surrounding climate policy in the United States. Climate science is complicated, and no one can say with high confidence precisely how climate will change in the future—we are in uncharted territory. But fundamental aspects of climate change science inform us about likely futures and make clear that choices we make today will affect climate decades from now. I am also painfully aware of how poorly scientists have done in communicating some of these fundamental aspects of climate change science to many nonscientists and public officials, who really do need to be aware of the consequences of ignoring this science.

Part of the problem is that very few scientists have had good training in how to communicate with the public. When scientists talk to one another, we tend to focus on the parts of our research we find most interesting: namely, what we don't know and what further research is needed to fill these gaps in our understanding. Good scientists are always questioning everything they have been taught or have themselves discovered. We train our students to go beyond what we can teach them—to use newer methods for gathering evidence, to subject their data to ever more sophisticated analyses, to always keep their minds open to other views in order to advance, in the most genuine sense of the word, the science that intrigues us. In this way, scientific knowledge is always evolving—our understanding of complex science will never be perfect, but it is constantly being improved. Unfortunately, this vital aspect of the scientific endeavor can be confusing to those who are looking for the clearest scientific findings that can be used in the formulation of policy. But at the most fundamental level, we now know unequivocally that climate change is occurring. We also know that by dramatically reducing our emissions of heat-trapping gases we can avoid some very serious consequences for the natural and built environment upon which all of human society depends. This book is important because it is informed by the very latest scientific understanding of the problem and pairs this knowledge with clear and effective strategies.

Unfortunately, it is also true that some people think that when a scientist comments on the implications of scientific findings for policy, this means that the expert has strayed into advocacy and diminished his or her objectivity. This misperception ignores the fact that scientists have a responsibility to share their knowledge, especially when it bears on pressing problems of the day. Given the magnitude of the climate problem we face, climate scientists have a responsibility to use every opportunity we have to share our understanding of climate science with the public and with policy makers across the land and to work with them to arrive at solutions. Here again, this volume makes an important contribution: a collection of expert analysts have teamed up with professional science writers and communications specialists to present the material in an engaging and action-oriented manner that is easy for each of us to understand and implement. It inspires me to take yet another look at my own personal habits to see what more I can do and to share this book's advice with others.

Finally, because global warming is occurring on a planet-wide scale, the solutions can seem overwhelming. To address this issue, we need to work at scales where we can have success. Not long ago, I served on a committee in Boston tasked to address how the city could reduce its emissions of greenhouse gases. We looked into making a 20 percent reduction by 2025 and realized that such a reduction wouldn't be all that difficult to achieve. So, with a go-ahead from Boston's mayor, Thomas Menino, we decided to reach higher—developing a plan for reductions of 25 percent in the same time period. Mayor Menino accepted this plan, and he and his staff found in meeting after meeting that there was wide public support for this trajectory for the city of Boston.

In fact, common-sense suggestions to address climate change have found similar reception across the country. Working for citywide reductions in emissions is on a scale that works. And not just in so-called blue states. Where options for alternative climate futures are clearly presented, people understand that changes are needed and that these make sense. At this level, there is much less opportunity for a variety of confounding special interests to block progress.

We very much need this kind of thinking on the state, national, and international levels as well. But we also need to make changes in our own personal actions. As this volume explains, individuals cannot solve the problems of a warming planet on their own. And yet it is also true that we can never hope to have success without changing our individual behavior to reduce our emissions of greenhouse gases. This, too, is on a scale at which we can have discernible success. And this book gives each of us the information and inspiration we need to get started.

James J. McCarthy
Alexander Agassiz Professor
of Biological Oceanography
Harvard University

PART I

THINKING ABOUT
YOUR CLIMATE CHOICES

CHAPTER 1

Can One Person Make a Difference?

Nobody made a greater mistake than he who
did nothing because he could do only a little.

—Edmund Burke

This book is about the steps you can take and the choices you can make to combat global warming.

Global warming presents one of the most enormous challenges humanity has ever faced. It threatens to affect nearly every aspect of our lives—our health, the availability of freshwater, the future of many coastal communities, our food supply, and even government stability as nations around the world begin to confront the adverse consequences of climate change.

More than a century ago, a Swedish scientist named Svante Arrhenius recognized that burning fossil fuels would create a thickening layer of carbon dioxide in the atmosphere, thus trapping a growing proportion of the sun's heat and causing Earth to warm up.

There's been a lot of misinformation about climate change in recent years. But political spin doesn't change the facts. Since Arrhenius's time, tens of thousands of scientists have studied and measured the climate in great detail and from many vantage points. And the more they learn, the more certain they are that the planet is warming at an alarming rate, that the warming is caused by human activity, and that if this warming is left unchecked, we are on a dangerous and unsustainable path toward disruptions in Earth's climate.

The overwhelming majority of the world's experts on every aspect of climate science have concluded that we need to make swift and deep reductions in our emissions of carbon dioxide and other heat-trapping gases to avoid the worst consequences of global warming.

We will review some of the most important scientific details in chapter 3, but this book is not primarily about the science and consequences of global warming. It's about how *you* can help solve the problem by making thoughtful, effective decisions in your daily life. The fact is, global warming is a human-caused problem, and it is within our power to solve. Individual actions can and do make a difference.

Maybe you're already committed to doing everything you can to reduce your contribution to global warming. If so, that's great. Our team of experts has compiled the information in this book to help you determine which actions you can take to be most effective.

It may be, however, that you haven't taken steps to combat global warming. After all, climate change is occurring on an almost unimaginably vast scale, and you are just one of the world's nearly 7 billion inhabitants. It is natural to feel dwarfed by the numbers. This book will help you see that while the world's reliance on fossil fuels is the basis of our problem, the choices each of us makes every day have enormous consequences. Our goal in these pages is to show you how changes you can make right now—multiplied many, many times over—can make a *real* difference in helping forestall the worst consequences of global warming.

To appreciate this point, consider the "penny parable," based on the real-life experience of someone named Nora Gross. Today, Gross is a graduate student at New York University. But 20 years ago, as a young girl growing up in Manhattan, she told her father she wanted to give her penny collection to the homeless man they often passed on the street near their home. In her childlike way, young Nora reasoned that if everyone did what she was proposing to do, perhaps no one would be homeless. Her father might have told her that her pennies couldn't possibly make a dent in the widespread scourge of homelessness. But instead, touched by his daughter's compassion for a stranger, Nora's father encouraged her to follow through on her idea. The two of them soon founded an organization, called Common Cents, dedicated to harvesting spare pennies.

In the ensuing years, Nora Gross's idea has mushroomed beyond all expectation. Since its founding, Common Cents has, amazingly, encouraged more than a million children around the country to collect almost 1 *billion* pennies. That adds up to $10 million, enough money to alleviate the suffering of thousands of homeless people—people who would not have been helped if one young girl had thought she couldn't make a difference.

Fanciful though the example may be, Nora Gross's story offers an important lesson that is relevant to the problem of global warming. It demonstrates how small individual actions can reap huge dividends in the aggregate, even when the individual actions seem simple. Many of the changes you can make to combat global warming are as easy and painless as giving spare pennies to a good cause, and the cumulative effects can be dramatic. For example, the U.S. government's Energy Star program estimates that if we improved the energy efficiency of residential buildings in this country by just 10 percent (a goal easily met by existing technology), Americans would save about $20 billion and reduce global warming emissions by as much as if 25 million cars were taken off the road. Small individual improvements in energy efficiency, in other words, can make a very big difference.

Of course, you may feel that your hands are simply too full with work or raising your kids to get into the "saving the planet" business. If you are curious enough to look through this book, though, you will still find valuable information. Many of the choices offered in the following chapters won't just lower your emissions of carbon dioxide; they can also improve the quality of your life, save you money and time, and even improve your health.

That's what the people of Salina, Kansas, found when they entered

---

UCS Climate Team *FAST FACT*

According to the U.S. government's Energy Star program, if Americans improved the energy efficiency of their homes by just 10 percent, they could cut some $20 billion from their utility bills and remove emissions equivalent to taking some 25 million cars off the road.

a yearlong competition with neighboring cities in their state to see who could save the most on their energy bills. Many residents of Salina have doubts about the findings of climate science. Nonetheless, these Kansans say they don't like their nation's dependence on foreign oil; plus, like most Americans, they are thrifty and very much like saving money. During this contest, the entire city of Salina (population 46,000) was able to reduce its overall carbon dioxide emissions by 5 percent. Jerry Clasen, a local grain farmer, captured the prevailing sentiment, commenting, "Whether or not the earth is getting warmer, it feels good to be part of something that works for Kansas and for the nation."

As the folks in Salina discovered, the inefficient use of energy in the United States makes it easy for anyone seeking to reduce emissions to reap quick rewards. Did you know, for instance, that fossil fuel power plants typically release roughly two-thirds of their energy as waste heat? Or that less than 20 percent of the gasoline a car burns goes toward propelling it down the road? Even without changing to renewable power sources that can generate electricity with zero carbon emissions, we can dramatically increase the efficiency of our use of fossil fuels with cost-effective, off-the-shelf technology. By one estimate, technologies to recover energy from waste heat and other waste resources in the United States potentially could harness almost 100,000 megawatts of electricity—enough to provide about 18 percent of the nation's electricity.

But we don't have to wait for more efficiency to be built into the system. The chapters that follow show clearly that as end users of this energy, we have at our disposal a wide variety of simple techniques to squeeze much more out of our current energy use, saving money and reducing our emissions.

What this means for you is that you can probably make some simple changes that will yield real improvements in your energy efficiency. Not long ago, a Canadian utility company drove home this point in a much-lauded television commercial that urged its customers to conserve energy. The ad depicts individuals engaging in laughably wasteful behavior. One guy is wrapping his sandwich in aluminum foil, but instead of using one sheet, he keeps wrapping and wrapping until he has used the entire roll.

UCS Climate Team _FAST FACT_

Our energy systems are remarkably inefficient. On average, only about 15 to 20 percent of a gallon of gasoline goes toward propelling a car or truck down the road. And an average fossil fuel power plant turns only about one-third of the energy it uses into electricity.

A woman takes just one bite of an apple, then drops it on the ground and picks up a new one, repeating this mindless act until the camera zooms out to reveal the ground below her strewn with bitten apples. The spot ends with a family going out of their house without turning out any of its brightly burning lights. It leaves the viewer to ponder why this behavior isn't every bit as preposterous as the others.

In many ways, the issue really is that simple. If you live in the United States, on average your activities emit a whopping 21 tons of carbon dioxide into the atmosphere annually.* That's one of the highest per-person emission rates in the world and some _four times_ higher than the global average.

There's no getting around the situation depicted in the graph on page 8. Compared with our counterparts around the world, we are responsible for outsized emissions and outsized costs. The emission levels of the average American are roughly four times the global average, as noted above, and they are also roughly _15 times_ those of the average citizen of India. To be sure, poverty in many parts of India, as in many countries, keeps personal consumption—and associated emissions—far below the level currently found in the United States. But on a per capita basis, even most industrialized European countries—with standards of living similar to those in the United States—emit less than half the carbon dioxide the United States does.

When you do the math, it reveals that, on average as an American, your activities emit just over 115 pounds of carbon dioxide daily. Think

*A note about numbers and terms: Throughout this book, all discussions of emissions, unless otherwise noted, use pounds and tons (2,000 pounds in a ton)—the most familiar units of measurement to most U.S. readers. Similarly, discussions of "carbon emissions" refer to emissions of units of "carbon dioxide equivalent" (CO_2e), as will be more fully explained in chapter 7.

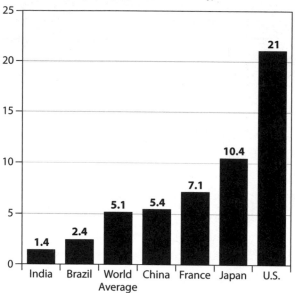

Figure 1.1. Global Carbon Dioxide Emissions
(Tons per Person Annually)

The United States' per-person carbon dioxide emission levels are about four times the world average. Source: UCS Modeling and World Bank, *World Development Indicators,* 2007.

about that for a moment: your actions are responsible for sending a fair portion of your total body weight up smokestacks and out tailpipes *every day*. And the heat-trapping carbon dioxide each of us is contributing is accumulating in the atmosphere to cause global warming.

Can we reduce our global warming emissions? Of course we can.

Bear in mind, for instance, that just two decades ago the chemicals in many common products, from refrigerators to hair spray, were eating away at the protective ozone layer in the atmosphere. The resulting ozone hole seemed to present an insurmountable global problem. Scientists and citizens alike were anticipating a future of unfettered ultraviolet radiation wreaking havoc on our skin and health. But with effective planning and innovation, we tackled the problem. Citizens, scientists, and government officials came together to phase out the harmful substances responsible for the problem. Today the stratospheric ozone layer is on a path to recovery.

An equally dramatic example is the story of the Cuyahoga River in Ohio. Today the Cuyahoga supports a wide variety of recreational opportunities, from kayaking to fishing, and boasts some 44 species of fish. Just a few decades ago, however, the Cuyahoga was one of the most polluted rivers in the United States. In the portion of the river from Akron to Cleveland, virtually all the fish had died. The situation seemed hopeless. But finally, when debris and chemicals in the Cuyahoga infamously caught fire in 1969, people were galvanized into action. Some have even called the public reaction to the Cuyahoga River fire the start of environmentalism, for that catastrophe helped spur a legislative response that included the Clean Water Act, the Great Lakes Water Quality Agreement, and the creation of the U.S. Environmental Protection Agency.

The point is that difficult problems aren't always as intractable as they seem. That doesn't mean they are easy to solve, of course, as any of the concerned citizens, activists, and government officials who fought to clean up the Cuyahoga River could attest. The problem seemed dire, and solutions were often elusive. In fact, the Cuyahoga actually caught fire more than a dozen times, the first time in 1868. It took until 1969—more than 100 years—to spur the necessary actions.

Let's be clear: global warming is much greater in scope than a burning river and more complex than a hole in the ozone layer. But as we said at the beginning of this chapter, people caused the problem, and people can solve it. We already have many of the tools and technologies we need to address global warming. The key is for each of us to begin to work toward solutions.

We all have examples of the power of individual actions. But the experience of a builder in Montana named Steve Loken is particularly worth recounting. One day some years ago, Loken visited a spot north of his home in Missoula where the forest had been clear-cut. The visit changed his life. At that moment, he says, he recognized the extent to which his work as a builder wasted precious resources. Loken didn't like the idea of contributing directly to the decimation of old-growth forests. "I realized I was part of the problem every time I blindly followed building practices that were inherently wasteful," he says.

Instead of continuing with business as usual, Loken decided to be part of the solution. He looked for ways to build that would be sustainable to the environment and the planet's climate. He began with an experiment: spending his savings to build a home for his family using exclusively recycled or salvaged materials. The result was extraordinary. The house Loken built looked and felt in every way like a handsome new suburban home. Visitors would never know that most of the wood in the house was a composite material made from the sawdust and shavings left over from the milling of lumber. They couldn't tell that the home's insulation was derived from recycled newspapers, that its ceramic floor tiles were manufactured from recycled car windshields, or that its carpets had once been plastic milk cartons.

At that time, it was not at all easy to find these new, unconventional materials and learn to use them, but Steve Loken demonstrated that houses could be built sustainably without sacrificing quality. And now, after years of researching new building technologies in the face of much skepticism from other builders, an amazing thing has happened: Steve Loken's house has helped spur dramatic changes in building techniques around the world. Much to his astonishment, many thousands of people, including leading architects and builders, have made the pilgrimage to Missoula to see his home. He founded an organization, the Center for Resourceful Building Technology, to help others find more environmentally sustainable ways to build. But his techniques caught on so quickly and were replicated so widely that he soon decided the organization wasn't needed anymore. Meanwhile, Loken's contracting business—

focusing on recycled materials and energy-efficient design—is booming as never before, with offers to build projects all around the country.

When you think about it, this story says a lot about how change occurs. Steve Loken is not that different from the rest of us. All he did was resolve to make some changes and then educate himself about how to do things in smarter ways. The changes reduced his family's environmental impacts, made him feel better about his work, inspired others, and helped his business prosper. When it comes to reducing your global warming emissions, you can very likely achieve similarly good results through your own efforts. And we've written this book so you don't have to do the research on your own, the way Steve did.

If there is any lesson that our fast-paced technological world reinforces over and over again, it is that change often happens more quickly and dramatically than we anticipate. Just over a century ago, only 8 percent of U.S. homes even had electricity, and Henry Ford had produced only a few thousand vehicles in his recently built car factory. Who could have imagined that by the mid-twentieth century, virtually every American home—and millions of others around the world—would have electricity or that the automobile would redefine American lifestyles and fundamentally transform the economy?

For an equally powerful example right at your fingertips, consider the cell phone. If it's a current model, it probably has a storage capacity of up to 32 gigabytes of information. That's more than *10 million times* the onboard computer storage capacity of the *Apollo 11* spacecraft when it traveled to the moon in 1969.

Who could ever have imagined then that such a dramatic increase in computing power would become so widely available the world over in a handheld wireless device?

The point is that it's hard to envision how dramatically—or how quickly—things could change as we wean ourselves off fossil fuels and move into an economy based on efficiency and renewable energy. One survey of nearly 50 past forecasts of future energy use in Europe and worldwide found that nearly all of the forecasts had underestimated the actual increase in renewable energy generation. In one example, the Inter-

---

UCS Climate Team *FAST FACT*

Global wind energy capacity has increased at almost twice the rate estimated by the International Energy Agency, reaching nearly 160,000 megawatts in 2009. China alone achieved a 20-fold increase in installed wind capacity between 2005 and 2009.

---

national Energy Agency (IEA) projected in its 2002 *World Energy Outlook* that global wind energy capacity would reach 100,000 megawatts by 2020. In reality, the wind industry passed this mark in early 2008 and is now close to achieving double the predicted capacity a decade ahead of the IEA's prediction. When it comes to wind energy, China alone shows how much can be done. In just four years, from 2005 to 2009, that nation achieved an astonishing 20-fold increase in installed wind capacity. The rapid pace of growth shows what's possible in the global shift to a cleaner energy supply.

You and your family aren't likely to be building new wind turbines to generate electricity. And you probably aren't in the contracting business like Steve Loken. Nevertheless, you can still go a long way toward weaning your household off fossil fuels and slashing your family's carbon emissions simply by making better choices about what you buy and how you live. The chapters ahead will show you how.

CHAPTER 2

Sweat the Right Stuff

Everybody talks about the weather,
but nobody does anything about it.

—Mark Twain

What are the most effective steps each of us can take to reduce our carbon emissions? This is the question the Climate Team at the Union of Concerned Scientists (UCS) set out to answer in this book. Of course, the best steps for you depend to some extent on how you live now. Some of us drive big cars, others ride the bus; some live in large houses, others in tiny studio apartments. The United States is a big country, and geography makes a difference, too: in colder climates, home heating naturally accounts for a far greater share of a household's emissions; city dwellers, meanwhile, tend to be less reliant on cars, with far fewer emissions in the transportation category than their rural counterparts.

While there is no single, one-size-fits-all solution to reducing carbon emissions, the first step is to look closely at your emissions and set a goal to reduce them. *Whatever your current circumstances, we suggest that you aim to reduce your carbon emissions by 20 percent over the coming year.*

Of course, you may find that you can make even deeper cuts. If so, great, because ultimately much deeper cuts in overall carbon emissions will be needed to dramatically slow the pace of climate change. But 20 percent is a meaningful—and achievable—goal to start with. It's large enough that, if adopted by enough Americans, it can make a significant difference to global warming. If all Americans reduced their emissions by 20 percent, the total of heat-trapping carbon dioxide entering the atmosphere each year would drop by well over *1 billion tons*. That's as much

13

carbon dioxide as 200 of the nation's average-sized coal-fired plants produce annually, or about half of the total U.S. carbon emissions from coal.

To avoid some of the most harmful consequences of global warming, a consensus has emerged among climate scientists that the world's nations must lower their emissions by 80 percent or more by the middle of this century, a goal that could be achieved by reducing global emissions by roughly 3 percent annually. Consider your personal commitment to reduce emissions by 20 percent as a down payment to help give the nation a healthy start along this path.

A big consideration for our team in adopting the 20 percent goal is that most Americans can achieve this. Toward that end, we offer a range of suggestions in this book—including many low-cost and no-cost solutions.

As we saw in chapter 1, the average American's activities are responsible for some 21 tons of carbon dioxide emissions annually. To lower that by 20 percent, you will need to find roughly 4 tons' worth of reductions. Of course, your personal contribution to global warming may vary significantly from this average figure. People who live in large houses, eat a lot of beef, or travel regularly may have considerably higher emissions than the national average, for instance. It will take a bit of effort to find the changes that best fit your lifestyle. But we are confident that by following the practical advice in this book, each of us can avoid emitting some 20 percent of the heat-trapping carbon dioxide we are each currently responsible for creating.

In our recommendations for steps you can take to reduce your carbon emissions, our team of authors has adopted a systematic approach. While many books and websites offer tips for lowering one's carbon footprint, we found that many of these tips have only a tiny payoff. In our quick review, we found recommendations ranging from staying out of elevators to starting worm farms in your basement and drinking locally brewed beer. None of those suggestions is likely to do any harm, but none of them will significantly reduce your carbon emissions.

To determine the most effective individual actions to combat global warming, we analyzed the climate impacts of hundreds of potential consumer decisions, from insulating your home to changing your diet. Our

UCS Climate Team Recommendation

Whatever your current circumstances, we suggest that you aim to reduce your carbon emissions by 20 percent over the coming year—a meaningful and achievable goal.

team used an input-output model that links detailed economic data about U.S. consumer spending in over 500 sectors with data on global warming emissions broken down by industry. By painstakingly allocating these emissions into the model's detailed consumption categories, we were ultimately able to derive both the direct and indirect emissions that resulted from every dollar spent by U.S. consumers. (For much more on the modeling methodology, see appendix C.)

This approach grew out of a pathbreaking earlier project. In the late 1990s, the Union of Concerned Scientists published *The Consumer's Guide to Effective Environmental Choices*. That book evaluated the environmental impacts of a variety of consumer activities and daily decisions. It pointed out that just a handful of consumer choices accounted for the bulk of an average person's environmental impact. It advised consumers not to worry about many inconsequential decisions that received a disproportionate amount of media attention: whether to choose paper or plastic at the grocery store, whether to diaper your baby in cloth or disposables. What turned out to be more effective from a practical standpoint was to focus on a handful of common purchases and behaviors. In other words, that book argued, "stop sweating the small stuff" and focus on the decisions that have the greatest impact.

As the following chapters will show in detail, much the same advice holds for global warming. Whenever possible, we feature choices that provide the greatest payoffs. We also present some smaller-scale suggestions whose ease and practicality make them worthwhile.

To start, take a look at the pie chart on the next page. Because it is based on average emissions, it may vary substantially from your personal numbers. Nevertheless, it's useful for thinking about the problem.

The first thing to notice is that the biggest share of Americans' emissions comes from transportation. For this reason, we begin our analysis

**Figure 2.1. Where the Average American's
Carbon Emissions Come From**

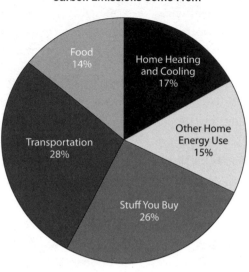

Food
14%

Home Heating
and Cooling
17%

Other Home
Energy Use
15%

Transportation
28%

Stuff You Buy
26%

*The breakdown in sources of carbon emissions for
the average American shows that transportation is
the largest single category.* Source: UCS modeling.

with this sector, which is overwhelmingly dominated by the emissions from driving our cars. As explained in chapter 4, many of us could achieve most or all of our first-year 20 percent reduction in carbon emissions simply by trading in our current car for a more energy-efficient model. In fact, switching from an average vehicle getting about 20 miles per gallon (mpg) to one getting 40 mpg would, in one fell swoop, *reduce your emissions by nearly the four tons annually needed to meet the goal.* No matter when you plan to purchase your next car, it will surely be one of the most important decisions you make in terms of your overall impact on global warming.

As the chart also shows, the two sectors that make up household energy usage—heating and cooling, plus lighting and the electricity for appliances and home electronics—account for about one-third of our average emissions. This is another area with great potential for reducing carbon emissions. Installing and using a programmable thermostat, if you haven't done so already, can reduce home-heating costs—and heating-related emissions—by about 15 percent, for a savings of more than a half ton of emissions annually on average. Dollar for dollar, this may be one of the most effective single actions you can take. You can probably find other good ways to drive down heat-trapping emissions without remodeling your home. However, if you are able to remodel, the possibilities are far greater.

Take the experience of Ann Luskey, a mother of three in Bethesda, Maryland. Luskey wanted to reduce her environmental impact, so she moved from an enormous suburban home to one less than half its size. But she wanted to do even more. So, working with a local contractor, she invested in retrofitting a "zero-net-energy" home—one that produces as much energy as it consumes. Zero-net-energy homes are beginning to spring up around the country. Luskey's is built with ultratight insulation and an array of solar panels on the roof. It required a significant investment of time, but the total price, including the retrofits, was not substantially higher than that of other homes in her new neighborhood. And now, after her initial outlay, Luskey has no monthly utility bills to pay. She says she prefers her new home's smaller, well-designed spaces and loves that it's close to schools and recreational spaces where her children can ride their bikes. Most of all, though, Luskey says that her experience with "green building" made her realize that energy-smart choices "really don't have to involve sacrifice."

As we each search for the reductions that best fit our personal circumstances, it is helpful to remember Luskey's insight. Despite some stories in the press, reducing our carbon footprint doesn't mean that we have to go to extremes. A recent article in the *New York Times* described the lengths to which a family in upstate New York had gone to achieve a green lifestyle. They had unplugged their refrigerator, turned their home's thermostat to a frosty 52 degrees in winter, and didn't allow one son to play on a Little League baseball team because of the emissions the extra driving would cause. This example gives a false impression. In fact, we don't have to shiver in our homes or read by candlelight to make serious reductions in our carbon emissions. Instead, we each just need to make smarter use of energy resources.

Step 1: Look Closely at Your Current Energy Usage

When we begin to look at Americans' energy usage, it is amazing to see how much energy we waste on average. Considering that we know how to make energy-efficient homes and manufacture cars that burn a fraction of the fuel that most current gas-guzzlers consume, and with the costs of energy already high and very likely to go higher, it is hard to understand why most Americans don't already make more energy-efficient choices.

Part of the answer is that many of our energy expenditures are relatively invisible to us. Most people simply aren't aware of how energy inefficient many of their choices are. Sure, we see the dollars mounting in a speedy blur when we fill the tank at a gas station. But when we turn up the thermostat or switch on the lights, most of us have very little sense of the consequences of those actions in terms of energy usage or excess carbon emissions.

Try this thought experiment: do you know where your home's electricity comes from? Do you know which of your appliances use the most energy? Or where your home's biggest heat losses are?

If your answer to any these questions is no, you are certainly not alone. A 2010 study published in the *Proceedings of the National Academy of Sciences* highlighted how inaccurate public perceptions tend to be on the subject of energy usage. More than 500 people from across the United States were asked a series of questions about what they thought were the most effective strategies for conserving energy. They were asked to estimate how much energy was used in various routine household activities and how much they thought they might save if they made certain changes. The respondents not only underestimated how much energy they could save; their estimates were also, on average, *nearly three times lower* than the actual savings they could achieve.

As the researchers analyzed the results, they noticed that the inaccuracies followed a pattern: people tended to favor turning off appliances and lights (what the researchers call "curtailment" efforts) over making improvements in efficiency. For instance, people were five times more

UCS Climate Team FAST FACT

In a 2010 study, Americans dramatically underestimated how much energy they might save by implementing a variety of energy efficiency measures at home. Their estimates were, on average, *nearly three times lower than the actual savings they could achieve.*

likely to choose turning off lights as a strategy for saving energy than switching to more energy-efficient lightbulbs, even though replacing old-fashioned incandescent bulbs can often result in savings of 75 percent or more in electricity costs. Of course, turning off lights when they are not in use is a great way to save energy, but think about that for a moment: you would have to turn off your lights entirely for *three out of every four days* to achieve comparable savings. The point is: people tend to underestimate how powerful it can be to use energy more efficiently.

Along the same lines, the study found that people were twice as likely to favor curtailing their use of appliances rather than using more energy-efficient ones. In open-ended questions, only 12 percent of the respondents even mentioned efficiency improvements. The fact is, making changes to improve efficiency often yields far greater savings in energy and emissions than trying to curtail or do without.

As the study's authors note, their results show that all too often people "believe they are doing their part to reduce energy use when they engage in low-effort, low-impact actions instead of focusing on changes that would make a bigger difference." In the chapters ahead, we will tackle many of these issues to help avoid this pitfall. By improving our "energy literacy," each of us can understand more precisely where our personal emissions are coming from.

The first step is to review your energy usage. Save and review your gas receipts and calculate your fuel economy. Look closely at your home's utility bills. Some utility companies now provide information showing how your energy usage stacks up against that of your neighbors. And many websites can help you calculate your carbon footprint. One well-respected example is a carbon calculator developed in conjunction with the Lawrence Berkeley National Laboratory, available at http://cool climate.berkeley.edu/uscalc. Websites such as this one ask visitors to enter specific information about their energy usage, such as how many miles they drive annually and what kind of home they live in. On the basis of the data provided, the websites offer an estimate of the amount of carbon an individual or household emits.

Carbon calculators are valuable tools, but estimating your total carbon emissions is only one piece of the picture. It is also important to find out where the biggest energy hogs in your home and your lifestyle are hiding. Before you buy a major appliance, read the labels and specification sheets to learn how much energy it consumes. Invest $20 in an appliance electricity meter that you can use to see which of your appliances are energy hogs. A wealth of this kind of information can be found through the federal government, for instance, at www.energysavers.gov, a website run by the U.S. Department of Energy. Review your travel patterns, and think about how you handle home activities such as lawn care. You might be surprised at what you find when you consider energy usage and emissions related to the many choices in your life.

As you learn more about the sources of your personal contribution to carbon emissions, you will most likely find yourself thinking differently about some of your choices. The fact is, when people realize they're being wasteful, most want to make some changes in the way they do things.

A 2002 psychological study demonstrated how information about energy usage can affect consumer behavior. In the study, 100 participants were shown an ultramodern washing machine and told they would be helping the engineers design a next-generation control panel. Using a simulated computer control panel, the participants made choices about 20 consecutive loads of laundry. All the control panels were the same—with one exception: some included a simple "real-time" meter purporting to show the amount of electricity the washing machine was using at different settings. At the end of the experiment, the people with the real-time energy usage information were found to have voluntarily set their washing machines to settings that used some 21 percent less power than their counterparts' settings. In other words, even though the participants wouldn't derive any personal savings from their choices, simply having information about the electricity the machine would use inclined them to use it wisely.

As you begin to think about your energy usage, don't forget to consider transportation and purchasing choices and even your diet. As we discuss in later chapters of this book, when each of us becomes more aware of the emissions that result from all the various choices we make, we are far more likely to discover ways in all these arenas to lower our carbon footprints.

Step 2: Make a Plan

Once you have learned where your personal carbon emissions are coming from, you can better decide which areas of your life offer the best reductions. Part II of this book will help you make these choices.

Chapter 4 looks at the average American consumer's global warming emissions from transportation, mainly from our cars. This chapter can help you make transportation choices that will get you where you want to go while driving down your share of these carbon emissions.

Chapter 5 addresses household heating and cooling, which accounts for a significant share of the nation's carbon dioxide emissions and, depending upon where you live, up to half of your total emissions at home. Making thoughtful choices about heating and cooling can greatly reduce your emissions while still allowing you to live comfortably and save money on your energy bills. In this chapter, we explain which changes will make the most difference in reducing your carbon emissions. And we review some of the latest advances in green building technology as well as the ins and outs of purchasing electricity from renewable energy sources.

Next to home heating and cooling, the biggest sources of residential carbon emissions are lighting, laundry and kitchen appliances, and the rapidly growing category of consumer electronics: televisions, computers, and other electronic devices. Chapter 6 explores the most effective strategies for lowering the emissions from each of these sources. It discusses ways to monitor your home's electricity usage and answers such questions as whether it is better to use a microwave or a conventional oven, when to replace your refrigerator, and what to look for in a new one.

In chapter 7 we tease apart the climate consequences of our food choices by tracking the heat-trapping emissions from farms, the industries that supply farmers with chemicals and equipment, and the long chain of processing, transportation, and distribution stretching from farm to table. Not all foods have the same global warming impact: this chapter discusses the outsized impact of meat consumption, emissions related to bottled water and other beverages, and the extent to which eating locally produced food reduces your global warming emissions.

Finally, chapter 8 focuses on the emissions caused by the stuff we buy: the clothing, furnishings, toys, books—everything we accumulate and often throw out much too soon—which accounts for roughly 10 percent of our personal carbon emissions. This chapter also reviews the services we buy, from health care through legal assistance, insurance, visits to hotels, movie theaters, and even the car wash, which together account for another 16 percent. Here you will find plenty of information about the climate consequences of the purchasing decisions you make every day.

Step 3: Look Around and Connect

By following the advice in part II, you will figure out the best changes you can make to reduce your emissions by 20 percent (or perhaps even more) this year.

While individual actions matter, they aren't sufficient. As individual consumers, we simply don't have control of all the decisions that must be made in tackling global warming. While we can take responsibility for our part of the problem, we also need to call on elected officials and corporate leaders to create better policies to reduce emissions. People like you, who have taken action in your own lives, have a vital role to play. The smart personal choices you have made will help you be a leader in your community and in your workplace or school, demonstrating how feasible and beneficial change can be.

Part III shows you how to step up, connect with others, and share the knowledge and experience you've gained. Family and friends are the best place to start, and chapter 9 shows you how. Chapter 10 explains how to apply what you've learned in your workplace. This chapter documents some of the most promising changes now underway in a variety of workplaces, from small firms to large companies, as well as at colleges, churches, and municipal facilities.

Chapter 11 shows how to make your voice heard beyond your local community. From our cities and towns to our state governments, officials make many decisions about how our tax dollars are spent. The taxes we pay can be used to continue on our current, recklessly unsustainable path of energy usage—or they can be used to improve our energy future. Many of the most important planning decisions about transportation and utilities are made at the state and local levels. Meanwhile, at the federal level, in Washington, DC, a wide variety of consequential policy decisions are made and, there, lobbyists for the fossil fuel industry are pushing hard for continued support of policies that perpetuate our dependence on coal and oil, block renewable energy, and delay energy efficiency measures. This chapter highlights a number of successful local, state, and federal programs and offers ideas about how to get involved.

Finally, chapter 12 presents a vision of the low-carbon future that you can help create. This is no high-tech sci-fi scenario. Our neighborhoods will look and feel much the same as they do now. But you'll see solar panels on many rooftops, and wind turbines will dot the countryside, generating plenty of electricity. Our homes will look much the same, too, just retrofitted for much greater energy efficiency. And our home appliances, along with whatever new gizmos have come along, will do the same jobs they do today, using far less energy. Cars will run much more efficiently and will fill up on biofuels, electricity, or hydrogen, while cities will boast more and better mass transit. And a robust mix of residential and commercial development, combined with a network of high-speed railways, will reduce our dependence on cars.

The good news is that we already have many of the tools and technologies we need to lower our carbon emissions. We just need to get moving in the right direction. The imminent threat of global warming means we need to act fast. But across the country and around the world, a sea change has begun in the way many people think about their carbon emissions. International agreements and many U.S. federal policies have lagged, but all around us positive signs abound—proverbial green shoots.

These changes are visible when we begin to look for them. A recent report found that in the northeastern United States, some 60 percent of all planned new electricity-generating projects for the region—about 17,000 megawatts of capacity—involve renewable energy, including solar and wind power. That's the equivalent capacity of more than two dozen average-sized coal-fired plants.

Green building projects are fast becoming the norm. In Washington, DC, for example, the city planning department reports that all of the 200 large buildings planned or under construction have been designed to meet aggressive new energy efficiency standards. Meanwhile, scores of major companies are starting to reduce their carbon footprints. In just one example, Walmart recently pledged to make 22 million tons' worth of reductions in its global warming emissions by 2015. That's the equivalent of taking nearly 4 million cars off the road.

The U.S. military, a huge energy consumer, is beginning to address the issue too: in 2010, U.S. Secretary of the Navy Ray Mabus set the ambitious goal of deriving half of all the power used by the U.S. Navy and Marines from renewable energy sources by 2020—a figure Mabus says will include energy for bases as well as the fuel used for vehicles and ships. Among other benefits, the military considers its energy plan as a way to save lives. A 2007 report found that one U.S. military person is killed or wounded for every 24 military fuel convoys run in Afghanistan.

The fuel economy of new cars is also finally starting to change. Fuel economy was stuck at about 25 miles per gallon for decades, but it has been rising very slowly since 2005. Starting in 2012, progress kicked into high gear as new fuel efficiency standards and the first-ever national greenhouse gas standards for cars began to push new vehicles to significantly increase fuel economy and cut carbon emissions.

Taken together, these kinds of efforts are already adding up on a global scale. According to the United Nations Environment Programme (UNEP), 2008 was a watershed year globally for investment in renewable sources of energy such as wind and solar power. For the first time ever, "green energy" investments exceeded total investments in coal, oil, and carbon-based energy, constituting some 56 percent of all money invested in the energy sector. Including businesses focused on energy efficiency and building retrofits, the total climate-related business sector had global revenues in 2008 even larger than those of the aerospace and defense industries, according to a report by HSBC Global Research, one of the world's largest financial institutions.

These important glimmers of hope indicate that once we get going, we can make changes happen quickly. That's good, because we need to act fast. For those with any doubts or questions about the pace and scope of global warming, chapter 3 provides a quick grounding in the science behind climate change that can help you spot and address some of the most egregious misrepresentations of the scientific evidence, which unfortunately have proliferated in the media and in our often polarized political discourse.

Reducing our global warming emissions is easier than you may think. A low-carbon future is within our reach, but only if all of us take steps toward it in our own lives and push for changes in the world around us. Though the task may sound huge, the transformation we need begins with each one of us, starting now.

CHAPTER 3

The Weight of the Evidence

How We Know the Planet Is Warming

It is fair to say that global warming may be the most carefully and fully studied topic in human history.

—Ralph Cicerone, president of
the National Academy of Sciences

You have undoubtedly heard a good deal about global warming. But if you're like most Americans, you feel somewhat confused about the topic. According to a national survey in 2010, only one in every 10 Americans feels very well informed about the causes of global warming and how Earth's climate system works. In other words, 90 percent of us consider ourselves a little shaky on the particulars.

Since we are recommending that you make some significant changes in your daily life, it is worth taking a few moments to review how the climate system operates and what has led the world's credentialed scientists to be so certain that we must act now to combat global warming.

Too Much Carbon

Scientists know that certain gases trap heat and act like a blanket to warm the planet. One of the most important of these gases is carbon dioxide. When we burn gasoline to drive our cars or burn coal, oil, or gas to heat our homes and power our lives, we release carbon dioxide, which is now overloading our atmosphere. Carbon dioxide is also released when trees are burned, as is occurring on a vast scale in the Amazon rainforest to make room for agriculture and development. As we pour more and more carbon dioxide into the atmosphere, this blanket of gas gets thicker and keeps heat from escaping into space, causing Earth to warm up.

From a scientific standpoint, there is really no question about this process. Scientists understand virtually every step of it and have a wealth of overwhelming evidence that global warming is well underway. Let's walk through some of the basics of what scientists know and how they know it.

To start, let's consider one of the biggest sources of people's confusion about global warming: the distinction between the weather and the climate. The weather, as we all know, varies. One moment it is sunny and mild, while the next can bring rain that lasts for days. In the north, questions about global warming usually come up after a cold spell or a big winter snowstorm. We can't help but wonder: How can scientists claim the planet is warming when we're having weather like *this*? The question could not be more natural. After all, we tend to base our understanding of the world upon firsthand observation, and in a really cold winter, for example, our observations seem at odds with the warming we associate with climate change.

However, our weather observations are really not at odds with global warming. In fact, while global warming is often described as a theory, our understanding of climate change is based on careful observations and measurements not far different from your observations of your local weather. The key is that weather and climate are not the same. That's because climate is the analysis of weather averaged over time, such as over the span of decades. Weather, on the other hand, is an extremely variable local phenomenon. It describes such things as temperature and precipitation in a given place at a particular moment in time. It is true that the weather varies from day to day. But when scientists observe Earth's climate, *they can see that it is unmistakably getting warmer.*

We Know Global Average Temperatures Are Rising

People have been recording temperatures regularly and reliably in many parts of the world since the mid-1800s—and even earlier at some locations in Europe and Asia. This vast cache of recorded local temperature data gives scientists a powerful way to track broad shifts in the planet's climate over time. Trends in temperature readings from around the world provide scientists with clear data that global warming is taking place; by adding

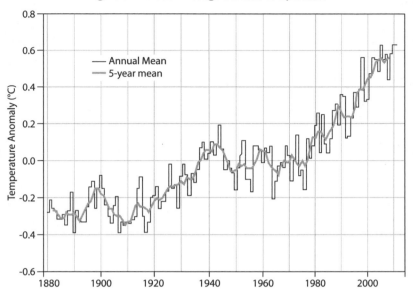

Figure 3.1. Global Average Surface Temperature

Drawing upon precise measurements of local temperatures from thousands of locations around the planet, this graph shows that the global average temperature is rising. Source: NASA/GISS, 2010.

up and averaging all the temperatures worldwide, they can see that the global average temperature is rising.

Here's how it works. To determine the global average temperature, scientists compile detailed temperature readings at thousands of locations around the globe. To see how the current year compares with previous years, they look at the average of yearly temperatures over a span of several decades or more and compare the new annual average to that baseline. This method requires a lot of data, but the concept is really quite simple. By averaging all the recorded day-to-day temperatures from the disparate locations, these scientists are able to average local weather variations to discern the overall trend in the global climate.

A number of independent teams of researchers around the world, using slightly different approaches in data and technique, have calculated the global average temperature over time, and all of the teams have found

---

UCS Climate Team FAST FACT

In 2008, for the first time, global investments in renewable sources of energy such as wind and solar power exceeded total investments in carbon-based energy. According to one financial assessment, when businesses that are focused on energy efficiency are factored in, the climate-related business sector now has global revenues even larger than those of the aerospace and defense industries.

---

that the planet's temperature is on the rise. It has gone up on every continent, including North America, and on the surface of the world's oceans as well. Averaging the numbers shows that the temperature has risen by about 1 degree Fahrenheit in the past century, which may not seem like much, but that 1 degree turns out to be a very significant number. After all, 18,000 years ago, at the last ice age maximum, the global average temperature was only about 9 degrees cooler than today.

Here's what stands out most dramatically in the data on global average temperatures: using this uniform method for comparing year-to-year temperature trends, the years 2010, 2005, and 1998 are roughly tied as the warmest years since reliable measurements began 130 years ago. The pattern is unmistakable: *15 of the past 16 years have ranked as the warmest ever.* And despite minor variations in the data, all the major research teams have determined that 2001–2010 was the hottest decade on record. With all the averaging involved, this is not a matter of localized variation. Statistically speaking, the chance that a stable climate would display such a strong trend is vanishingly small. That's one of many reasons why scientists are certain that something must be forcing the climate to get warmer. And as we will see, the evidence is overwhelming that warming temperatures are a result of human activities that are changing the atmosphere.

We Know Human Activity Has Changed Earth's Atmosphere

An important part of the story of global warming begins with the Second Industrial Revolution in the latter half of the 1800s, when people began to burn an unprecedented amount of coal and oil. With the advent of coal-fired steam engines and oil-fired combustion engines, a fast-growing global economy depended largely upon the burning of carbon-based fuels.

Carbon is a key building block in virtually all of the planet's life forms. A particularly versatile element, carbon is abundant in the sediments and rocks near Earth's surface and is a major component of everything from trees and plants to insects, mammals, microbes, and fungi. Earth has a natural recycling system for carbon, known as the carbon cycle. As plants and animals grow, they extract carbon from the environment. Plants do this through photosynthesis, while animals do it by eating plants or other animals. When living organisms die and decompose, carbon normally is released into the atmosphere or is buried in sediments. A good deal of the carbon emitted by living humans and animals through respiration is also absorbed by the oceans. Carbon dioxide moves through the atmosphere every day as part of this carbon cycle. For many millennia before the Industrial Revolution, Earth's natural carbon cycle was in balance, soaking in roughly as much carbon as it released.

Starting in the Industrial Revolution, however, people invented all kinds of ways to put fossil fuels to work. As more and more industrial processes depended on the burning of coal and oil, we began to release vast quantities of carbon into the atmosphere so quickly that plants and oceans were not able to absorb it all. The carbon cycle fell out of balance: carbon dioxide began to build up in Earth's atmosphere.

Recent surveys of Americans' understanding of global warming reveals some basic confusion about this fundamental aspect of the problem. It is really quite straightforward. When we burn something that was once alive, the carbon it contained is released into the atmosphere. Today's major energy sources—coal, oil, and natural gas—are called "fossil fuels"

UCS Climate Team FAST FACT

Researchers compiling local temperature records to determine the planet's global average temperature over time have documented that 15 of the past 16 years have ranked as the warmest ever recorded and that 2001–2010 was the hottest decade on record.

because they are the fossilized remains of formerly living plants and organisms buried in sediments millions of years ago.

Coal consists primarily of the remains of huge trees that proliferated on Earth tens, or even hundreds, of millions of years ago. When the trees fell into the swamps where they grew, they didn't decompose but eventually were compressed and transformed into the coal we burn today. A similar marine process created Earth's patchwork of oil and natural gas deposits from the remains of tiny organisms called plankton. Since all three of these fossil fuels—coal, oil, and natural gas—are made up of formerly living things, they contain fairly concentrated amounts of carbon. This makes them a potent source of energy. But burning fossil fuels combines their carbon with oxygen to form carbon dioxide.

The important point is this: Ever since the Industrial Revolution, we have powered our world by burning vast storehouses of prehistoric carbon. In the process, huge amounts of carbon that had been stored for many millions of years are now overloading the atmosphere.

Burning carbon might not be such a big deal on a small scale. But we rely on this fundamental process to fuel our cars, heat our homes, and run everything from our hair dryers to our cell phones. With billions of people living in an industrialized world powered largely by ancient carbon, which goes up our smokestacks and out our tailpipes as carbon dioxide, it is really no surprise that we have overwhelmed the absorptive capacity of Earth's natural carbon cycle and created a carbon overload in our atmosphere.

So, why are the rising levels of atmospheric carbon dioxide a big deal?

Because scientists have known for more than a century that carbon dioxide plays a vital role in keeping the planet warm. Earth is just far enough away from the sun that without heat-trapping gases such as carbon dioxide, our planet would most likely be a frozen, lifeless wasteland. Even though the amount of carbon dioxide in the air is relatively small compared with the amounts of nitrogen and oxygen, carbon dioxide is so effective at trapping the sun's heat that it works as a kind of invisible blanket, letting sunlight in but preventing much of the resulting heat from escaping back into space.

Which leads us to the second reason why scientists know that global warming is underway: *they can observe that the amount of carbon dioxide in the atmosphere is increasing.*

We Know Carbon Dioxide Levels Are Rising

Scientists know how much carbon dioxide is in the atmosphere because they have been carefully measuring it for more than a half century. It is not a matter of a theory or model but is the result of direct observation.

Many research teams around the world now track carbon dioxide levels. But one of the most respected sources of data began with the work of a meticulous American scientist named Charles David Keeling. Back in the 1950s, Keeling became the first person to develop a highly accurate technique for measuring the amount of carbon dioxide in the atmosphere, and he made it his life's work to measure the gas over time. To do the job, Keeling used a new weather-monitoring facility in Hawaii, far from industrial sources that might skew the results. He began taking measurements in 1957 as part of the first worldwide program, known as the International Geophysical Year, to send scientists out in the field to measure practically everything on the planet, including carbon dioxide.

Today the Mauna Loa Observatory, where Keeling set up his experiment, continues to make hourly measurements of the carbon dioxide in the atmosphere. Since Charles Keeling's death in 2005, his son Ralph, a scientist at Scripps Institution of Oceanography, has overseen the monitoring. The measurements are so precise and have been handled so consistently that they have long been considered the gold standard in the field of climate studies. And the measurements over the years show a steady and indisputable buildup of carbon dioxide in the atmosphere. Charles Keeling's work eventually earned him the National Medal of Science, the nation's top honor for a scientist. His Keeling Curve, as it is now known (shown on the next page), is considered such an important contribution to our understanding of the planet that it is actually engraved on the wall of the National Academy of Sciences headquarters in Washington, DC.

A close look at Keeling's data on the concentration of carbon dioxide in the atmosphere offers a number of important insights into global warm-

Figure 3.2. Atmosphere CO$_2$ at Mauna Loa Observatory

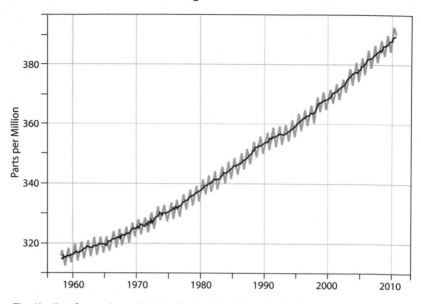

The Keeling Curve shows the steady rise of carbon dioxide in the atmosphere between 1958 and 2011. Source: Scripps Institution of Oceanography/NOAA Earth System Research Laboratory, February 2011.

ing. Its pattern of regular oscillations was the first conclusive evidence that atmospheric carbon dioxide levels vary with the seasons. As we now know, the levels are lower during spring and summer in the Northern Hemisphere because this half of the globe has more overall land mass than the Southern Hemisphere, and growing plants absorb more of the carbon dioxide. The carbon dioxide levels rise in the fall, when decaying leaves emit more of the gas than is removed in the winter, when most plants in the Northern Hemisphere are dormant.

Keeling's data also confirm that the overall percentage of carbon dioxide in the atmosphere is very small. After all, the graph measures *parts per million* of carbon dioxide in the atmosphere—basically a trace amount compared with the 78 percent nitrogen and 21 percent oxygen that make up most of the air we breathe. Measured that way, carbon dioxide accounts for less than *four one-hundredths of a percent.* One might imagine that such

Aren't There Other Heat-Trapping Gases Besides Carbon Dioxide?

Carbon dioxide (CO_2) is the most abundant, long-lived heat-trapping gas, and it is responsible for most of the global warming that has occurred over the past 50 years. Because we emit so much CO_2, and because it stays in the atmosphere for many decades (with 20 to 30 percent of it lingering as long as 2,000 years), CO_2 is building up in the atmosphere and warming our climate. But other atmospheric gases also play a role in global warming. The degree to which each gas contributes to global warming is a combination of its heat-trapping ability, its abundance, and its longevity in the atmosphere.

Methane (CH_4) is released when organic material decomposes in the absence of oxygen. Sources include livestock, wetlands, and landfills. A molecule of CH_4 released into the atmosphere traps a significant amount of heat—at least 20 times more than a molecule of CO_2—but methane is far less abundant and remains in the atmosphere less than a decade before breaking down into CO_2 and water. Chemically, it is the same as the natural gas mined by energy companies and used to heat our homes. When burned, methane emits CO_2.

Nitrous oxide (N_2O) is a gas some may know from their dentists' offices, but more common sources of N_2O are combustion of fossil fuels, some industrial processes, and fertilizers. Molecule for molecule, nitrous oxide traps far more heat than either methane or CO_2, but it is far less common than either. Like CO_2, nitrous oxide stays in the atmosphere a long time, lingering for about a century.

Several other gases play a minor role in global warming. Some examples are **hydrochlorofluorocarbons (HCFCs)**—such as refrigerants—which are strong heat trappers but not abundant; ground-level ozone (O_3), which traps heat locally but stays in the atmosphere for less than a month; and **water vapor (H_2O)**, which is, of course, common in the atmosphere but lasts for only days. The higher temperatures we expect from global warming will probably mean higher humidity because warmer air holds more water vapor—think of the humidity that builds up in a closed bathroom when you take a hot shower.

These are the chemicals people refer to when they talk about "greenhouse gases," global warming gases, or heat-trapping gases. We focus primarily on carbon dioxide because of its predominant role in global warming.

tiny amounts of carbon dioxide in the atmosphere must be insignificant, but the opposite is true: carbon dioxide is such a potent heat trapper that it plays a leading role in managing Earth's heat balance. Along with water vapor and a few other gases, the presence of carbon dioxide even in such small amounts keeps Earth's temperature in a livable range.

And that fact is why Keeling's data are so alarming: the steady, inexorable rise in concentrations of this potent, heat-trapping gas in the atmosphere makes it virtually certain that Earth will continue to get warmer. When Keeling first measured carbon dioxide levels over an entire year, in 1958, the average annual level was about 315 parts per million. As of 2011, the average annual level has risen dramatically, to 390 parts per million, an almost 25 percent increase in just 53 years. And the increase in carbon dioxide shows no signs of abating. In fact, the pace seems to be accelerating.

We Know the Past Makeup of the Atmosphere from Ice Cores

From the global average temperature record and measurements of carbon dioxide levels in the atmosphere, scientists have compelling direct evidence that the planet is warming. But what about long-term fluctuations in Earth's climate? After all, we know, from the geologic evidence of glaciers and many other sources, that the planet has had many ice ages in the distant past. How can we be sure that the current warming trend is not an entirely natural planetary cycle?

One ingenious method scientists have developed to understand the past climate record is to measure the composition of prehistoric air bubbles trapped in polar ice cores. Amazingly, these air bubbles have survived, locked in ice buried far below the surface. At some locations on Earth, the ice has remained frozen for millennia, with each year's snowfall burying it ever deeper. The preserved air bubbles serve as time capsules, documenting the composition of the atmosphere at the time they were captured in frozen ice and snow.

Cameron Wake, a climate scientist at the University of New Hampshire, is one of scores of scientists who gather ice cores from remote glaciers and bring them back to unlock the clues they contain about the climate record. As he puts it, "If you put out a call for engineers to design a system that stored pristine samples of the atmosphere for hundreds of thousands of years, I doubt they could design a better system than glaciers."

As Wake explains, chemical compounds in the air bubbles offer an exact record of the atmosphere at the moment the ice froze around them. Exhuming the long-buried air bubbles, scientists can track the unmistakable increase in heat-trapping gases such as carbon dioxide over time. The deeper the researchers dig, the older the bits of preserved atmosphere they find. Wake continues to marvel at the information the air bubbles contain; to him and his colleagues, reading their chemical traces is almost like perusing a stack of old newspapers frozen in the ice. The sudden appearance of traces of radioactive cesium, for instance, marks the advent of aboveground nuclear tests by the United States and the Soviet Union prior to the 1963 Nuclear Test-Ban Treaty. And even in the ice of the planet's most remote glaciers, Wake says, you can see the surge in trace levels of lead (from leaded gasoline) as cars became our dominant mode of transportation. The levels of these substances in the air bubbles are unmistakable, he says, "like a baseball bat hitting you on the head."

Wake says the evidence of global warming in glacial ice has been clear to him and his colleagues for decades. Ice cores have been unearthed that date back hundreds of thousands of years. And they show that until the 1800s, carbon dioxide levels hovered in the range of 250 to 280 parts per million. That's *more than one-third* less carbon dioxide than researchers find in the atmosphere today.

The scientists' key finding from the ice-core data is this: despite some variation in levels over the millennia between ice ages and warmer periods, *for the 800,000 years for which we have clear ice-core data, carbon dioxide levels in the atmosphere have never been anywhere near as high as they are today.* That means we know with a high degree of confidence that carbon dioxide levels are higher than they have been since about the time our distant human ancestors began migrating out of Africa.

So let's review. We have unmistakable hard data to show that carbon dioxide levels are rising and are higher than they have been for as long as we have detailed records (some 800,000 years). We have known for a century that rising levels of carbon dioxide in the atmosphere irrefutably cause the planet to warm. And we know from temperature data that a warming trend is already underway.

But how do scientists know that human activities—namely, the emissions from our tailpipes and smokestacks—are responsible for the warming? As it turns out, just as criminals leave hard evidence such as fingerprints and DNA at the scene of a crime, the various causes of climate change leave distinct signatures or patterns that climate scientists can identify if they look carefully enough.

Global Warming's "Climate Fingerprint" Reveals Humans' Role

One of the most powerful tools scientists have to find out if humans are responsible for the current increase in global warming is a technique called "climate fingerprinting." In much the way detectives analyze forensic evidence, climate scientists can study carbon molecules and gradations in temperature in the atmosphere to determine where the carbon came from.

A carbon molecule in carbon dioxide emitted by the burning of fossil fuels has a subtly different fingerprint from that of a carbon molecule in carbon dioxide from any other source; the nucleus contains fewer neutrons. By analyzing the revealing fingerprints—isotopes—of carbon in the atmosphere, scientists can definitively tell that the burning of fossil fuels *accounts for the largest increase in atmospheric carbon dioxide since the Industrial Revolution.*

Not only is the carbon itself distinctive, but also the temperature patterns created in the particular way the atmosphere heats up offer key evidence of the warming's source. Benjamin Santer, a climate scientist at the Lawrence Livermore National Laboratory in California, is one of the researchers who first explored the implications of climate fingerprinting. The key insight of Santer's research is straightforward: The factors that might account for global warming—what climate scientists call "forcings"—operate in observably different ways. If the warming were caused by increased energy from the sun, for instance, careful temperature measurements of all levels of the atmosphere would reveal it warming from the top straight down to Earth's surface. If massive volcanic eruptions were a significant factor, their influence would show up with a distinctly different profile. The dust produced by an erupting volcano often reaches the upper portions of Earth's atmosphere and can remain there for several years. Because volcanic dust absorbs incoming sunlight, preventing much of it from reaching Earth's surface, the data would show heating in the stratosphere (the upper layer of the atmosphere) but cooling in the troposphere (the layer closest to Earth's surface).

But, Santer points out, the actual temperature measurements show neither of those profiles. His research, now replicated by many other researchers around the world, instead documents a telltale warming of the lower atmosphere—the troposphere—and a cooling of the upper layer of the atmosphere, or stratosphere. This is the precise fingerprint scientists expect if heat-trapping carbon dioxide from fossil fuel emissions is building up in the atmosphere.

In the decades since Santer first published his groundbreaking research, the evidence that human activity is causing global warming has become stronger than ever, and it is now accepted by the overwhelming majority of scientists who study the topic. Our understanding of climate fingerprinting has also become far more sophisticated and now shows human causation in measurements of change in ocean temperatures, Arctic sea ice, precipitation, and atmospheric moisture, among many other indicators.

All of the climate-fingerprinting research to date, Santer explains, has arrived at the same conclusion, namely, that "natural causes cannot provide a convincing explanation for the particular patterns of climate

---

UCS Climate Team *FAST FACT*

Scientists can tell that human activity is responsible for global warming because of the distinctive pattern, or "fingerprint," of the warming, which differs notably from the fingerprints of other possible causes, such as an increase in the sun's energy output.

change we see." That, he says, is why scientists "have come to have such confidence in our understanding of what is happening—because of the breadth of scientific work and reproducibility of the results."

Overwhelming Data from Disparate Fields

Santer's point about the breadth of scientific work holds not just for climate-fingerprinting research but also for the burgeoning number of scientific fields focusing on diverse aspects of our warming planet. We will review just a sampling here, but the striking feature is that in virtually every field, from atmospheric science to zoology, scientists are finding compelling evidence of global warming—evidence that Earth is warming fast, with serious consequences for people and the planet.

MELTING ICE

Many parts of Earth's polar regions—including the Antarctic Peninsula and immense regions of the Arctic—are heating up much faster than other parts of the globe. You may have seen pictures of stranded polar bears and heard that global warming is causing the melting of Arctic sea ice—the floating ice on the ocean's surface. Like most people, you might think that this distant phenomenon is occurring gradually, over a centuries-long time frame. In fact, the work of many researchers, such as Julienne Stroeve, a climate scientist at the National Snow and Ice Data Center in Boulder, Colorado, shows that dramatic changes are taking place right now—far faster than most experts anticipated and with enormous consequences for the whole planet, not just the Arctic region.

For instance, the smallest amounts of Arctic sea ice area *ever measured* during late summer have all occurred in recent years. As Stroeve explains, "Since 2002, we have seen one pronounced record minimum after another. The data all point to a strong warming signal." Stroeve says that highly reliable data on the extent of Arctic sea ice have been collected since 1978. In just over 30 years, Stroeve estimates, *some 40 percent of the region's ice has been lost.*

Shrinking ice is not confined to the polar regions, either. Researchers who track glaciers around the world find that they are shrinking and retreating almost everywhere, from the Alps to the Himalayas to the Andes, the Rockies, and Alaska.

A wealth of research data show that other large ice masses are also shrinking. To assess this kind of melting, teams of researchers make direct measurements in the field. But they also use specially designed, sophisticated satellite equipment that can accurately measure Earth's land—or ice—masses as the satellite orbits overhead. The data show that Greenland's vast ice sheet is melting at a dramatic rate. Between April 2002 and February 2009, the Greenland ice sheet lost roughly 385 cubic miles of ice. That's more than twice the volume of water in Lake Erie.

Melting ice on this scale has enormous consequences. Glaciers—and their cousins, winter snowpacks—provide critical water storage. More than two-thirds of the planet's freshwater is held in glaciers, so their retreat can be devastating to communities that depend largely on glacier-fed sources for drinking water, electric power generation, and irrigation. Here again, the evidence is unmistakable. In one especially dramatic example, Chacaltaya Glacier in the South American Andes, a major source of water for La Paz, Bolivia, lost more than 90 percent of its volume from the 1940s to the late 1990s.

In 2009, Chacaltaya disappeared completely.

RISING SEA

Not surprisingly, all this melting ice on land, as well as the expansion of the ocean as it warms, inevitably leads to rising sea levels. Researchers who track global sea levels have documented a rise of about 6.7 inches over the past century. The rate in the past decade, however, has accelerated significantly. Left unchecked, these rising sea levels threaten coastal communities and island nations around the world.

The graph shows a trajectory that could displace millions of people in coastal areas in coming decades. A good portion of the rise in sea level is due to thermal expansion: water expands as it warms. But the rapidly melting ice sheets in Greenland and the Antarctic are also a major factor

Figure 3.3. Trends in Global Average Absolute Sea Level

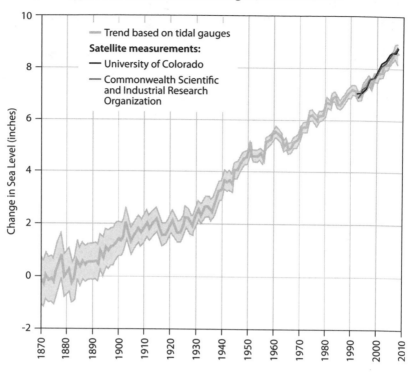

Detailed measurements over the past century show that the sea level has risen by more than eight inches since 1870 and continues to rise as the planet warms and major ice sheets melt. Source: CSIRO, 2009; University of Colorado at Boulder, 2009.

now, having become the most important contributors to the faster rise of sea levels over the course of the first decade of this century.

TROUBLE FOR OCEANS

The rise in sea level is hardly the only effect of global warming on the oceans. We know from careful scientific measurements that surface sea temperatures are rising, affecting weather patterns around the globe and causing steep declines in coral reefs, with dire consequences for some tropical fish populations.

But something else is going on, too.

As part of the carbon cycle, the world's oceans have long absorbed

UCS Climate Team *FAST FACT*
As the world's oceans absorb more carbon dioxide, they become more acidic, threatening the ocean's coral reefs and some of the plankton that form the base of the aquatic food chain.

roughly one-third of all the carbon dioxide emitted by human activity, thereby slowing the buildup of heat-trapping gases in the atmosphere and staving off a more dramatic warming of the planet. But as the oceans absorb excess carbon, they become more acidic. In fact, current measurements indicate that Earth's oceans are already about 30 percent more acidic than they were before the Industrial Revolution.

Ocean acidification poses a dire threat to marine ecosystems. The increasing acidity is likely to be devastating to fisheries around the world, but its impact is even bigger because of the threat to the ocean's phytoplankton—the microscopic plant organisms at the base of the aquatic food chain.

Some scientists are charting the toll ocean acidification is already taking on the world's coral reefs, which have struggled to survive the assaults of overfishing, pollution, and sediment-laden runoff from other human activities. John Guinotte, a coral specialist at the Marine Conservation Biology Institute in Bellevue, Washington, says that what keeps him awake at night are the profound changes in ocean chemistry he is seeing, which may be among the most devastating effects of the rising levels of carbon dioxide in the atmosphere. As it worsens, Guinotte explains, ocean acidification corrodes coral reefs, causing cascading problems up the marine food chain. He says, "From the standpoint of the oceans, there is simply no escaping the fact that we are going to need major reductions in our carbon dioxide emissions."

TROUBLE ON LAND

Scientists studying plant and animal life on land are seeing dramatic evidence of global warming, too. Longstanding natural processes are being disrupted as plants bloom and animal species breed earlier in the year.

Some plants and animals are being forced to migrate northward or face extinction. Of 561 European plant and animal species studied over the decades between 1970 and 2010, roughly 78 percent shifted their characteristic spring patterns (blooming, seasonal migration, and so on) to earlier in the season. Biologists are discovering that in some places these changes are causing fatal mismatches; for example, the preferred type of caterpillar that certain birds feed on may have already metamorphosed into butterflies when the birds arrive in their spring breeding areas and thus are no longer available as food. These kinds of changes place an increasing number of species at risk of extinction.

One researcher, Camille Parmesan, an ecologist at the University of Texas at Austin, conducted pathbreaking field observations of butterfly populations, which provided compelling evidence of how climate change is already affecting our living planet.

In the early 1990s, Parmesan spent four and a half years tracing the known habitats of one butterfly species, the Edith's checkerspot, across its entire range in western North America, from Baja to Banff. Living primarily out of her car and closely observing the nonmigratory butterflies in the field, Parmesan sought to determine whether they were an example of local extinction on a warming planet. Her painstaking fieldwork paid off. Parmesan's landmark 1996 paper in the British science journal *Nature* was one of the first definitive caterpillar's-eye views of the effects of global warming on a living species. Even discounting sites where urban sprawl or other human interference might have impinged upon the butterflies' habitat, Parmesan showed that *80 percent of the populations of Edith's checkerspots had already died out* at the southern edge of their range in Mexico and southern California, leading to reasonable concern that they could be early indicators of trouble for many species.

UCS Climate Team *FAST FACT*

Analyzing research on nearly 1,700 separate wild species, scientists have found strong scientific evidence that some 52 percent of the species studied to date show signs of having been affected by global warming.

Since completing that research, Parmesan and other researchers have determined that nearly two-thirds of some 57 species of nonmigratory European butterflies are similarly dying out on the southern edges of their ranges. Of course, the implications of this research go far beyond butterflies. Broadening the scope, Parmesan teamed up with the economist Gary Yohe at Wesleyan University to analyze a profusion of new biological studies she helped inspire. Combing the literature and applying stringent criteria to data on nearly 1,700 species of plants and animals, Parmesan and Yohe found strong scientific evidence *that some 52 percent of all the wild species studied to date showed signs of having been affected by global warming.* The evidence, Parmesan says, is "more pervasive and widespread than almost any biologists expected." Parmesan and Yohe's 2003 paper in *Nature* is still one of the most widely cited articles in the field of ecology, providing some of the strongest statistical evidence yet that global warming is having a broad impact on Earth's life forms. Research such as Parmesan's shows that accelerated global warming may lead to possibly irreversible consequences and even the extinction of many species.

Standing at the Crossroads

As even this brief review shows, the evidence that global warming is underway is not just persuasive, it's overwhelming—the scientific equivalent of a slam dunk. Anyone who says otherwise is full of, well, hot air. The more we learn, the more we recognize that humanity really does stand at a crossroads today. Our failure to address this problem will imperil us all. The evidence is accumulating from diverse disciplines and from research teams in every corner of the globe. It is worth noting that the great majority of the scientists conducting this research do so out of passion for their subject matter, not as part of any political policy debate. Most of them would love nothing more than to find evidence that global warming is abating. But as we have seen, that is emphatically not the case.

That's why it is so important—not just to our environment but also to our democracy—for each of us to learn as much as we can about the facts of global warming. The widespread lack of public understanding causes

45

problems in several ways. First, it creates a gap between the nation's citizens and the experts who study the problem on their behalf. Some climate scientists are so immersed in their specialized research they may forget that the public is not as conversant as they are with "carbon sinks" and "radiative forcings." They don't realize that most of us have never had a strong grasp of the basics.

But there is a more insidious problem, too: the lack of public understanding allows some powerful interests to milk the confusion so they can keep profiting from business as usual. This is not some wild conspiracy theory; it's documented fact. A report published by the Union of Concerned Scientists in 2007, for instance, clearly demonstrates how ExxonMobil has, for years, poured millions of dollars into purposefully manufacturing uncertainty on climate change by underwriting the work of discredited spokespersons whose work couldn't pass muster in legitimate, peer-reviewed scientific journals. Drawing on techniques perfected by the tobacco industry in the 1960s, ExxonMobil has worked behind the scenes to create or fund organizations with legitimate-sounding names—like the Committee for a Constructive Tomorrow or the Center for Science and Public Policy—specifically to publicize discredited views that are not supported by the science and to make their handpicked faux experts available to the media.

Of course, ExxonMobil is not the only player to employ this cynical tactic. But unfortunately for all of us, the disinformation has been remarkably effective in encouraging many people to believe there is some controversy or doubt among scientists about global warming when, in fact, there has been an overwhelming consensus for many years that the burning of fossil fuels by humans is driving disruptive climate change.

Thankfully, there's an easy way to thwart overt disinformation. People who are informed about the facts won't be misled by Exxon-style campaigns.

And as we put together the big picture from the disparate strands of evidence about global warming, it becomes increasingly clear that with carbon dioxide emissions on track to increase by some 43 percent above

2007 levels by the year 2035 (according to the U.S. Energy Information Administration), doing nothing is really not a viable option.

For one thing, evidence is mounting that global warming is leading to an increase in the incidence of extreme weather events. With rising temperatures, strong data already link global warming trends to an increase in the number and severity of heat waves. But the evidence also shows that the severity of intense precipitation events is increasing as well. This is because global warming is causing more evaporation of ocean water into the atmosphere as well as increasing the amount of water vapor the atmosphere can hold. High levels of water vapor in the atmosphere in turn create conditions more favorable to heavier precipitation in the form of intense rain and snowstorms. According to a recent assessment, for instance, between 1958 and 2007 the amount of rain or snow falling in the heaviest storms in the northeastern United States *increased, on average, by 67 percent.*

Similarly, while the data are still evolving on the link between global warming and hurricanes, the latest science suggests that hurricanes developing on the Atlantic Ocean are likely to diminish in total number but increase in intensity and drop more flood-producing rains inland, making it more likely for them to cause damage to populated regions.

There is no question that we will need to undergo a major transformation to contend with climate change. To be sure, there are many hopeful signs of this transformation. But given the number of powerful interests standing in the way, it is unlikely to happen quickly enough to avert the most devastating results of a warming planet unless there is pressure from the ground up on governments and corporations. They will need to step up and do more, but they are unlikely to do so until they see this groundswell. Making changes in your life to reduce your emissions sends an important signal to many others near and far. In other words, you have the power to make significant changes. And there's no time to waste.

PART II

MAKING EFFECTIVE
CLIMATE CHOICES

CHAPTER 4

Driving Down Emissions

If all the cars in the United States were placed end to end,
it would probably be Labor Day Weekend.

—Doug Larson

There's no point in searching your house for the largest contribution you make to climate change: the culprits are most likely parked in your driveway. If you are like the average American, driving accounts for about one-quarter of your total carbon emissions. There is simply no getting around the fact that our cars are a sizable piece of the global warming problem.

Today in the United States, there are roughly 240 million cars and light trucks on the road, traveling a mind-boggling 2.7 trillion miles annually. *That's enough miles to make more than 14,000 round-trip voyages to the sun.* And almost every one of those miles is driven by burning gasoline made from oil—with all of its serious drawbacks, from price spikes that spur recessions to reliance on a world oil market that entangles our nation in the politics of some of the most volatile regions of the world. Little wonder a string of U.S. presidents, stretching back at least to Richard Nixon, have lamented the nation's "addiction" to oil.

Not surprisingly, our national dependence on automobiles that burn gasoline has also inflicted some of the most consequential and damaging impacts on our planet. Each year in the United States, our cars are responsible for emissions of about 1.6 billion tons of carbon dioxide and other heat-trapping gases into the atmosphere. All by itself, this amount represents a significant share of the entire world's global warming emissions.

And if the sheer scale of heat-trapping emissions from Americans' cars weren't enough, the story gets worse in the larger context. Compared

Figure 4.1. Emissions from Transportation

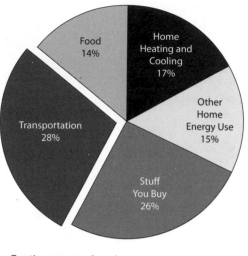

*For the average American, car use accounts for
more than one-quarter of total carbon dioxide
emissions.* Source: UCS modeling.

with the rest of the world, the gas-guzzling cars in this country represent
one of the planet's most lopsided resource hogs. According to one 2006
study, the United States, with less than 5 percent of the world's population, is responsible for about 45 percent of the world's automotive carbon
dioxide emissions.

It is almost impossible not to feel dwarfed by the immense scale of the
global warming emissions from our cars. But as vast as the problem is,
it results from a myriad of individual decisions—including the ones *you*
make every day. With the help of the recommendations in this chapter,
each of us can take care of our personal share of this global problem and
start to become part of the solution.

The first thing to consider is that when all stages of production and
combustion are counted, every single gallon of gas a car burns emits
nearly 25 pounds of carbon dioxide and other global warming gases
into the atmosphere. About 5 pounds of that come from the extraction
of petroleum and the production and delivery of the fuel. But the great

---

How Can a Car's Emissions Weigh More Than the Gasoline That Went into the Tank?

In considering all the emissions that vehicles cause, from the production of oil to the use of fuel, the UCS Climate Team calculates that the average vehicle emits nearly 25 pounds of carbon dioxide for each gallon of gasoline it uses. Of this amount, oil drilling and the refining and distribution of gasoline account for nearly 5 pounds of global warming pollution per gallon; burning the gas in your car's engine emits another 19.6 pounds of carbon dioxide directly from the exhaust pipe.

Since a gallon of gasoline weighs only about 6 pounds, how can it possibly produce more than three times its weight in emissions? The answer relates to the fact that gasoline is densely packed with carbon. When gasoline burns, its carbon is released into the air, where it combines with oxygen to form carbon dioxide. In CO_2, each carbon atom bonds with two oxygen atoms (as you remember from high school chemistry, that's what the "2" stands for). Oxygen has a higher atomic weight than carbon, so in a molecule of carbon dioxide, most of the weight comes from the two oxygen atoms. As a result, the heat-trapping carbon dioxide weighs just over three times more than the carbon it contains.

---

bulk of automobile heat-trapping emissions—more than 19 pounds per gallon—comes right out of a car's tailpipe.

As the box explains, it is a fact of chemistry that a gallon of gasoline weighing just over six pounds can release more than three times that amount of pollutants into the air. An average driver is responsible for about twice his or her own weight in carbon dioxide for every tankful of gas used. That's several hundred pounds of heat-trapping emissions the atmosphere would be far better off without.

A car that is driven 12,000 miles per year (about the national average) and that gets roughly 20 miles per gallon, or mpg (also about the real-world national average), is responsible for *more than seven tons of carbon dioxide annually*. That's approximately three and one-half times the car's weight in heat-trapping emissions into the atmosphere each year. And those seven tons per year are harming the planet.

So that's the bad news.

The good news is, you can do something about it. The cars we buy and our driving habits are so resource inefficient that they represent some of the "lowest-hanging fruit" available to those of us seeking to reduce our emissions. Many of us could go a long way toward the first-year goal of a 20 percent reduction in our carbon footprint just by making some simple changes in how we get around. If you are serious about reducing your carbon emissions, the vehicle you drive and your driving habits are great places to start.

While the gas-powered automobile is deeply embedded in Americans' current way of life, it hasn't always played such a central role, and its present status need not be permanent. In the United States, we've had a longstanding love affair with automobiles for the convenience, mobility, and autonomy they offer (not to mention the aura of glamour they hold for many people). Today, it is hard to remember that less than a century ago railroads were the backbone of the U.S. transportation system, and not just for freight. In 1920 (the peak year of U.S. train ridership, aside from a brief surge during World War II), the average American took some 150 trips per year on local rail systems and another 12 train trips from one city to another.

Since that long-ago time, we've become more dependent on our fleet of cars than ever. And there are a lot more of them than ever before, too. As recently as 1950, there were only enough cars on the road for 28 percent of the population to drive one. Today, there are twice as many Americans, but the number of vehicles is equal to some 80 percent of the population—that's more cars than there are people licensed to drive them.

Even more than the number of cars we own, our automobile dependence is reflected in the statistics on how much we drive. Commuting offers a good example. In 1960, just 64 percent of Americans commuted to work by car, while 22 percent took public transportation or walked. By

---

UCS Climate Team FAST FACT

On average, your car emits seven tons of carbon dioxide into the atmosphere each year—about three and one-half times the vehicle's weight.

2009, the number of public transit users and walkers had fallen to 8 percent, with 92 *percent* of Americans driving to work each day. Even carpooling is down: according to the latest figures, more than three-quarters of all American workers drive to work each day alone in their cars, while only 10 percent carpool—half of what it was 30 years ago.

The good news is that some things are starting to change. For one thing, requirements are now in place to deliver a boost of roughly 25 percent in new car fuel economy by 2016, and automakers are on record supporting a proposal to nearly double fuel economy by 2025. At the same time, we stand on the verge of an exciting transition in the auto industry. The battery-electric Nissan Leaf and the gas-electric, plug-in hybrid Chevrolet Volt are now on the showroom floor, and most major car companies have announced plans to offer models driven partially or completely by batteries or fuel cells within the next few years. We will discuss these choices in more detail shortly, but the important thing to remember is that while electric-drive vehicles—battery, fuel cell, and plug-in hybrid electric cars—won't take over the car market overnight, they could combine with fuel economy improvements and better fuels as part of a revolution that helps to dramatically cut urban smog-forming pollution, reduce U.S. global warming emissions by 80 percent or more, and effectively end our addiction to oil.

Such a change will very likely take decades, but revolutionary changes in transportation have happened surprisingly quickly before. It is worth remembering that American consumers were still skeptical about gas-powered cars back in 1908, when Henry Ford unveiled his company's Model T. Within just six years, however, Ford had produced more cars than all other automakers combined, and the era of gas-powered vehicles had swept the nation.

What You Can Do

Starting now, you can make many changes, large and small, to lower your transportation emissions. None is especially hard. Most will save money; some will even improve your health. This chapter will review four overlapping strategies to reduce your personal contribution to global warming. But let's start with the big-ticket item that could probably make the most dramatic difference.

BUY A FUEL-EFFICIENT CAR

It doesn't happen often, but once every several years you make a decision that has an enormous, lasting impact on your energy use and carbon emissions: you buy a car. Whether you are buying a car for the first time or replacing one you currently own, think long and hard. The choice you make in the showroom or on the used car lot will determine your emissions for as long as you own and drive that vehicle. Of course, we all know that some cars get better gas mileage than others. But if you're like most Americans, this fact has not played a big enough role in your car-buying decisions in the past. This time around, it should. This section shows what a big difference a fuel-efficient car can make to the environment—and to your pocketbook.

Let's walk through the data.

The 240 million cars and light trucks on the road in the United States today consume about 130 billion gallons of gasoline annually. That puts a big burden on our climate when it comes to global warming emissions. But in a good year for the auto industry, about 16 million of those cars and light trucks are replaced with new ones, and about two and a half times as many exchange hands in the used car market. So every year there are about 55 million opportunities for Americans purchasing a car to influence the automobile market and emissions for decades to come.

What does this mean for you? Well, when it's time to buy a car, choose the most fuel-efficient model that meets your *ordinary* transportation needs. Sure, you'd like to be able to haul a heavy trailer if you move to a new apartment, and you'd like to have room for your entire extended family when you take a vacation. But on those occasions, you can rent a pickup truck or an extra-large SUV. Buying a vehicle for those infrequent needs is expensive and will waste a lot of fuel along the way.

When we think about it, we probably don't all need to drive a three-ton behemoth to complete our routine tasks, such as getting to work and picking up groceries. Unless we have a big family or a home-based business, most of our routine tasks can be accomplished with a modest-sized, fuel-efficient car. Not only will it dramatically reduce emissions, it will save money every time we drive over the life of the car.

Remember, too, that while the size of the car is important, it is not the only factor affecting fuel efficiency. The diminutive Smart Car, distributed by Mercedes-Benz, may be the best choice for squeezing into tight urban parking spaces, for example. But it may not be the smartest choice for saving gas: in 2011 the U.S. Environmental Protection Agency (EPA) rated the tiny two-seater at 36 mpg, while the Honda Civic Hybrid, with seating for five and more than twice the passenger volume, was rated at 42 mpg.

The key point to remember is that all other things being equal, a more fuel-efficient car pollutes less. When you start looking at the data, you may be surprised by the difference fuel efficiency makes to the environment. The U.S. Department of Energy and the EPA publish official estimates of city, highway, and average gas mileage for each model of car sold in the United States. The accuracy of these mileage estimates has been debated, but they provide a useful standard of comparison. For the latest information on fuel efficiency, be sure to visit the agencies' joint website at www.fueleconomy.gov before purchasing your next vehicle.

A review of the site's data about commonly purchased cars in the 2011 model year reveals that you could buy anything from a Toyota Prius, rated at 50 mpg—the highest fuel economy gasoline car—to a GMC Yukon four-wheel-drive SUV, rated as the year's worst SUV on fuel economy, at 12 mpg.* The difference in emissions between these vehicles is much larger than you might imagine.

Assume the car is driven the average American's 12,000 miles a year. If the car is a Prius, rated at 50 mpg, it will emit less than 3 tons of carbon dioxide per year; if a GMC Yukon (or a similar large SUV) drives the same distance, it will emit 12 tons per year—*four times* more. The difference is 9 extra tons of carbon dioxide emitted every year for the lifetime of the car.

---

*Most pickup trucks (and some oversized vans, as well as a few high-end luxury sports cars) are not included in these figures, and many get in the range of 9 to 11 mpg. From the standpoint of carbon emissions, your best bet is to avoid driving a pickup truck unless your livelihood depends on it.

But Aren't SUVs Safer?

Large, heavy sport-utility vehicles, looming over smaller cars on the road, aren't inherently safe, even if they look like they should be. It seems like common sense: from the point of view of protecting the passengers, isn't it better to be inside a big, heavy hunk of metal rather than a smaller, lighter one?

The data suggest that bigger and heavier does not mean safer. One large-scale study of children injured in motor vehicle accidents found that the most important variables for kids' safety are proper use of seat belts and keeping the children out of the front seat. The study found that the increased tendency of SUVs to roll over offset any benefit of their greater weight, such that children's injury rates were about the same in SUVs and in cars.

In fact, a detailed statistical analysis of traffic fatalities and serious injuries from 2000 to 2007 found that vehicle design and other factors (e.g., driver age, rural driving) had much larger roles in vehicle safety than did size and weight. For example, the drivers of compact crossover vehicles (car-based vehicles that ride lower to the ground and have the functionality of SUVs) had a lower risk of a fatality or serious injury than the drivers of bigger and heavier SUVs. Making matters worse for SUVs, the same study found that they also put other drivers at a greater risk of fatality.

The National Highway Traffic Safety Administration tests vehicles to make sure their designs are safe, and it provides a simple five-star rating system available at www.safercar.gov. So, when you are in the market for a vehicle, keep your eyes on the safety stars, not the size and weight of the vehicle. And when you are on the road, make sure everyone is buckled up and in the right seat, and drive defensively.

The foregoing example is an extreme one: the Prius is, of course, quite a bit smaller than the Yukon. But even switching from a more modest-sized SUV to a Prius or another fuel-efficient hybrid car could easily cut your emissions in half. Either way, the reductions in emissions—and savings in gasoline costs over the life of the car—are dramatic.

How dramatic?

To keep the numbers simple, let's compare one car that gets 40 mpg with another that gets 20 mpg. In 2011, some seven models reached or exceeded 40 mpg, and the number of such new fuel-efficient models

Figure 4.2. Vehicle Emission Comparison

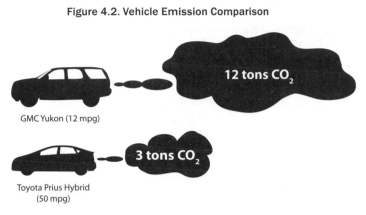

GMC Yukon (12 mpg)

12 tons CO$_2$

3 tons CO$_2$

Toyota Prius Hybrid
(50 mpg)

By trading in that SUV for a Toyota Prius or another fuel-efficient hybrid, you'll emit just one-quarter to one-half as much carbon dioxide when you drive—keeping some six to nine tons of carbon dioxide out of the atmosphere every year for the lifetime of the car. Source: UCS Modeling.

will almost surely grow in the future. The alternative, 20 mpg, is around the national average for old and new cars combined; in 2011, you could buy that level of relative fuel inefficiency in many new models of pickup trucks and SUVs and even in cars such as the Ford Fusion all-wheel drive, rated at 19 mpg, or the Subaru Outback, rated at 20 mpg, not to mention virtually any car with a V8 engine, such as the Ford Mustang, which even in 2011 weighed in at 17 mpg.

First, let's compare how much gas the two cars will use. At 12,000 miles per year of driving, the 40-mpg car will need

$$\frac{12{,}000 \text{ miles}}{40 \text{ mpg}} = 300 \text{ gallons}$$

For the same amount of driving, the 20-mpg car will need

$$\frac{12{,}000 \text{ miles}}{20 \text{ mpg}} = 600 \text{ gallons}$$

If you buy the 40-mpg car instead of the 20-mpg one, you will save 300 gallons of gasoline every year. That's enough to avoid almost 3.8 tons of emissions per year, nearly reaching your 20 percent goal with just one

---

Can the Auto Industry Make More Fuel-Efficient Cars?

The short answer is *yes.*

Increasing the fuel efficiency of new cars and trucks is a critical step toward cutting America's oil dependence and reducing carbon emissions. Expert assessments from the Massachusetts Institute of Technology (MIT); the University of Michigan; the University of California, Davis; and the EPA show that we have the know-how to put the needed technology to work. The studies by researchers at MIT and UC Davis show that if manufacturers applied basic clean car technologies to all cars (such as improved engine efficiency and aerodynamics), they could reduce today's average vehicle fuel use and emissions by 45 percent over the next 20 years; making use of hybrid vehicle technology could achieve reductions of 60 percent over the same period. In both cases, the vehicles would deliver the same size, safety, and performance consumers enjoy today.

While automakers have the technology to increase fuel efficiency and reduce global warming pollution, they've often needed to be pushed, not just by consumers but also by government standards, to get this technology off the shelf and into the showroom. That's why the Union of Concerned Scientists has long been in the forefront of the movement for stronger federal fuel efficiency and global warming pollution standards, with current analysis urging standards that would cut new vehicle fuel use and emissions at least in half by 2025.

---

major purchase. Of course, the car will keep consuming gasoline until it is scrapped, perhaps 15 years or so after it is purchased. If you plan to own and drive the same car for 15 years, you're looking at a lifetime savings of 4,500 gallons of gasoline.

Even if you figure that the price of gas will stay around $3.50 per gallon over that time (an unlikely prospect because gasoline prices will probably rise in coming years), that's worth more than $15,000 during the life of the car. If gasoline prices rise to $4.50 per gallon, that would equal more than $20,000—either way, it represents a fair portion of the price of the vehicle. And at nearly 25 pounds of carbon dioxide emissions per gallon, the difference between these two vehicles amounts to a whopping *55 tons of emissions* over the lifetime of the vehicle.

Many people make decisions based on shorter time horizons. But even if you count only the fuel used in the next five years, the difference of 300 gallons per year means a total savings of 1,500 gallons. That will keep some 18 tons of emissions out of the atmosphere and save more than $5,000—and that's not counting the higher resale value of more efficient vehicles, according to the latest figures.

Whichever way you do the arithmetic, the 40-mpg car will save thousands of dollars at the gas pump and keep many tons of global warming emissions from the atmosphere. It's well worth remembering those numbers when you are ready to purchase your next car.

THINK BEFORE YOU DRIVE

As we have seen, fuel efficiency makes a huge difference in your share of carbon emissions from transportation. Still, no matter what kind of car you own, one of the smartest ways you can drive down your emissions is by *driving less*.

At least until the economic downturn in 2008, the statistics on our driving habits suggest that people have been doing precisely the opposite. Figure 4.3 tells the story. Since 1950, the U.S. population has doubled, and the number of cars on the road has more than quadrupled. But the biggest increase by far can be seen in our collective annual vehicle miles traveled, or VMT in transportation lingo. Since 1950, our VMT has increased more than six-fold. In other words, we don't just have a lot more cars; we're also driving them more than ever.

Americans' ballooning VMT is especially worrisome because unless we reverse the increase in miles driven, we will threaten the gains we might achieve from improved fuel efficiency.

When you look at the data, one fact jumps out: Americans are more dependent on cars than just about any other people on the planet. In the United States, more than 80 percent of all trips are taken by car and light truck, compared with 60 percent of all trips in Germany and 45 percent in the Netherlands. Sure, our country is big and spread out, with sparse public transit options in many areas. But a closer look at our habits reveals a good deal about how we rack up all that VMT. According to the latest

Figure 4.3. U.S. Increase in Vehicle Miles Traveled (VMT)

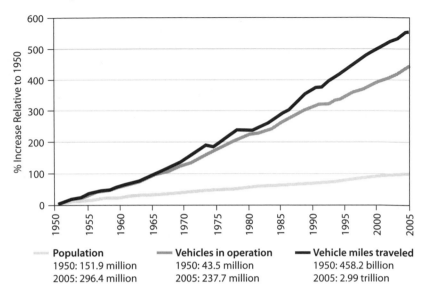

Population
1950: 151.9 million
2005: 296.4 million

Vehicles in operation
1950: 43.5 million
2005: 237.7 million

Vehicle miles traveled
1950: 458.2 billion
2005: 2.99 trillion

In the United States, the number of vehicle miles traveled has risen more than six-fold since 1950, faster than the growth in population or the increase in cars on the road. Source: UCS, adapted from Davis and Diegel, U.S. Department of Energy, *Transportation Energy Data Book*, 2007.

data from the U.S. Department of Transportation, more than 60 percent of all trips by car cover no more than six miles—and many are far shorter.

We've all done it: hopping in the car for a quick trip to the nearest mailbox and then, shortly after returning home, driving to the grocery store for that missing dinner ingredient. A simple strategy for driving less is "trip chaining"—the fancy term for taking that trip to the store or post office on your way home from work rather making a separate trip after you get home. Remember, every car trip not taken reduces your overall emissions and saves money on gasoline.

Suza Francina, a former mayor of Ojai, California, adopted a more dramatic strategy years ago to cut down on short trips. "When I learned that half of all car trips were less than three miles in length," Francina says, "I made a vow that, except for emergencies, I would make all trips within a three-mile radius on foot or bicycle." To follow through on her pledge, Francina purchased a bicycle trailer big enough for her weekly groceries. She says the benefits to her health alone have been well worth the extra effort.

Another strategy for driving less is for a family to try to share one car instead of owning two. Gina Diamond, a Seattle resident, made this choice in 2007. She and her husband junked one of their two cars—the older, gas-guzzling one they had inherited—and Gina, who works mostly at home, made the commitment to walk the mile and a half to take her daughter to and from preschool. She says she has sometimes had second thoughts about her decision on cold or rainy days. But the weather has never dampened her enthusiasm for the extra exercise and the relaxed time to chat with her daughter along the way.

Of course, a growing number of people, especially city dwellers and those near colleges, are finding that they can get along fine—and save a lot of money—by not owning a car at all. Their decision has been greatly aided in recent years by the growth of car-sharing companies such as Zipcar, which in 2011 boasted some 560,000 members and 8,000 vehicles in 60 U.S. cities and about 230 college campuses. A car sharer can easily locate the nearest Zipcar online or with a mobile phone app and rent it on the spot by the hour. This is a great option for those who make only occasional trips by car. Unlike car owners, users of such car-sharing services pay only when they use a vehicle. Not surprisingly, perhaps, one recent study found that regular users of car-sharing services traveled one-third fewer miles than their car-owning counterparts, who pay for their vehicles (in car payments, insurance premiums, and excise tax) whether they drive them or not.

Even if you don't want to switch to walking or biking for short distances and would rather not get rid of your car, you might consider simply leaving it at home one day a week and finding another way to get to work, such as carpooling or biking. The city of Boulder, Colorado, in conjunction with local businesses, is a proponent of that idea. Since the summer of 2010, Boulder's Driven to Drive Less program has enlisted residents to pledge to give up driving at least one day per week. In exchange, participants receive special perks and discounts from local stores and restaurants.

UCS Climate Team *FAST FACT*

In a program begun in Boulder, Colorado, in 2010, some 500 residents have pledged to leave their cars home one day per week. In return, they receive perks and discounts from local merchants. At average driving rates, this effort alone could keep some 500 tons of carbon dioxide from the atmosphere annually.

Aaron Kennedy, a Boulder restaurant owner, is both a participant in and a sponsor of the program. "It's liberating to leave my car at home," he says. "I don't have to find and pay for parking, watch my speed to avoid tickets, sit in stop-and-go traffic, or fill up my gas tank as often." Kennedy says he loves the exercise he gets by riding his bike and notes that it takes him only 20 to 30 minutes more to make his commute than it did in a car. He is so taken with the program that he has begun to leave his car home several days per week. And he is not alone. Within its first three months, this local program in a relatively small city had enlisted nearly 500 residents.

If you're thinking of leaving the car home one or more days per week, you might also talk to your employer about telecommuting. Recent figures show that the number of Americans who work from home is rising significantly. According to the U.S. Bureau of Labor Statistics, some 24 percent of the nation's workforce work from home at least one day per month, and as many as 9 percent work from home full-time.

Of course, telecommuting provides an environmental benefit by eliminating a round-trip vehicle trip and the emissions it would have caused. One analysis found that if over the next 12 years, the number of U.S. workers telecommuting full-time increased to 14 percent of the workforce, it could eliminate 136 billion vehicle travel miles annually, resulting in a 5 percent reduction in the nation's total car emissions.* So consider telecommuting at least part of the time as one possible strategy for driving less. Given that the average daily round-trip commute by car takes 48 minutes,

---

*Of course, working at home leads to emissions as well if you normally adjust the heat and keep lights off when nobody is home, but if you follow the tips in chapters 5 and 6, you can keep that to a minimum, guaranteeing real emissions savings.

working from home won't just save gasoline and reduce your emissions; it will save you precious time as well.

FILL 'ER UP WITH PASSENGERS

As noted earlier, another long-term trend in American vehicle use is how often we drive alone. As the number of cars has increased, average vehicle occupancy has declined. According to the U.S. Census Bureau's Journey to Work Survey, the proportion of single-occupant commuter trips increased from 64 percent in 1980 to 73 percent in 1990 and almost 76 percent in 2000. The number of people carpooling, meanwhile, has dropped. In 1980, nearly 20 percent of Americans carpooled to work. By 2009, the proportion using carpools had fallen to 10 percent.

The fact is, shared use of vehicles has declined in all categories of personal car travel. Across all automobile trips for all purposes, the average number of occupants per vehicle in 2009 was 1.7 persons, down from 1.9 in 1977.

If you're looking for one of the quickest and easiest ways to cut your transportation emissions in half, here it is: buddy up with friends and family and share rides.

Each additional car passenger adds only a small percentage to the vehicle's total weight, fuel use, and emissions. So with two people in a car, emissions per passenger-mile are only slightly more than half the amount with one person in the same car.

Of course, the same principle applies many times over on a bus or train, with an added bonus. When you decide to drive, you are putting an additional vehicle on the road. If you take a train or bus, in most cases you are occupying a seat on a vehicle that would have made the same trip without you. In that sense, you are contributing very few, if any, additional emissions to the environment.

Despite its decline in popularity, carpooling remains a smart and easy option, saving money and dramatically cutting carbon emissions. Interestingly, while the overall numbers of carpoolers are down, some new twists on the idea are gaining popularity. One is Internet-based ride sharing. Companies such as eRideShare.com and ride-sharing listings on www.craigslist.org make it more convenient than ever to find rides and riders, especially for longer trips.

Some pilot projects are even taking web-based ride sharing to new technological heights. One such nascent effort, called Avego, offers a smartphone app that allows "real-time ridesharing." In a pilot project begun in January 2011 in Seattle, the Washington State Department of Transportation is working with Avego to allow 250 drivers with GPS-enabled smartphones to offer the empty seats in their vehicles to some 750 similarly equipped riders along State Route 520. If a member of the program is driving on the highway, the software identifies anyone in the network who is looking for a ride at that moment and links the two. Once a match is made, the software facilitates the pickup and drop-off and even allows for electronic micropayments to allow riders to share the cost of the journey.

A lower-tech version of real-time carpooling, called "slugging," is also gaining popularity in some parts of California and around Washington, DC, which is notorious for its rush-hour traffic congestion. Commuters seeking a ride line up at designated spots known as slug lines. Cars pull up to the slug line if they need additional passengers to qualify for the three-person high-occupancy vehicle (HOV) lanes. The sluggers display signs or simply call out their destinations, which are always a generally understood drop-off point near a subway stop. No money is exchanged. The "sluggers" get a quicker ride for free, while the drivers get access to the less congested HOV lanes—and cut their carbon emissions by two-thirds.

With any ride-sharing program, personal safety is an important consideration, and participants should exercise caution. However you go about it, though, safely putting extra passengers in your car makes sense as a strategy to combat global warming.

DRIVE SMARTER

"Use your gas wisely." This slogan, which appeared on World War II ration cards, is still relevant today. Out on the not-so-open road, though, it is not always easy to carry out. We've all been there: bumper-to-bumper stop-and-go traffic; unexpected delays for road construction or accidents; way too many red lights; a car in front of us going inexplicably slowly on a day when we're running late and hoping to make up some time.

An all-too-common response to traffic congestion is to drive frenetically, a strategy that rarely gets us to our destination any faster. And it is surprising to learn how much gasoline it can waste. On the highway especially, stressed-out driving, such as repeated braking followed by sudden acceleration, can lower a car's gas mileage by as much as 30 percent, according to the EPA. Driving too fast will also cause your car to guzzle gas. Data from Oak Ridge National Laboratory's *Transportation Energy Data Book* indicate that driving at 75 miles per hour reduces your car's fuel economy by more than 20 percent compared with driving at 60 miles per hour. Smarter driving techniques can certainly help save gas and reduce emissions for most drivers. In case you have doubts, the city of Denver has the quantitative data to prove it.

In Denver's 2009 Driving Change program, the city outfitted some 400 local cars, including 160 city vehicles, with an Internet-based system that kept close track of how much gasoline each car was consuming as it operated. Participating drivers received detailed, individualized online information at their home computers about how they could improve their driving to reduce their carbon emissions. During the year the program was in operation, Denver found that on the basis of the feedback the system provided, participants cut their cars' overall carbon emissions by 10 percent.

One of the most notable findings of Denver's Driving Change program was that the feedback on emissions helped participants decrease their cars' idling time by more than one-third. According to one estimate, voluntary idling adds up to more than 100 million tons of carbon dioxide

---

UCS Climate Team *FAST FACT*

A high-tech Internet-based system tested in 2009 by the city of Denver offered real-time feedback to some 400 drivers about the emissions they were causing. Armed with the information, the drivers were quickly able to improve their driving— especially their idling—habits enough to reduce their emissions by 10 percent.

emissions annually in the United States alone, so it's easy to see the cumulative power of driving smarter.

Denver's tracking system gave participants a lot of valuable information. But you really don't need a fancy online readout to help you pay more attention to your driving habits. Here are six steps to smarter driving that can make a real difference to the climate:

1. *Keep your vehicle well tuned.* Simple maintenance—such as regular oil changes, air filter changes, and spark plug replacements—will lengthen the life of a vehicle as well as improve fuel economy and minimize emissions.

2. *Check your tires regularly.* Low tire pressure reduces a car's fuel efficiency by increasing the resistance its engine must overcome. Keeping your tires properly inflated will save fuel and lower your emissions. Also, when it's time to replace your tires, consider getting a set of low-rolling-resistance (LRR) tires. These tires may cost slightly more than traditional replacement tires, but by reducing rolling resistance by 10 percent, they can improve the gas mileage of most passenger vehicles by 1 to 2 percent.

3. *Speed up and slow down gradually.* Avoid jackrabbit starts. When coming to a stop, take your foot off the gas early so that you're slowing down even before you hit the brakes. On the highway especially, this technique can increase your car's fuel efficiency significantly.

4. *Remove the empty roof rack.* Don't leave luggage carriers or bike racks on the car when they are not in use. Cars are designed for aerodynamic efficiency; anything that changes the overall shape and creates air resistance will decrease gas mileage. According to the EPA, a roof rack can decrease a car's fuel economy by as much as 5 percent.

5. *Be weight conscious.* Items inside the car accelerate along with the car, and that means more fuel consumption. It's a good idea to remove unnecessary items from the trunk or backseat. For every 100 pounds of extra weight in a vehicle, fuel economy decreases by 1 to 2 percent.

ASK THE EXPERTS

Open the Windows or Turn On the A/C?

Maybe you have had this debate: the environmentalist in your car wants to turn off the air conditioner in hot weather and open the windows instead, arguing that the air conditioner draws extra power from the engine, using more gas and thus increasing your emissions. Is it true? Will the car use less gas without the air conditioner, or will opening the windows create enough aerodynamic drag to offset any savings?

Technically, the environmentalist may be right. A road test in a Honda Accord by *Consumer Reports* in 2008 found that the air conditioner reduced gas mileage by about 3 percent at 65 miles per hour, while open windows had no measurable effect on gas mileage. As a practical matter, though, neither choice will make as much of a difference as most of the other recommendations in this chapter, especially in a newer car. Automotive air-conditioning has become more efficient in recent years, and new models use considerably less power than older ones did. So in this case, don't sweat it either way. Save gas in other ways and cool your car by whichever method helps you drive most comfortably and carefully.

---

6. *Don't idle.* During start-up, a car's engine burns some extra gasoline. But letting an engine idle for more than a minute burns more fuel than turning off the engine and restarting it. Today's fuel injection vehicles (which have been the norm since the mid-1980s) can be restarted frequently without engine damage and need no more than 30 seconds to warm up even on the coldest winter days.

Fueling Our Future

Although the overwhelming majority of cars on America's roads run on conventional unleaded gasoline, there are other fuel options currently available, with a wider array of choices on the horizon. Let's take a moment to see how some of these fuels stack up in terms of carbon emissions, starting with conventional fuels and working up to exciting emerging options such as cars powered by electricity from batteries or hydrogen fuel cells.

Conventional gasoline usually comes in three octane grades—87, 89, and 91—more commonly known as regular, midgrade, and premium. From a climate perspective, the only misconception to clear up is that premium gas will not help your car achieve better fuel economy. Gone, too, are the days when premium gasoline was the only grade to contain detergents that were supposed to help maintain an engine. The fact is, premium-grade gas costs more, and producing it typically uses more energy, so it may actually raise overall emissions slightly. The bottom line: use the grade of gasoline that the manufacturer recommends for your vehicle.

Diesel is no longer the "dirty fuel" it was several decades ago. An increasing number of car models running on today's diesel boast better efficiency and higher fuel economy than equivalent gasoline-powered cars. If you are in the market for a new car, these vehicles could be a good choice, especially if you do a lot of highway driving, where their fuel efficiency tends to excel. From a climate perspective, however, there is an important catch: diesel is more carbon intensive than conventional gas, so a car running on diesel will cause carbon emissions 10 to 15 percent higher than a car running on conventional gas that has the same gas mileage. To compare diesel models with those that run on regular gas, in other words, discount the fuel economy of the diesel vehicle by 10 to 15 percent to estimate the amount of carbon emissions it will produce, or just get the actual data from www.fueleconomy.gov. When you do that, you will see that many diesel cars are still a good choice as far as global warming is concerned, although there may be efficient gasoline, or gas-electric hybrid, options that will do just as well or better.

With either gasoline or diesel, however, you should be aware that when it comes to carbon emissions, both of these fuels are getting dirtier. We've tapped most of the easy-to-reach oil, so to keep up with rising demand we are pumping oil from deeper wells and separating oil from tar sands. Turning the latter into gasoline and burning it in a car results in roughly 15 percent higher carbon emissions than using conventional oil does. Even worse, some companies are now pushing to essentially squeeze oil from rocks—oil shale and coal—which would lead to twice the carbon footprint per gallon of today's gasoline.

Natural gas is an option for some car models on the market in 2011.

The Honda Civic, for instance, comes in a natural gas model that delivers about a 15 percent reduction in global warming emissions (based on data from www.fueleconomy.gov)—about half the benefit of the Civic hybrid. Natural gas is cheaper than gasoline, but the vehicles that run on it are more expensive than their gasoline and hybrid counterparts. Also, there's not much infrastructure for fueling these vehicles, making them a better option for fleets of cars or trucks with a dedicated refueling station. An added consideration is that natural gas is increasingly produced by hydraulic fracturing techniques, popularly known as "fracking," that pose real potential risks for increased leakage—natural gas, with its high methane content, is significantly more potent than carbon dioxide when it is released directly into the atmosphere—as well as potential impacts on groundwater. If you are an average consumer and want to focus on benefits to the climate, natural gas will deliver real benefits but is probably not your best vehicle choice.

Biofuels could play an important role if the technology for sustainable "low-carbon" biofuel works out. The driving idea behind biofuels is that they can—theoretically, at least—offer a carbon-neutral fuel source because the emissions caused by burning them are offset by the carbon dioxide taken up by the crops grown to make the fuel in the first place.

At many gas stations across the country, biofuels—in the form of ethanol made from corn—are already mixed into conventional gasoline at levels of up to 10 percent (and soon 15 percent for more modern cars). Some cars can also run on E85, a blend of 85 percent ethanol and 15 percent gasoline. But because there are very few fueling stations now offering this product, few of the consumers who buy those cars currently fill up with it. *Ethanol* has for some time been touted as an answer to the nation's growing demand for automotive fuel. The United States is, after all, spectacularly good at growing corn. Before the ethanol boom of recent years, U.S. farmers produced more corn than anyone wanted to buy, depressing prices and leading to expensive government subsidies for growers.

Unfortunately, despite the appeal of using excess corn to create a renewable fuel, corn-based ethanol hasn't lived up to its hype. For one thing, American agriculture itself runs on fossil fuel. Fertilizers and pesticides are produced in energy-intensive facilities, using petrochemicals. Farm machinery burns diesel fuel, as do the trucks that transport materials to farms and harvested crops to markets. (For more about emissions from agriculture, see chapter 7.) As a result, corn-based ethanol today leads to the same global warming emissions as, or even more than, gasoline.

Yet another challenge is that we don't produce nearly enough corn to power our vehicles. We already turn about one-third of our corn into ethanol, and even if we used the entire U.S. corn crop, it could replace only about 20 percent of the gasoline we use for transportation today. Long before that point, increased production of corn-based ethanol threatens to eat into food supplies and force up food prices, especially in a global market. As it is, there are serious concerns about the extent to which the ethanol boom is helping drive up global food prices, which are already stressed by floods, droughts, and increased demand for carbon-intensive products such as meat.

A better long-run vision for biofuels involves a new technology known as *cellulosic biofuel*. This offers the promise of creating fuel from garbage, wood wastes, and fast-growing plants such as switchgrass, which can be grown on land unsuitable for food production. Unfortunately, the cellulosic biofuel manufacturing process is still in its infancy, so it will take time for this fuel to have an impact on transportation emissions. Still, cellulosic biofuel does offer significant potential to lower our transportation-related carbon emissions, and it could well become a more viable fuel option in the years to come.

Electricity is, without doubt, the most exciting fuel option coming to the American car market. With the Nissan Leaf and Chevrolet Volt leading the way, electric-drive vehicles could be the start of a revolution, helping to dramatically reduce U.S. global warming emissions and effectively end our oil addiction. But to make such a revolution a reality, we will need patience, consumer interest, and smart government policies. Electric-drive vehicles won't solve global warming overnight. But their long-term potential is so great that they are worth careful consideration when you think about purchasing your next vehicle.

Electric vehicles are, at present, expensive to buy, but they can save a lot of money on fuel—around $15,000 over the life of the car, compared with a 20-mpg gas car at $3.50 per gallon. State and federal tax breaks can make electric vehicles even more affordable. In the longer term, as the technology takes hold, research and economies of scale are likely to lower their sticker prices substantially. If you are considering one of the electric vehicles that need to plug in, bear in mind, however, that most American homes will need to upgrade at least some of their electric wiring to effectively support it.

Battery-electric vehicles, such as the Nissan Leaf, have a limited range on a single charge of their battery packs, but they could be a great option for commuting and city driving, especially as a second car for families that need two vehicles. The potential for fast charging could extend the range of battery-electric vehicles but would require significant infrastructure investments and may compromise some of the advantages. Their global warming benefits are superior to those of a good hybrid if the electricity is generated from natural gas, and they are emission free when recharged with electricity produced from renewable resources such as wind and solar power. If you live in a region that gets its electricity primarily from coal, however, a good hybrid will do more to cut emissions.

Plug-in electric hybrids, such as the Chevrolet Volt, still have a gasoline engine, but they also have an electric motor and a large battery pack so they can run on electricity from the power grid. This means that they have a great range because when their batteries get low, they can run on gas and operate just like a more conventional hybrid, with similar emissions. On the other hand, their gasoline usage will vary considerably, depending on which fuel they use. Like their all-electric counterparts, their potential for reducing emissions will depend on how the electricity used to recharge is produced. As long as you live in a region where electricity is not produced predominantly by coal, however, you can maximize your fuel efficiency impact by running these vehicles on electricity as often as possible, using them primarily for short and medium distances.

Fuel cell electric vehicles, such as the Honda Clarity, are expected to come to the broader car market by 2015. Instead of recharging batteries from the grid, they use fuel cells to combine hydrogen with air to generate electricity and water with no tailpipe emissions. The infrastructure to support them is starting to be built in southern California, where pilot programs are underway. There are a number of ways to create hydrogen, although many use fossil fuels and thereby create some amount of carbon emissions. Much as with battery-electric vehicles, using natural gas would lead to larger reductions in global warming emissions than would a good hybrid, while using renewable electricity, such as wind power, would nearly eliminate global warming emissions from cars. At this point, however, fuel cell vehicles are not an option for most car buyers.

One other thing to note as you consider an electric vehicle is that the otherwise very helpful www.fueleconomy.gov website does not yet give global warming information about these vehicles. Unfortunately, the government offers only a "miles-per-gallon equivalent," which tells little or nothing about the cars' global warming emissions. Although cars running on electricity don't emit carbon from the tailpipe (the Nissan Leaf famously doesn't even have a tailpipe), they are only as clean as the grid or the hydrogen from which they get their electricity.

We've tried to offer some rules of thumb to help you think about the potential global warming emissions benefits of electric-drive vehicles, but as we discuss further in chapter 5, the emissions generated from the production of electricity vary significantly, depending on where you live. Still, there is little question that when it comes to global warming, electric vehicles are likely to pave the way to a cleaner future.

Reduce Your Long-Distance Travel

American society is famous for its mobility and dynamism. Many families are spread out over long distances, and people frequently move to take jobs in different regions. Of course, this leads to a lot of long-distance travel. According to the U.S. Department of Transportation's Bureau of Transportation Statistics, Americans annually make some 2.6 billion trips of 50 miles or longer, which add up to a whopping 1.3 trillion person-miles of long-distance travel.

All of this long-distance travel causes a lot of carbon emissions. After all, a single round-trip flight from Los Angeles to New York emits around a ton of carbon dioxide per passenger—equal to the amount an average American SUV driver would be responsible for emitting in a month of average driving. What should you do if you want to cut your long-distance emissions?

First of all, consider any long-distance travel plans carefully. If you are flying for pleasure, perhaps you might take a vacation closer to home. If your destination is set and the distance is not too great, perhaps you can find a more environmentally benign alternative to air travel. Going by bus is among the least carbon intensive ways of traveling, and trains are comparatively carbon friendly. On a per-passenger basis, a train trip can emit as little as one-quarter the emissions of an equivalent journey alone in a large car. You might consider reducing your emissions by making fewer long trips to visit family and staying longer when you go.

Figure 4.4 compares carbon emissions for many modes of transportation used for longer trips, clearly highlighting the benefits to the climate from having more passengers regardless of the mode of transport.

As the graph shows, the only option for longer trips that beats taking an intercity bus is driving a Prius with a total of four people in the car. The next best choices are taking an Amtrak train if it runs as full as the airlines (shown as "Amtrak potential" in the graph) or driving a Prius with two people on board. Of course, if you are just commuting to work or around town and you have access to an urban bus or transit system, that may well be the best choice.

At the other extreme, the worst ways to travel, in terms of emissions per passenger-mile, are driving alone in a typical car and driving alone or with one other person in a typical SUV. These choices cause more emissions than flying the same distance, even in a less efficient regional jet.

When you do fly, consider that all types of air travel are not equal. A report by the Union of Concerned Scientists, "Getting There Greener," shows this clearly with an analysis of the emissions from various vacation travel options. Flying a family of four in first class from Chicago to Orlando for a vacation at Disney World, for instance, probably results in

Figure 4.4. CO$_2$ Emissions per 100 passenger miles

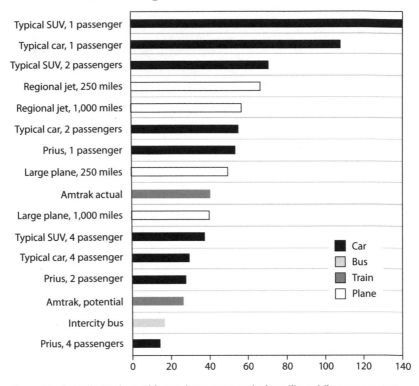

On a mile-for-mile basis, nothing reduces your emissions like adding passengers. This chart compares per-person carbon emissions for different modes of transportation on a 100-mile trip. Source: UCS modeling.

more carbon dioxide emissions than both parents would normally emit in a year's worth of commuting to and from work by car.

First-class and business-class seats, of course, take up a larger share of the plane's passenger space and are therefore responsible for a somewhat larger share of the plane's emissions. Flying coach or economy class is better for the environment. And, as the "Getting There Greener" report found, flying in economy class often results in lower emissions per mile than driving with one person in the car. And these days, the airlines tend to pack most flights as close as possible to capacity, which lowers the relative per-person emission rates even more. At least that's something to console yourself with the next time you are feeling squeezed on an over-crowded flight.

An option of growing popularity when traveling by air is to purchase so-called carbon offsets—essentially paying someone to engage in an activity, such as maintaining forested areas, that absorbs as much carbon dioxide as your flight will emit. We address the topic of carbon offsets in more detail in chapter 8. Suffice it to say here that offsets are a good idea; in general, however, the best strategy is to try to find ways to reduce your own emissions as much as you can.

Of course, realistically speaking, for long trips there is often no viable alternative to flying. And travel is an important component of both work and play; it is one of the ways we learn about the world and make connec-tions. Staying close to home is not always a reasonable option or a helpful recommendation.

Notably, even Colin Beavan, who in 2009 went to great lengths to live carbon neutral for a year, documenting his efforts in his blog, book, and documentary, *No Impact Man*, finally broke down when it came to visiting family for the holidays. For the entire year, Beavan, a Manhattan resident, had ridden his bike everywhere and even given up elevators in a city of skyscrapers. But he made an exception for a flight to Minneapolis with his wife and daughter.

For all the understandable fretting in the environmental literature over the carbon emissions from air travel, and despite the enormous amount of emissions a single airplane causes, it is worth remembering that passenger air travel accounts for less than 3 percent of total U.S. global warming emissions and less than 8 percent of household travel emissions. Even for long-distance travel, Americans still drive far more than they fly. Still, given the emissions involved in the average airplane trip, it pays to consider your options carefully.

As you consider the climate impact of your long-distance travel, one sector potentially ripe for reductions in carbon emissions is business travel, which represents over 40 percent of all long-distance trips. Ameri-

Figure 4.5. Breakdown of Transportation Emissions

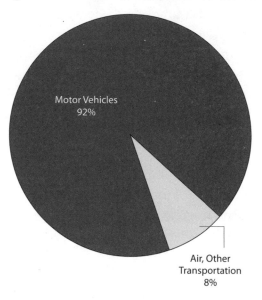

This chart shows the breakdown of total U.S. emissions in the transportation sector. Even for long-distance travel, Americans still drive far more than they fly. Source: UCS modeling.

cans take more than 405 million long-distance business trips per year. If you are flying a lot for work, you might find it relatively easy to reduce your emissions. Think about it. Are all your business trips really necessary? Maybe you could cut back on some trips or combine them to minimize your air travel. If a conference is not too far away, perhaps you could carpool with a coworker, greatly reducing your emissions.

Here again, technology is beginning to change the picture significantly. Advances in videoconferencing can dramatically reduce the need for business travel. As most firms know, sending a worker on a two-day trip to attend a meeting 500 miles away can easily cost $2,000 or more, taking into account the costs of accommodation, travel, and meals. Not only can high-quality videoconferencing save time and reduce those per-person costs by 90 percent or more; it can also greatly reduce the emissions caused by today's business travelers.

The Future of Transportation: It Needs to Look Different

The choices described in this chapter can help you lower transportation emissions, whether by buying a more fuel-efficient—or even electric—car, driving less and smarter, or flying less often and seeking lower-impact modes of long-distance travel.

But even if everyone followed all this advice, the choices currently in front of us are not enough. To prevent the worst outcomes of climate change and create a sustainable future, we need to build a transportation system for our grandchildren that looks very different from the one we have today but still allows people to go about their day-to-day business.

Transportation choices are closely linked to patterns of housing and urban development. Unlike many high-income countries, the United States is projected to have a growing population for the next several decades, so we will need to build new housing and new communities. The way these homes and communities are designed will make all the difference in our future transportation emissions. We'll discuss some of these bigger-picture considerations in later chapters. But there is no question that we must focus on creating cities that are centered on public transit and are bicycle and pedestrian friendly. We must develop highly efficient surface transportation between metropolitan areas that can minimize the need for air travel. Better planning is needed every step of the way, from local municipalities to the federal level.

A study in 2011 by the urban planning experts Ralph Buehler at Virginia Tech and John Pucher at Rutgers University shows that we already know how to make many of the changes needed to reduce our transportation emissions, and we know these changes can work to build thriving, sustainable communities. Buehler and Pucher closely studied the transportation choices made over the past 40 years by Freiburg, Germany. A city of 220,000 in the southwest of the country, Freiburg is known throughout Germany as the nation's most sustainable city. It offers a model that American cities could emulate. Over the past three decades, Freiburg has created a transportation system in which the number of bicycle trips has nearly tripled, public transport ridership has almost doubled, and the

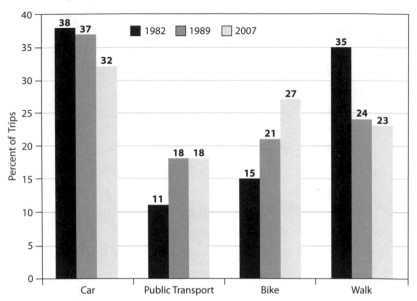

Figure 4.6. Transportation Modes in Freiburg, Germany

Shown here are trends in the percentages of trips made by car, public transportation, bicycle, and walking in Freiburg, Germany, between 1982 and 2007. Source: Adapted from Beuhler and Pucher, 2011.

share of trips by automobile has declined to 32 percent. The city has experienced strong economic growth and a dramatic drop in per capita carbon dioxide emissions from transport. To accomplish this, Freiburg officials created car-free pedestrian zones and restricted cars in the center of the city, upgraded suburban rail and regional bus services, and created more than 70 miles of bike paths.

Some U.S. cities, perhaps most notably Portland, Oregon, have already adopted a number of sustainable transportation and land use policies similar to the ones in Freiburg and many other cities.

Other trends from abroad are catching on in the United States as well. Amsterdam has long been famous for its high percentage of bicycle riders, and recently Paris has begun a high-profile bike-sharing program, which is catching on rapidly. Even the Parisian program, however, is dwarfed by the gargantuan bike-sharing program in Hangzhou, China, a city with a population nearing 7 million. Hangzhou's program boasts some 50,000 bikes at over 2,000 bike-share stations. With these bicycles, according to the program, Chinese riders now make an average of 240,000 trips each day.

Meanwhile, in 2008 Washington, DC, began Capital Bikeshare, the largest bicycle-sharing program to date in the United States, already boasting some 5,000 members. And New York City recently announced plans for a bike-share program with some 10,000 bikes and 600 kiosks.

Of course, we aren't suggesting that bicycles alone can solve the planet's global warming problem. One way or another, however, we need to create not only sustainable downtowns but also livable, walkable, bikeable suburban neighborhoods with transit connections to the rest of the metropolitan area and energy-efficient, high-speed intercity ground transit.

Getting to 20

In transportation, as in all areas where we need to reduce emissions, the long-term key is farsighted planning and decision making. As we work toward these goals, however, each of us needs to consider what we can do right now to move toward a sustainable future. We've already explained why reducing our emissions by 20 percent this year is an important goal. Since transportation accounts for such a large share of the average American's emissions, almost all of us will need to seek sizable reductions in the personal choices we make about how we get around.

Most of us can literally save tons of emissions (for years to come) with a single action: replacing an existing car with a far more fuel-efficient one. If that step is not practical this year (or your car already is fuel efficient), you can still get a long way toward the 20 percent goal by combining several strategies from this chapter that reduce the miles you travel, such as trip chaining, carpooling, leaving your car at home one or more days per week, changing your driving habits, and reducing your long-distance travel. By examining your own transportation choices and seeking out the best ways to reduce your emissions, you've already embarked on that journey.

CHAPTER 5

Home Is Where the Heat Is

What's the use of a fine house if you haven't
got a tolerable planet to put it on?

—Henry David Thoreau

Americans emit more carbon dioxide into the atmosphere by heating and cooling their homes than by any other single activity besides driving their cars. All told, residential heating and cooling systems in the United States emit about 500 million tons of carbon dioxide into the atmosphere each year. That's equivalent to the emissions of more than 100 midsized coal-fired plants.

All these emissions from heating and cooling also cost a lot. Most American households have annual energy costs of roughly $2,200, half of which goes toward heating and cooling. It is not uncommon, especially in colder climates, for the heating bill to make up two-thirds of a household's total energy expenditures. And many homeowners, especially those in larger, older houses, greatly exceed the national average, which includes condos, apartments, and other small dwellings.

The good news is, no matter where you live or what size home or apartment you have, you can reduce your emissions from heating and cooling and save money at the same time. A number of easy steps can pay quick dividends, lowering emissions and costs. And beyond these initial steps, various kinds of retrofitting can reduce heating and cooling emissions even more, making it possible to achieve a good portion of our suggested 20 percent reduction in your overall emissions in this category alone.

Figure 5.1. Emissions from Heating and Cooling

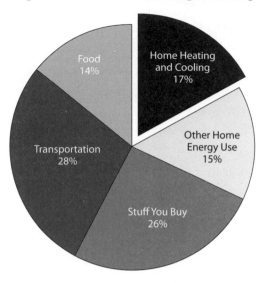

Household energy use accounts for roughly one-third of your total carbon dioxide emissions, and, on average, more than half of household emissions derive from heating and cooling. Source: UCS modeling.

In chapter 4, our first recommendation, given that most Americans are very dependent on their automobiles, was to purchase a more energy-efficient car. When it comes to heating and cooling, however, the same logic does not apply. It may well be time to replace your aging furnace or central air-conditioning system with a more efficient model. But most American homes are so leaky and energy inefficient that you can begin by taking some simple steps to address that issue. They won't cost a lot and will reduce your emissions right away.

The key is that it's not just a furnace or an air-conditioning system that keeps you and your family at a comfortable temperature; it's the whole house. In cold weather, a house functions as a building-sized blanket, offering insulation from the freezing temperatures outside. In hot weather, a home shields you from the worst of the heat and humidity outside.

The benefit of considering your whole house as an energy system is that we have long known that by building homes in smart ways and with enough insulation, we can greatly reduce heating and cooling costs. Homes that prove this have been built for many decades. Engineers at the Massachusetts Institute of Technology constructed a number of demonstration homes in the 1950s—*more than a half century ago*—that showed indisputably that solar energy alone could provide the bulk of a home's space-heating and water-heating needs, even in the Northeast, with its often cold temperatures and cloudy days.

The oil crisis of the 1970s spurred much more innovation in efficient building techniques. Among the projects undertaken were many varieties of so-called passive solar houses—well-insulated homes that used no solar photovoltaic panels but rather captured the sun's energy by means of the house's orientation, insulation, and window placement. In the early 1980s, a federal government study closely monitored the energy usage in some 70 passive solar homes that had recently been built. The study confirmed that heating these houses cost an average of 70 percent less than heating comparable conventionally designed homes. In 1979, an enterprising contractor named Eugene Leger built a nonsolar, conventional-looking home in East Pepperell, Massachusetts, using large amounts of insulation to save on heating costs. Leger's "superinsulated" home deservedly garnered a lot of attention for its annual natural gas heating bill of just $50 (about $160 in today's dollars).

Since those early successes, much more progress has been made in the United States and around the world in energy-efficient building techniques.

Take, for instance, the "tale of two houses" built in Lakeland, Florida, in 1998—one of scores of similar efforts around the country. To evaluate the potential of the latest green building techniques at the time, the Florida Solar Energy Center, a research institute of the University of Central Florida, built two homes side by side. Each was constructed by the same builder with the same floor plan and the same basic amenities, including air-conditioning. One of the homes, however, was the builder's standard model, while the other made use of energy-efficient materials and design. The energy-efficient house included more wall insulation, a

---

UCS Climate Team *FAST FACT*

We already have the technology we need to dramatically reduce emissions from heating and cooling in most residential and commercial buildings in the United States. If we committed ourselves to this task on a national scale, we could ultimately eliminate roughly 1 billion tons of carbon dioxide emissions into the atmosphere—enough to close roughly 215 polluting coal-fired plants.

---

white roof, a solar water heating system, a high-efficiency heat pump for heating and cooling, and a 4-kilowatt photovoltaic system, among other features. When the homes were completed and occupied, energy usage at each was monitored closely. After a year, the energy-efficient home's consumption from the electric grid was found to be *92 percent lower than that of the conventional house next door.* Although the efficiency and solar features added substantially to the construction cost, the experiment demonstrated the potential to radically reduce home energy usage with today's technology.

As these examples show, we have the technology we need right now to sharply reduce costs and emissions from heating and cooling in most residential and commercial buildings in the country. If we committed ourselves to the endeavor on a national scale, we could eliminate upward of 1 billion tons of carbon dioxide emissions into the atmosphere per year, which would allow us to shutter roughly 215 average-sized coal power plants altogether. Best of all, we would sacrifice nothing in the way of comfort; we could live and work in the same places we do now and be every bit as warm in the winter and cool in the summer.

Right now, in every part of the United States, from Maine to southern California, people are building new homes and retrofitting old ones to use little or no fossil fuel for heating and cooling. These "deep-energy-reduction" and "zero-net-energy" homes establish a new standard and an exciting goal that we can all move toward. Of course, they entail some substantial upfront expenditures. But the benefits are real and enticing: these buildings will virtually eliminate almost all heating and cooling costs—and emissions—from now on. Period.

Investing in Energy Efficiency

The potential of deep-energy-reduction houses provides a helpful yard-stick to measure the changes each of us could make in our own homes. We conventionally talk about the "payback period," the length of time it will take for the savings from improvements in energy efficiency to cover the upfront cost. This technique is helpful for prioritizing particular improvements. But a better way to think about these projects is as an investment, pure and simple. After all, the improvements do more than simply recoup the initial costs; most continue to pay dividends in energy savings for as long as you own your home and even make your home more valuable and desirable when it comes time to sell.

Few of us can choose to drive our heating and cooling costs to zero all at once. But no matter what our personal circumstances are, each of us can take steps toward energy efficiency that will make a big difference. If you have any doubts about that, just ask Anthony Malkin. He oversaw a retro-fit job, completed in 2010, that reduced his utility bill by nearly 40 percent.

In Malkin's case, though, that 40 percent reduction resulted in a yearly savings of *$4.4 million* in energy costs. That's because the building he ret-rofitted was the Empire State Building in New York City.

By employing up-to-date, energy-efficient materials and design, Malkin (whose firm manages the Empire State Building for a holding company) was able to adapt a 1930s energy hog of a skyscraper into one that ranks among the top 10 percent of all buildings in the nation for energy efficiency. And through this single effort, the Empire State Building's annual emissions of carbon dioxide will be reduced by more than 100,000 tons.

Granted, with some 2.7 million square feet of space, the building Malkin oversees is a bit bigger than your home. But the principles are exactly the same. Malkin's retrofit included installing heat reflectors behind the building's radiators and replacing windows (some 6,500 of them). He invested $18 million in energy efficiency. But not only will his investment be repaid in energy savings in the first four years, *it will continue yielding significant economic and environmental dividends for decades to come.*

UCS Climate Team *FAST FACT*

A 2010 retrofit of the Empire State Building in New York City, including replacement of the building's 6,500 windows, resulted in a 40 percent reduction in energy usage, saving $4.4 million—and 105,000 tons of carbon dioxide emissions—annually. The job will recoup its costs in just four years and continue to pay dividends in energy and emissions savings for decades to come.

To understand the power of Malkin's investment, look at it from a 10-year perspective. Even if energy costs stay flat (a highly unlikely assumption), Malkin will have turned his $18 million investment into $44 million worth of energy savings a decade from now—$44 million he would otherwise have had to spend. From that perspective, Malkin earned an annual return on his investment of more than 9 percent, or nearly $12 million more than he would have made from a 10-year bond yielding a 6 percent annual return. Plus, he modernized his building, making it even more attractive to tenants. Malkin understands all this, of course. He says he is happy for the environmental benefit, but he emphasizes that the changes made sense on purely economic grounds. As he put it, "It would have been bad business not to do this."

What You Can Do

Starting right now, you can make changes large and small to lower your carbon emissions from heating and cooling. The job begins by assessing your home heating and cooling systems and gauging their current level of energy efficiency.

Step one is to amass some basic information, starting with your utility bills and basic information about your home. What kind of fuel do you use to heat and cool your home? How much do you spend each year? Is your home insulated? Are your home's heating and cooling units efficient and up-to-date? The answers to these kinds of basic questions will start you on the path to energy savings.

To a large extent, the answers to basic questions about the way each of us heats and cools our home depend in part on where we live. While

Figure 5.2. Household Heating Systems in
the United States, by Type

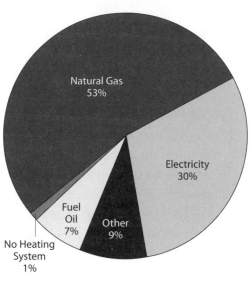

*Natural gas is the most common fuel for heating homes
in the United States, but different regions of the country have widely different profiles. The "other" category
includes homes heated with wood, propane, and renewable sources such as geothermal heat pumps and solar
energy.* Source: Adapted from U.S. Department of Energy, EIA.

natural gas is the most commonly used fuel for heating nationwide, there
are significant regional variations. In the South, for instance, electricity is
used for nearly all cooling and for heating in 44 percent of homes. Home
heating oil is hardly used at all except in the Northeast, where it is used
in some 36 percent of homes. Interestingly, though, despite the regional
differences in types of fuel, households in each part of the country spend
(very roughly) the same amount for heating and cooling.

Natural gas, the most commonly used fuel for furnaces, boilers, and
water heaters, has generally lower carbon dioxide emissions than other
heating fuels. When it comes to electricity, however, emissions vary tre-
mendously, depending on whether the electricity is produced by burning
coal (which emits the most carbon), oil, or natural gas. Electricity pro-

duced from renewable energy sources, of course, has the lowest emissions. We'll look more closely at electricity in the next chapter, including ways to buy green energy.

The next step is to assess your home's energy efficiency. The best way to do this is by arranging for a professional home energy audit, which can provide specific information about where the house is losing its heated or cooled air and what are the cheapest and easiest efficiency projects you might undertake. A professional energy audit can often be done free of charge or at a greatly reduced rate through your utility company or state energy office. If a free energy audit is not available, try the federal government's locator tool for energy-efficient builders in your area, most of whom could conduct an audit. Listings are available at www.energystar.gov.

There are also ways to get a sense of your home's energy efficiency on your own. One crude method is to tally up your energy bills for the past 12 months and divide by the square footage of livable space in your house (excluding your unfinished basement or attic). If you find that you're spending anywhere near $1 per square foot on total household energy, very likely you can do a lot to increase your energy efficiency. Some of the most efficient homes today have annual rates closer to 10 cents per square foot. Of course, fuel costs vary enough that you should not rely on this method as anything more than a very rough gauge.

More precise assessment methods can be found online. One offered by Efficiency Vermont, a Vermont-based energy efficiency agency, for instance, follows much the same method as outlined above but with a downloadable worksheet that helps convert your utility bills to compute how many Btu (British thermal units) your house uses per square foot.

A website with a notably different approach was developed at the Lawrence Berkeley National Laboratory in conjunction with the U.S. Department of Energy. This website (http://hes.lbl.gov/consumer) walks you through a series of questions about your home's location and age, the kinds of windows and insulation it has, and so on. On the basis of the information you provide, the online calculator estimates how much you spend on energy and also how much you could save from energy efficiency improvements. This more sophisticated approach is helpful if you have accurate information about your house, but if you don't, you can still get a reasonable estimate of your home's efficiency from one of the simpler tools listed above.

Having good information about your home's efficiency will help you decide how to reduce your heating and cooling emissions. The best ways to do this will depend on many factors, including the age of the house, the amount of insulation it has, and the age of the heating and cooling units. If you rent your living space, your choices for improvements will be more limited; after all, you're not going to replace your landlord's furnace to lower your heating bills. Still, there are a number of improvements that may be worth making, especially if you are paying the utility bills and care about lowering your emissions.

Broadly speaking, there are three overlapping strategies you can employ:

1. Changing your heating and cooling practices
2. Reducing heating and cooling losses by tightening up and insulating your house
3. Upgrading your heating and cooling systems

We will consider these strategies separately to highlight some of the specific reductions each one can offer.

Upgrade Your Thermostat—and Your Thinking

Let's start by addressing your heating and cooling habits. Do your thermostat settings accurately reflect the way you use your home? Are you needlessly heating or cooling the house while you are away or asleep? A programmable thermostat will allow you to set the temperature in your home to reflect your needs throughout the week, and installing one is very easy—you can probably do it yourself. This is one of the least expensive and most cost-effective steps you can take to lower your carbon emissions.

According to the latest available figures, only about one-third of the homes in the United States have programmable thermostats; if you don't have one, we urge you to make this modest investment, even if you rent your apartment but pay for utilities. Some of the latest models are Wi-Fi enabled, allowing you to control your home's heating and cooling from your laptop or smartphone; one new model from a California-based startup called Nest Labs even includes sensors to tell when you are in the house and claims to automatically learn your habits and adjust accordingly.

For many years, books and websites on energy efficiency have touted programmable thermostats as a way to save 15 percent on home heating bills. But those savings can be realized *only if occupants actually use the device to lower the heat (or reduce the cooling) while they sleep or are away from home.* It sounds obvious, of course, but the data indicate that a significant portion of people who have programmable thermostats don't take full advantage of their potential.

A much-discussed study in 1999 surveyed heating and thermostat use by residents of some 300 single-family homes in Wisconsin. While roughly one-third of the homes surveyed had programmable thermostats, study participants who did have them reported hardly any energy savings from them. Why? Follow-up interviews determined that many of those who had the devices weren't programming them to substantially lower the temperature at night, and fewer still were using them to lower the temperature while they were away during the day.

More recently, research by the U.S. Environmental Protection Agency (EPA) has found that even though roughly half of all American homes are empty during the day, nearly 60 percent of residents report leaving the heat or the air-conditioning on while they are away during working hours, and only 46 percent report adjusting their thermostats for the hours when they sleep.

Some people mistakenly believe that heating their house at a constant temperature around the clock takes the same amount of energy as bringing the temperature back to a comfortable point after the thermostat has been adjusted. For virtually all types of heating and cooling and all housing types, that is emphatically *not* the case. All you'll do by running the furnace or air conditioner while you are away is heat or cool the furniture. Your pets won't mind slightly cooler or warmer temperatures either.

Many people who leave their heating system or air conditioner at a constant setting would probably reconsider their habits if they realized how much money they could save. As a rough rule of thumb, each degree Fahrenheit that one adjusts a thermostat downward (for heating) or upward (for cooling) yields a 1 percent saving in heating or cooling costs over a seven- to eight-hour period, with a comparable reduction in carbon emissions.

During winter, in other words, if you lower the thermostat from 68 degrees Fahrenheit (a comfortable temperature during the hours when you are using your home) to 60 degrees for seven hours during the night and for the eight hours you are away during the day, you will lower your heating bill and heating-related emissions by about 15 percent. Considering that the average American spends about $1,100 on heating annually, this simple action can save you $180 this year alone while reducing your carbon emissions by more than half a ton. (If you have a big home in a northern state, you could save considerably more.) Best of all, you'll be every bit as warm as usual during the waking hours you spend at home.

A similar rationale applies for cooling. A setting of 78 degrees Fahrenheit is optimal during the hours you are occupying your home, and the EPA recommends settings of 85 degrees when you are away during the day and 82 degrees (or higher) during the night.

So, if you don't have a programmable thermostat, perhaps this analysis will encourage you to purchase one right away. Do it to lower your emissions, or do it because it will pay for itself within a few months and continue to save you money for years to come. And if you are one of the millions of Americans who have a programmable thermostat but have never bothered to set it correctly, now is a perfect time to do so. If you

---

UCS Climate Team FAST FACT

You can save 15 percent or more on your heating and cooling costs and lower your carbon emissions by more than half a ton annually just by using a programmable thermostat to adjust your home's temperature during the night and while you are away at work during the day.

aren't sure how, you can find step-by-step directions on the Internet for almost every model. If you're reading this book at home, seize the moment right now: head over to your thermostat and program it to work to its maximum potential. If it is already programmed, try adjusting it by a few more degrees for additional reductions in your carbon emissions. You can use the money you'll save to give yourself a reward. Or, better yet, invest the money in additional energy efficiency improvements to drive down your emissions even further.

While we're on the topic of heating and cooling habits, we should mention that another good way to reduce heating and cooling emissions is to heat or cool only the part of the house that you are using. It doesn't make much sense to heat or cool rarely used guest rooms and storage spaces. This "heat only what you use" attitude is widespread in many other parts of the world. In Japan, for instance, even affluent households heat only the main living area. In the bedrooms, small space heaters are turned on only when needed. This practice is one of the reasons Japan's per capita carbon dioxide emissions are half those of the United States.

If you heat with radiators, shut them off in rooms that aren't being used. Small electric space heaters are a good way to heat little-used rooms; just be sure to use them judiciously and to buy a model that automatically shuts off if it tips over, to avoid a fire hazard. Similarly, a room air conditioner can be turned on to cool an unused room only when guests arrive. Depending on the type of heating system you have, it might be worth retrofitting to create separate zones with their own thermostats so you don't have to heat the whole house when you are using only part of it. Ask your plumber or energy auditor if this is feasible in your home.

Tighten Your Home: a.k.a. Don't Heat (or Cool) the Neighborhood

Now that you've adjusted your thermostat, it's time to take the next step: eliminating the air leaks in your home. Doing this is easier—and more effective—than it sounds.

Hot air leaking out of our homes in winter and coming in during summer wastes more energy than most of us would ever imagine. Even in reasonably tight homes, air leaks may account for 15 to 25 percent of the heat our furnaces generate in winter or that our homes gain in summer. If you pay $1,100 a year to heat and cool your home, you might be wasting as much as $275 annually. Do you really want to use that much energy to heat and cool your neighborhood? You wouldn't try to hold water in a leaky bucket, and you wouldn't keep trying to blow up a balloon with holes in it. But that's exactly what each of us does when we pump heated or cooled air into a leaky house.

By one estimate, an average unweatherized house in the United States loses as much air as it would if a good-sized window were left open year-round. Another estimate, by the American Council for an Energy-Efficient Economy, puts a dollar value on all this lost energy, estimating that each year in the United States about $13 billion worth of energy in the form of heated or cooled air escapes through holes and cracks in residential buildings.

Depending on how your home is constructed, you may be able to quickly reduce your carbon emissions and save money simply by caulking, sealing, and weatherstripping all seams, cracks, and openings to the outside. In fact, dollar for dollar, plugging these leaks is likely to be one of the most cost-effective energy-saving measures you can take.

Many home improvement books and websites offer detailed tips on how to seal a home, but the following chart shows where the leaks come from in most homes.

As you can see from the chart, air finds many places to escape. A lot of hot air leaves a house through the attic, especially if it's uninsulated. Ducts can be big culprits, as can the gaps where plumbing pipes come

---

UCS Climate Team *FAST FACT*

Some $13 billion worth of energy in the form of heated or cooled air escapes through holes and cracks in residential buildings, according to one reputable estimate. Put another way, as much as one-quarter of the carbon dioxide emissions from heating and cooling your home are caused by your furnace or air conditioner working extra hard to heat or cool your neighborhood.

Figure 5.3. Where Air Escapes from Your Home

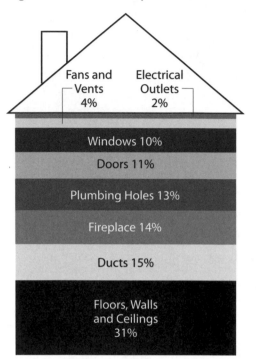

Shown here are the greatest sources of air leaks in the average home. A major source, in homes with fireplaces, is an improperly damped chimney. Source: EERE, 2009.

up from an unheated basement. And if your home has a fireplace, your chimney can suck vast amounts of heated or cooled air straight up to the outside, especially if the damper is left open or doesn't close snugly. (See the box for ways to make a fireplace tighter.)

A good professional energy audit will show exactly where your home is leaking air. Auditors often use an infrared detector to see where heat losses are occurring. Also common is a test aptly known as a blower door test, in which a strong fan is sealed into a doorway to pull air out of your house. This depressurizes the space inside, causing outside air to flow in through all the cracks and crevices. The energy auditor can then tell

Does My Fireplace Contribute to Global Warming?

Yes, but perhaps not in the way you think. Burning wood creates higher direct carbon emissions than any of the major fossil fuels, but its overall carbon profile depends on the sustainability of the wood sourcing.

Even without considering the carbon equation of the actual wood burning, the traditional fireplace is a global warming problem because it loses more heat from your home than it creates. According to the U.S. Department of Energy, a blazing fire can send 24,000 cubic feet of air per hour up the chimney, along with about 90 percent of the heat produced by the fire and some of the heat produced by your furnace. And most fireplaces are a big source of air leaks when they're not in use.

Luckily, if you love the cozy feel of a fire, there are several good ways to increase your home's energy efficiency and reduce the pollution created by traditional wood fires. One option is to fit a woodstove (or gas stove) insert into your existing fireplace. These units usually have a tempered glass front so you can see the fire burn. But unlike a traditional open fire, they actually heat your home. And because they burn so much hotter, they create far less air pollution. If you don't want to purchase an insert, you can still reduce your carbon footprint for relatively little cost by installing tempered glass doors in front of your fireplace and making sure to keep them (and the flue) firmly shut when the fireplace is not in use. Or, if you use your fireplace rarely or not at all, you can put inflatable inserts into the chimney to seal air leaks.

where the leaks are by feeling for air flow with her hand or by using a "smoke pencil," which visually shows air currents. Then she can advise you on which home sealing jobs will be most cost-effective to do first.

If you are a do-it-yourself type, basic weatherizing is pretty easy. You can do your own low-tech test for air leaks by carefully walking around inside your home on a windy day; some efficiency manuals suggest holding a lit incense stick as you go, paying special attention to windows, doors, electrical boxes and outlets, plumbing fixtures, ceiling light fixtures, attic hatches, and other locations where there may be an air path to the outside. Wherever the smoke stream indicates a draft, you have found an air leak that can be caulked, sealed, or weatherstripped.

One dedicated homeowner in Montana named Gary Reysa closely

documented his efforts in 2010 to cut his carbon emissions and overall home energy use in half. Sealing air leaks was one of Reysa's first priorities. In an online account of his efforts, he reports that he spent a total of about $50 on tubes of good-quality caulking and cans of polyurethane foam; he then spent about eight hours one weekend sealing air leaks. His one-time effort (augmented perhaps by his subsequently increased attention to energy efficiency) lowered his heating bill for the year by more than $150. If energy prices rise by 5 percent a year (a steep increase but not an unreasonable assumption), Reysa's investment will save him nearly $1,900 over 10 years and, he estimates, will reduce his carbon emissions by roughly 5 tons over the same period. Not bad for a single $50 weekend project.

There are many other strategies to increase your home's energy efficiency, and there are numerous books, articles, and websites that offer advice. We offer here some of the most important steps that have proven effective.

One of the cheapest and easiest strategies for cold climates is to add reflective barriers or insulation behind the radiators in your home, especially those that stand against outside walls. You can find reflective insulation in most home improvement stores. Or you can make barriers from any material that reflects heat: sheets of metal, even pieces of cardboard covered with aluminum foil. Installing reflective barriers was a key component of the Empire State Building retrofit job, and it can be part of your strategy at home as well.

Insulating your home is one of the cheapest and best ways to reduce your heating and cooling emissions. A home energy audit can provide professional advice tailored to your individual needs. If your walls are not insulated, an auditor might advise you to hire a contractor to blow loose cellulose or fiberglass insulation into them. Insulating the basement is a very good idea as well. These approaches are relatively inexpensive, recoup their costs quickly, and increase the comfort of your home immediately.

Even if your home is already insulated, you can probably save money and energy by adding more. One easy project is to add additional insulation to an unfinished attic. Given that rolls of fiberglass insulation cost

UCS Climate Team *FAST FACT*

According to data collected by the federal Energy Star program, if every American household added insulation to the attic, we would save more than $1.8 billion in annual energy costs and prevent nearly 12 million tons of heat-trapping emissions, equivalent to the emissions from 2 million cars.

around $20 each, the job should pay for itself in energy savings within a few seasons. In fact, according to the federal government's Energy Star program, if every American household added insulation to the attic, the nation could save more than $1.8 billion in annual energy costs and keep more than 12 million tons of carbon dioxide out of the atmosphere each year, the equivalent of emissions from some 2 million cars.

In warm climates, you can get a relatively quick return on your investment by turning your roof into a "cool roof," using materials or coatings that reflect the sun's energy away from the surface. While traditional roofs absorb as much as 95 percent of the sun's energy, cool roofs reflect up to 90 percent. That means they can lower the roof's surface temperature by as much as 100 degrees Fahrenheit, which reduces the heat transferred into the building below. This can be especially helpful in buildings that are not well insulated. The materials for flat or low-slope roofs are mainly bright white, but other cool-roof colors are becoming available as well. Cool roofs can be applied in a variety of ways, depending on your existing roofing material, either on top of your existing roof or as a low-profile coating that is brushed or sprayed on.

According to studies at the Lawrence Berkeley National Laboratory, switching to a cool roof can reduce the energy needed to cool your home by as much as 20 percent. A 1,000-square-foot cool roof could reduce your carbon dioxide emissions by half a ton per year, especially in a sunny, warm climate. In fact, as U.S. Secretary of Energy Steven Chu, a Nobel laureate, noted in 2010, "Cool roofs are one of the quickest and lowest-cost ways we can reduce our global carbon emissions."

Moving up the ladder in terms of upfront costs, replacing single-paned windows and older frames with double- or triple-paned windows and insulated frames can be a good investment. There is little question about their energy savings. One study found that replacing single-paned windows with double-paned windows and insulated frames could reduce heating costs by 36 percent in a Boston winter and lower cooling costs by 32 percent in a Phoenix summer. New energy-efficient windows are quite expensive, but their so-called low-e coatings (which reduce radiant heat transfer) help keep you warmer in winter and cooler in summer, and energy savings should repay your investment in 5 to 10 years. Lower-cost options include applying sheets of clear plastic tightly over the inside of old windows, hanging insulated curtains or shades, and adding or replacing storm windows.

Upgrade Your Heating (and Cooling) Equipment

Once you have curbed the worst excesses of your heating and cooling habits and taken some modest steps to improve your home's energy efficiency, you may want to consider replacing your air conditioner, water heater, furnace, or boiler with a newer, more efficient model. These changes involve fairly substantial upfront costs, but the energy-efficient replacements will reduce your emissions right away and eventually save you money. Plus, you may well be eligible for tax credits or local utility rebates that can help recoup your out-of-pocket expenses more quickly.

The most important guideline for buying any major heating or cooling equipment is to consider not just the price tag but also the lifetime operating costs: despite their higher purchase price, the most efficient units are almost always more economical in energy costs down the line. It may take a number of years to recoup your initial investment, but in conjunction with better insulation, air sealing, and thermostat settings, today's most efficient equipment can help you cut the energy you use for heating and cooling in half, with a comparable reduction in your emissions.

COOLING

Overall, air conditioners may be the best candidates for replacement because they have become much more efficient over the past 15 years. Top-rated models are now up to 50 percent more efficient than even the

---

UCS Climate Team *FAST FACT*

Air conditioners have become much more efficient over the past 15 years. Top-rated models now boast efficiency levels up to 50 percent higher than the current average.

---

current average. Especially if you now have an older, inefficient model, you may be able to replace it with a unit that cools your home using far less energy and with substantially fewer emissions, making the higher price tag worth it. Even an air conditioner with the minimum efficiency allowed by federal energy regulations can reduce your cooling costs and emissions by 20 percent over an older model. Check for a model's efficiency rating, called a SEER rating (seasonal energy efficiency ratio): the higher the number, the more efficient the unit.

If you are ready to replace your air-conditioning unit, you should also consider the even deeper reductions in emissions you could achieve from cheaper, lower-energy cooling choices such as ceiling fans, a whole-house exhaust fan, or, in drier climates, an evaporative cooler (often called a swamp cooler). Even if you still need air-conditioning, these options can greatly reduce the energy you use by allowing you to buy a smaller air conditioner and run it less often. In addition, passive solar solutions, such as planting trees or bushes and installing awnings or shades to keep out the summer sun, can be attractive and cost-effective ways to reduce your need for air-conditioning.

FURNACES AND BOILERS

You should think about replacing your furnace or boiler if it is more than 20 years old, if it has a continuously burning pilot light rather than electronic ignition, if it isn't heating your home comfortably in the winter, or if your heating bills seem particularly high. The kind of heating system you now have—whether forced hot air, hot-water radiators, steam heat, or something else—will most likely constrain your replacement choices. Unless you are undertaking a major remodeling, it is rarely cost-effective to change your entire heating system. Still, replacing your furnace or boiler will give you an opportunity to significantly reduce your emissions and cut your costs in the long run, especially in a relatively energy-efficient house.

Every model of furnace or boiler sold in the United States is given an AFUE (annual fuel utilization efficiency) rating that tells you how much of the unit's energy is converted to heat. (Water heaters have AFUE ratings, too.) The ratings also tell you the projected dollar savings per $100 of your present fuel bills. For example, let's say your current furnace's AFUE rating is 65 percent and you plan to install a high-efficiency natural gas system with a 90 percent AFUE rating. According to the rating data, your projected savings will be $27 per $100. If your annual fuel bill is near the norm of $1,100, then your total yearly savings in energy costs should be about $27 × 11 = $297.

That's a lot of savings each year. And even though a new furnace or boiler will not be cheap, and it will very likely take 10 years or more to recoup the initial purchase and installation costs, you will reduce your heating-related carbon emissions by 25 percent right away. According to the federal government, if just 10 percent of U.S. households replaced their old heating and cooling equipment with properly sized and installed Energy Star–qualified models, they could prevent the emission of *some 7 million tons of carbon dioxide per year*, equivalent to taking some 1.2 million cars off the road.

WATER HEATERS

Water heaters are responsible for about 15 percent of your home energy usage and emissions. Like air conditioners, they have benefited from successive waves of government requirements for greater efficiency; the most advanced models today are a lot more efficient than their predecessors. If it is time to replace your water heater, look at a range of options, including the highly efficient tankless (or on-demand) water heaters, which quickly heat water as needed rather than keeping it constantly hot in a tank; water heaters that use efficient air-source heat pump technology; and solar water heaters, which can be expensive to install but heat your water with zero carbon emissions and zero fuel costs. All of these options can be more expensive to install than a conventional water heater, but you will have the satisfaction of knowing you're helping combat global warming, and your investment will be paid back over time.

If you have an older water heater and can't replace it now, you could add a layer of insulation to reduce energy loss. (Newer water heaters have plenty of insulation built in.) In addition, setting the water temperature somewhat lower will save money and energy and can reduce the risk of scalding as well as avoid mineral buildup and corrosion in your heater and pipes. An ideal temperature is 120 degrees Fahrenheit: that's the temperature threshold needed to prevent the growth of bacteria in your hot-water system.

HEAT PUMPS

If you are building a new home or retrofitting an existing energy system, heat pumps are an innovative and energy-efficient technology for both heating and cooling. Like a refrigerator or an air conditioner, a heat pump sends coolant around a loop that goes through two regions of different temperature. The coolant absorbs heat in one region (inside your house, for example) and releases it in the other region (outside). Heat pumps can be set up to reverse direction so that they provide both summer cooling and winter heating.

Heat pumps come in two types.

Air-source heat pumps rely on the difference in temperature between indoor air and outside air. Though relatively inexpensive, they are less efficient when the outdoor temperature drops to freezing or below, so they work best in regions that have moderate winters. These days, more and more central air-conditioning systems include heat pumps.

Geothermal or ground-source heat pumps draw heat from the ground or groundwater beneath a building. They are fairly expensive to install because the piping has to be sunk into the ground, but they use 30 to 45 percent less energy than typical new heating and cooling systems. In the United States, the use of geothermal heat pumps has increased dramatically over the past decade, with more than 100,000 systems installed in each of the past several years.

According to the U.S. Department of Energy, geothermal heat pumps

---

ASK THE EXPERTS

How Do Geothermal Heat Pumps Work?

Geothermal heat pumps (also known as ground-source heat pumps) draw heat from the ground or groundwater beneath a building. About eight feet below the surface, the earth stays about 50 degrees Fahrenheit year-round—cooler than the outdoor air in summer and warmer than outdoors in winter. In a geothermal system, either air or liquid antifreeze is circulated through a loop of pipes buried underground that travels up into the building. In summer, the system carries heat from the building into the ground. In winter, it does the opposite, taking advantage of the earth's natural warmth. In regions with temperature extremes, such as the northern United States, geothermal heat pumps are fast gaining in popularity because they are so energy efficient and environmentally clean.

---

can save a typical home hundreds of dollars in energy costs each year, with the system typically paying for itself in 8 to 12 years. Furthermore, recent policies offer strong incentives for homeowners to install these systems. The Emergency Economic Stabilization Act of 2008 included an eight-year extension (through 2016) of a 30 percent tax credit, with no upper limit, to all homeowners who install Energy Star–certified geothermal heat pumps. Such tax credits and other incentives can reduce the payback period for many homeowners to five years or less, making this efficient technology an increasingly attractive choice for heating and cooling buildings.

COGENERATION

Among the other heating and cooling possibilities available to homeowners is *cogeneration*, in which waste heat from a power plant provides space heating or water heating to nearby buildings—a system sometimes known as "district heating." Such systems, widely used in Europe, can offer substantial energy savings and emission reductions. In the United States, many large institutions, such as universities, operate cogeneration systems, with steam tunnels heating multiple buildings. But now *micro-cogeneration systems* (also known as micro-combined heat and power systems) are applying the same principle on a household scale, gaining increased efficiency by converting fuel (normally natural gas) into both electricity and heat in a single process on-site in the basement of a home or an apartment building. Japan and some European countries are well ahead of the United States in introducing these systems, but they are becoming more widely available in the U.S. market. Because they capture waste heat and normally generate electricity from natural gas, they are of greatest value in cold areas where electricity is expensive and natural gas prices are low. As the cost of micro-cogeneration comes down in the future, these systems will become increasingly attractive.

While the wide array of heating and cooling options may seem overwhelming, making changes in this sector can achieve deep reductions in your carbon footprint with little alteration in your lifestyle. Eventually, burning huge amounts of fossil fuel to heat and cool our homes will quite likely come to be seen as one of our nation's most wasteful habits, akin to burning dollar bills in the fireplace to keep warm. Every step we take toward making our homes more energy efficient is another dollar saved from this wasteful practice—another dollar that we will never again have to pay to a utility company or to a foreign country for fossil fuel. More important, every step toward smarter energy design permanently eliminates a major source of carbon emissions without requiring us to curtail our usual activities. Seen from that perspective, the move toward energy efficiency and renewable power in our homes seems more enticing than ever.

Going Deep: Approaching Zero

If you are interested in making deep energy retrofits to your home, bear in mind that the upfront costs will be substantial. With that said, virtually any home can be retrofitted to lower heating and cooling costs almost to zero. A growing number of contractors across the country are offering such services and gaining expertise in achieving deep reductions more cost-effectively.

In warm and cold climates alike, the principle of deep energy reduction is the same: the house must be well insulated and sealed very tightly.

In colder climates, the most cost-effective way to do this is to wrap a layer of rigid insulation around the outside of the house, essentially encasing it in a new shell. The advantage of this method is that the inside of the home remains largely untouched, retaining its existing character and finish detail.

The emergence of such deep-energy-reduction building techniques makes this a very exciting and dynamic time for those who want to reduce their carbon emissions and fight global warming. In almost every community around the country, homes and commercial buildings are being designed and built with impressively reduced energy needs.

In one dramatic example, the Cleveland Museum of Natural History in 2011 underwrote the construction of a so-called passive home, based on a building technique known as Passivhaus, pioneered in Germany. This attractive, conventional-looking home has triple-paned windows and walls more than 1 foot thick. Built to strict specifications, the house operates much like a Thermos bottle to insulate it in winter from the freezing temperatures outside. Instead of a furnace, the house needs only two ductless air-source heat pumps (one on each floor), which together consume only as much electricity as two hair dryers. Built in a prominent location downtown on the grounds of the museum, next to the botanical garden, the house was built originally as an exhibit that could be closely inspected inside and out by thousands of visitors. At the end of the special exhibit, the house was moved to a neighborhood a half mile away and sold as a private home.

Along with this exciting example of deep-energy-reduction building, a wealth of other energy-efficient projects and retrofits are being undertaken around the country. For instance, the Southwest Minnesota Housing Partnership renovated 60 dilapidated apartments in Worthington, a rural community in the southwestern part of the state, turning them into energy-efficient, affordable housing. The project, called Viking Terrace, drew on municipal and federal funding as well as low-income housing tax credits to incorporate many energy-saving features into the complex, including a high-efficiency geothermal heating and cooling system that is expected to pay for itself through energy savings in just a decade.

Projects such as Viking Terrace are still far from the norm, however, and require more time and research than projects using conventional construction techniques. On average, many builders say costs for green building now run 5 to 10 percent above conventional techniques. But as green materials and energy-efficient methods become more widespread and as energy prices rise, such projects will be more and more cost-effective.

A wealth of information about green buildings is available from the U.S. Green Building Council, online at www.usgbc.org. The EPA also offers a primer about green building techniques at www.epa.gov, and lists of local contractors who specialize in energy-efficient building can be found online, including a listing at www.greenbuilding.com. For people who want to reduce their global warming emissions and are able to take advantage of emerging green building techniques, this is an excellent time to get started.

Getting to 20

As we have discussed, almost everyone—homeowners and renters alike—can achieve significant reductions in their emissions from home heating and cooling. At the top of the list, two very inexpensive strategies can achieve immediate results. For about $50 you can buy and install a programmable thermostat. And for as little as $15 to $20 you can buy caulking, weatherstripping, or shrink-to-fit plastic to seal air leaks and leaky doors and windows. Homeowners can drive down emissions much further by adding insulation and upgrading to more efficient (or renewable-powered) heating and cooling equipment. All these techniques can help you make substantial progress toward the goal of reducing emissions by 20 percent over the coming year; some of them will most likely be included as we each find our preferred path to meeting that goal.

CHAPTER 6

Taking Charge of Electricity at Home

Knowledge is power.

—Francis Bacon

For convenience and versatility, electricity is hard to beat. It's no wonder that our per capita consumption of electricity has risen steadily ever since the technology became available. And just since 1970, U.S. residential electricity use has gone up by 39 percent, reflecting the overall trend toward larger homes and a greater variety of electronic gadgets in each one. We seem to become more and more reliant on electric devices, even for tasks—from brushing our teeth to reading books and magazines—that we used to do without electricity. According to the U.S. Department of Energy's *International Energy Outlook 2010,* worldwide electricity use is projected to rise by roughly 70 percent between 2010 and 2035.

While the overall rise in energy use in the United States and worldwide is, of course, a problem for global warming, the shift away from direct fuel combustion and toward electricity is also a positive development because it creates greater opportunities for efficiency and renewable energy. As we will discuss in more detail, most electric devices at home have become remarkably more efficient over time, and if the energy to power them is produced from clean, renewable sources, they cause no global warming emissions at all. The key, of course, is to be aware of how much electricity your appliances and electronics use and where that electricity is coming from.

Unfortunately, this is not always an easy task. The convenience of lighting a room with the flick of a switch or turning on entertainment

Figure 6.1. Emissions from Household

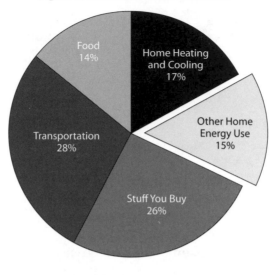

*Not counting heating, cooling, or energy for hot water
(all of which may use electricity), electrical appliances
and devices contribute about 15 percent to our
overall emissions, or more than three tons annually
for the average American.* Source: UCS modeling.

with the press of a button presents a challenge to those who want to
reduce their share of global warming emissions: electric devices work so
seamlessly, and the infrastructure that supports them is so hidden from
our view, that we hardly ever think about how much energy these devices
are consuming—or how much carbon they are emitting.

Polls show that Americans tend to be unaware of how much electricity they use, where it comes from, or how best to reduce the amount. It's
not really surprising. After all, how would we get that information? Our
electric bills can be tricky to decipher, and most of our electric devices
don't advertise how much electricity they consume. Think about it: Can
you name the three appliances in your home that use the most electricity?
Do you know how the electricity in your state or region is produced? If the
answer to both questions is no, don't worry. This chapter will tackle these
issues and many others.

Figure 6.2. Breakdown of Household Emissions

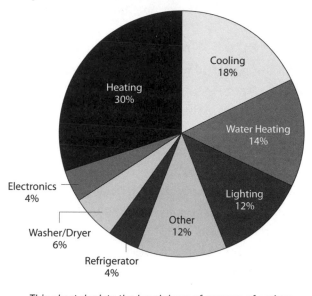

This chart depicts the breakdown of sources of carbon
emissions for the average American household.
Source: EERE, 2009.

So far, we've looked at ways to reduce emissions from transportation and home heating and cooling; electricity use in the home is the next largest segment of the average American's carbon emissions. As figure 6.1 shows, not counting heating, cooling, or energy for hot water (all of which may also use electricity), the myriad electric devices you use are responsible for roughly 15 percent of your total overall carbon emissions—some three tons' worth annually.

Here's the good news: most of us can easily shrink the amount of electricity we consume and the emissions we create in the process. The first step is to become more aware of exactly how much electricity we each use routinely. That means finding out which home appliances use the largest share of our electricity, where we can make significant savings—and which uses are small enough that they aren't worth worrying about.

If you pay closer attention and take time to master the details of where your electricity dollars are going, you'll be well on your way to lowering your electric bill and your associated carbon emissions from electricity use by 20 to 50 percent, with little or no change in your daily life.

Knowledge (about Power) Is Power

To get a sense of how powerful it can be to monitor your electricity usage, consider a pilot program established by the Salt River Project, a utility company in the Phoenix, Arizona, metropolitan area. Participants in the M-Power program were offered the opportunity to change the way they bought electricity. Their households were outfitted with digital electric meters that displayed a real-time readout of how much they were spending on electricity at any given time. In addition, participants in the M-Power program agreed to prepay for "chunks" of electricity, in much the way people purchase gasoline for their cars.

In this program, the electricity purchased is added to customers' accounts using cards that work much like ATM debit cards. More electricity can be added at ATM-like machines or by phone. When a home's "electricity tank" begins to run low, the system alerts the user; if the account happens to run out during the night, a "friendly credit" program allows the power to continue until the account can be replenished the next day.

The M-Power program does not explicitly involve energy efficiency guidelines or home energy audits or switching to low-carbon power sources. But changing the way people buy power and giving them a way to continually track their usage in dollars and cents made a stark difference in their electricity usage. In 2009, some 78,000 customers participated in the program. On average, they reduced their overall electricity usage by 12 percent.

UCS Climate Team *FAST FACT*

Some 78,000 utility customers in Phoenix, Arizona, participate in a pay-as-you-go program that includes a digital meter displaying how much the household is spending on electricity. Just changing the way they purchase electricity and receiving real-time information about their consumption has led participants to reduce their electricity usage by 12 percent on average.

So-called smart meters such as those used in the M-Power program are becoming more common for electricity customers around the country. In addition to offering detailed usage information, they can wirelessly transmit data to the utility company, negating the need for meter readers. As a component of a "smart electric grid," smart meters have received federal funding across the country and have even been mandated in some states, including Texas, which is currently phasing them in for all residential electricity customers.

In fact, you don't have to wait for your utility company. A growing number of manufacturers offer smart meters you can purchase, for about $120 for a stripped-down model, and install yourself. These units often come with software that allows users to easily track their home's electricity usage on their computer. Many users claim to have lowered their electricity bill by hundreds of dollars each year just by monitoring their usage carefully.

For those who don't want to go to the expense or trouble of buying a whole-house smart meter, a lot of the same information is available from a simple electricity meter; a variety of models are widely sold for $20 to $40. These meters plug into any wall socket and provide a readout of the amount of electricity used by any device or appliance plugged into it. For instance, you can measure how much electricity your refrigerator is using to help you gauge exactly how much you could save with a newer, more energy-efficient model. You can also see how much electricity your television and many other electronic devices use even when they are turned off—so-called phantom loads, which we discuss in more detail later in the chapter. Any of these meters—from the most high-tech to the most basic—could be well worth the investment as a tool to help track where your electricity dollars are going.

Only a power meter offers specific data about your home electricity use, but even without one, there are plenty of ways to educate yourself about electricity usage. This chapter identifies some of the biggest electricity hogs in most homes and suggests how to reduce the amount of electricity they use. As we walk through the data, we will also point out the smaller electricity wasters that are not worth fretting over. But first, let's take a moment to review some basics about electricity to help make sense of that electric bill.

The first point to emphasize is that different electric appliances and devices draw energy from the grid at *very* different rates. The rate of electricity consumption is measured in watts or kilowatts (1,000 watts). If you think of appliances and electronic devices as drinking electricity from the wires that come to a home, an appliance's wattage describes how fast they drink. Imagine wattage as the size of the straw that the device uses to sip electricity from the socket. Some devices, such as digital clocks, have wattage in the single digits—they sip electricity through a very narrow straw. High-wattage devices, such as heaters and hair dryers, may be rated at 2,000 watts or more. When they are on, they gulp electricity through a straw the size of a fire hose.

When looking for the energy hogs in your home, however, keep in mind that wattage is only one piece of the story. You probably use an iron or a hair dryer for no more than a few hours or so every month, whereas a refrigerator contributes much more to your monthly costs because it runs all the time. These differences are important, but they are obscured in an electric bill that reports only how much total electricity was consumed that month in kilowatt-hours (kWh).

We buy gasoline by the gallon, which is a pretty straightforward measure—after all, we see the size of a gallon every time we buy milk at the grocery store. The kilowatt-hour, however, is a much less obvious measurement. It describes the amount of electricity consumed by running a 1,000-watt device (for instance, a hair dryer) for one hour or the equivalent; if you kept a 100-watt lightbulb on for ten hours, it would use 1 kilowatt-hour's worth of electricity. According to the latest data, in 2009 the average American home consumed some 11,040 kilowatt-hours' worth of electricity, which works out to some 920 kilowatt-hours per month. A household's power consumption could be several hundred kilowatt-hours higher or lower, however, depending on whether electricity or some other energy source is used for space heating or water heating or both.

In this realm, it's all about knowledge and choice. As you learn where your household's electricity hogs are and follow some simple steps to reduce their intake, you should see the number of kilowatt-hours on your monthly electric bill drop substantially. Making simple changes in the kinds of electric devices you use and the way you use them can dramatically lower your electricity usage and reduce your carbon emissions.

Shedding Some Light

When we think about saving electricity from lighting, most of us focus on remembering to turn off the lights we aren't using. That's an important step, of course. But in this area, you will be surprised to learn how far you can get not just by trying to do without but also by doing more with less. After heating and cooling (and making hot water), lighting consumes the most energy in many homes, accounting for somewhere between 10 and 15 percent of the electricity used. It is a promising category for savings because you can reduce the amount of power you use, the amount of money you spend, and your carbon footprint all at once without giving up a thing.

Lighting is in the midst of a quiet revolution. The standard incandescent bulb long ago transformed our ability to illuminate our homes, but it didn't change much at all in the century after Thomas Edison's heyday. Incandescent lightbulbs have always been notoriously inefficient: some 95 percent of the energy input is emitted as heat rather than light (that's why incandescents are too hot to touch when they are turned on). Especially because of all that heat production, a 60-watt bulb drinks electricity through a pretty big straw.

The lighting picture began to change a bit in 1960 with the introduction of halogen lights, once considered the lighting of the future. But while they produced a pleasing, warm white light, they were only about 20 percent more energy efficient than incandescent bulbs, and the high-wattage bulbs burned even hotter than incandescents, posing a potentially serious fire hazard. A far more dramatic change came with the advent of compact fluorescent lightbulbs.

Compact fluorescent bulbs were actually invented in the 1930s and were even displayed at the 1939 New York World's Fair. But they became commercially available in the United States only in the mid-1980s. Since then, American homes equipped with compact fluorescent bulbs have enjoyed the same amount of light as those with incandescent bulbs while using just a fraction of the electricity. Compared with a 60-watt incandescent bulb, for instance, a compact fluorescent that generates an equivalent amount of light uses only about 15 watts. This means that switching entirely from incandescents to compact fluorescent bulbs will cut your lighting bill—and your emissions from lighting—*by 75 percent*.

Compact fluorescent bulbs are already displacing incandescent and halogen bulbs. The economic case for switching is a strong one: although they cost a bit more than incandescents, they can pay for themselves in electricity savings in less than a year. Given that compact fluorescents last up to six times as long as equally bright incandescents, they are a bargain for consumers on a life cycle basis.

That's why the U.S. government, in its 2007 federal energy bill, set efficiency standards for lighting designed to phase out the sale of today's inefficient incandescent bulbs beginning in 2012. (Some efficient incandescent bulbs will meet the new standards and thus will continue to be sold.) The United States is not the first country to go down this path; the European Union and Australia phased out inefficient incandescent bulbs in 2010.

Many people initially rejected compact fluorescent bulbs because their brightness and light quality did not seem to match the incandescent bulbs they were used to. But if light quality has been an issue for you, take another look; compact fluorescents now come in many different levels and qualities of light to match all kinds of preferences.

Today's compact fluorescent bulbs are much better than earlier models, but they do have some limitations. For one thing, turning them on and off frequently can shorten their life span. More important, though, compact fluorescents, like some other household products and unlike incandescents, contain a small amount of mercury, a potent neurotoxin. That is definitely a downside. The amount, however, is very small. On average, compact fluorescent bulbs contain about 4 milligrams of mercury sealed within the glass tubing. By comparison, older thermometers contain about 500 milligrams of mercury, or more than is contained in over

---

ASK THE EXPERTS

Don't Compact Fluorescent Bulbs Contain Mercury?

Yes, compact fluorescents do contain a small amount of mercury. Paradoxically, however, their use can actually reduce people's exposure to mercury overall.

These bulbs contain about 4 milligrams (mg) of mercury vapor, which, in the presence of an electric current, gives off visible light when it strikes the phosphor coating of the bulb. But that amount of mercury is only 1 percent of what was in an old-fashioned mercury thermometer. And some manufacturers have produced compact fluorescent bulbs with even less mercury.

Here's how compact fluorescent bulbs can actually *reduce* human exposure to mercury: The biggest source of exposure is coal-burning power plants, because mercury is a common contaminant in coal. A 13-watt compact fluorescent light-bulb (CFL), used for its rated lifetime of 8,000 hours, will result in 1.2 mg of mercury emissions from electricity production if coal-burning plants supply half of that electricity (the national average). By the end of the CFL's life, most of its mercury is bound to the inside of the bulb and is therefore harmless, but 0.44 mg of mercury could still be released if the bulb is broken during disposal. The total lifetime release of the CFL would then be 1.6 mg of mercury, even with improper disposal.

Under the same assumptions, using a 60-watt incandescent bulb, which produces the same amount of light, would release 5.5 mg of mercury from the burning of coal. So even if CFLs are not recycled and always break during disposal, their use still reduces overall mercury exposure, as long as at least 16 percent or more of the electricity used comes from coal, as is the case in almost every part of the country.

---

100 compact fluorescent bulbs. It is also worth noting that the energy efficiency of these bulbs is so great that, paradoxically, they will still reduce overall exposure to mercury, as the box explains.

Now, right on the heels of compact fluorescent bulbs, an exciting new lighting technology is making inroads in the global market: LED (light-emitting diode) lights. Semiconductors in LED lights glow when an electric current flows through them; no gas-filled or vacuum bulb is involved. There is no mercury in LEDs, and no other health hazards have been identified.

With LED lights, Americans will be able to cut their electricity consumption from lighting even further. LED lights offer a high-quality, warm white light, and they last 25,000 to 50,000 hours—that's at least *17 years* if the bulb is on for four hours each day. LED lights that draw about 7 watts of electricity offer the same amount of light as a 60-watt incandescent bulb. In other words, compared with incandescents, they are able to light a home using almost *nine times less electricity and releasing nine times less carbon dioxide into the atmosphere.*

LEDs are still relatively expensive, but judging by the fast-growing adoption of compact fluorescent bulbs and their consequent reduction in price, the cost of LEDs will very likely drop fast as they become adopted more widely. By some estimates, they will begin to dominate the market within just a few years.

Homes that still use incandescent bulbs are needlessly running up their electric bills and emissions. The size of the potential savings might come as a surprise. To find out just how big the savings can be, let's walk through the numbers.

According to the latest government figures, the average American home spends roughly $190 annually on electricity for lighting. With incandescent bulbs, at the national average price of electricity, you would spend roughly that much by burning 10 60-watt bulbs for eight hours each day. By changing all 10 of those 60-watt bulbs to compact fluorescents using just 15 watts for the equivalent amount of light, running the same 10 light fixtures for the same amount of time would reduce annual lighting costs from $190 to around $48 a year. Switching those same lights to LED bulbs using just 7 watts each would cut annual lighting costs in half again—*to just over $22.* In either case, not only would you save more than $140 in

Figure 6.3. Annual Electricity Costs by Lighting Source

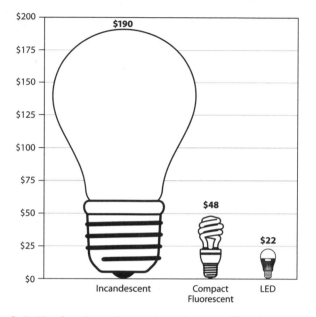

Switching from incandescent bulbs to more efficient compact fluorescent bulbs or newer LED bulbs can result in significant savings on your electric bill. This chart shows the difference in electricity costs from producing the same amount of light from each source. Source: UCS, 2012, adapted from 2011 EIA data.

operating costs annually, you would also lower your household's carbon emissions by more than half a ton!

Appliances 101

How significant are the emissions produced by home appliances and electronic devices? A good way to measure that is to look at the amount of electricity each one uses in the average household. Figure 6.4 shows some typical costs for the electricity to run selected appliances and devices in the average American household. As we will discuss, however, the amount you spend may vary significantly from these figures. Your numbers will depend on how efficient your lights, appliances, and electronic

Figure 6.4. Typical Annual Electricity Costs at Home (by End Use)

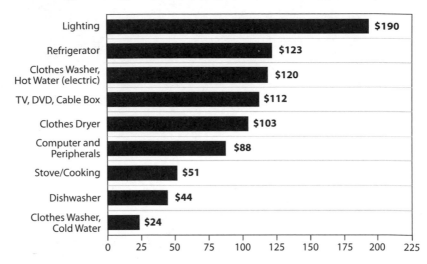

This chart shows some typical amounts spent by American households to run selected electric appliances and devices. Note that the washing machine is listed twice to highlight the difference between hot- and cold-water washes, on average. Sources: www.energysavers.gov and UCS modeling.

devices are, on the knowledge you bring to bear in using them, and on the price of electricity in your region.

As we have discussed, lighting makes up the largest category of electricity use (aside from heating and cooling, which were discussed in chapter 5). But next to lighting, a home's refrigerator probably uses more electricity than any other single device. So let's take a moment to look more closely at that appliance, a mainstay in almost all American homes.

Refrigerators, of course, must constantly cycle on and off to keep food cold, which is part of the reason that they cost the average household somewhere around $123 per year to operate. What this figure masks, however, is the strikingly large variation in the electricity consumption of different models.

The good news is that refrigerators have become much more efficient in recent years, as have most other major household appliances. Appliance efficiency standards introduced over the past few decades have helped speed this process along and brought down energy use per appliance dramatically, reducing *total* U.S. electricity consumption as of 2010 by an estimated 7 percent below the amount that would have been consumed without those standards in place. In fact, if every refrigerator, dishwasher, and clothes washer purchased in the United States this year had met the federal government's current Energy Star efficiency guidelines, we would have saved $700 million in annual energy costs while preventing the emission of 2 million tons of global warming gases each year, equivalent to the annual emissions from 350,000 cars.

Of all household appliances, refrigerators may have undergone the most impressive changes. Six rounds of progressively stricter standards for refrigerator efficiency took place from 1978 through 2003; the first three were initiated by California and then picked up by other states, while the later ones were adopted at the federal level. After the 2003 rule took effect, the average new refrigerator was 60 percent cheaper and 20 percent larger than its mid-1970s counterpart *and used 70 percent less electricity*. But even after these huge efficiency gains, the refrigerator remains one of the top energy users in most households.

The bottom line: it could well be worth your while to replace your refrigerator. How can you tell if the time has come? Well, as a recent article in the *New York Times* put it: if it's avocado, it's probably not green. If your refrigerator dates from before the 2003 efficiency standard or, even worse, from before the 1993 standard (when colors like avocado were in vogue), you can save a lot of energy by replacing it sooner rather than later. If you're replacing one of the older models, the savings in energy alone could recoup your out-of-pocket costs in as little as three years and get you a significant step closer to your first-year goal of reducing your emissions by 20 percent.

To find out how efficient your refrigerator is, try metering its energy usage. Or visit the government's Energy Star website (www.energystar. gov), which offers a calculator to do the job. Simply enter the age, size, and model of your refrigerator and the cost of a kilowatt-hour of electricity in your state (if you don't know your rate, the site offers a national average), and it will compute exactly how much you could save by replacing it with an up-to-date Energy Star product. Remember, you're not just saving money; you are also doing more with less—reducing your share of the emissions that contribute to global warming.

When you do purchase a new refrigerator, don't buy more capacity than you need, and, using the Energy Star ratings, choose the most efficient model you can afford. Remember that most of the fancy features, such as automatic ice makers and through-the-door water dispensers, often use significantly more energy; you'll be paying for these features for the entire life of the appliance, so think carefully about whether you really need them. Also, you may be able to get a government or utility rebate; refrigerators are perhaps the most common appliances for which rebates are offered. The Energy Star website offers a good tool for locating rebates in your area; check, too, to see whether your local utility company is sponsoring any rebates now or plans to do so in the future.

Also worth considering is the fact that 26 percent of all homes keep an extra refrigerator in the basement, garage, or bar, according to a U.S. Department of Energy (DOE) survey conducted in 2009. You can save dramatically by unplugging this unit except during the holidays or on other occasions when you are entertaining a crowd. If your second fridge is an older model, it is most likely using considerably more electricity than your main one. And you can probably find some room in your main refrigerator for that extra beer, soda, or whatever else you keep in there. The same advice holds for an additional freezer in the basement unless you use it a lot.

Most consumer guides suggest making sure that your refrigerator door seals well and that you periodically clean the condenser coils. Such maintenance will make your refrigerator run more efficiently, but the truth is, we cancel out many such gains when we succumb to the common habit of keeping the door gaping wide as we decide what to fix for dinner. Remember that even though the refrigerator stays on all the time, it maintains its cool temperature mostly through insulation; the less often the door is opened, the less often the motor has to kick on to cool down the interior.

Washing and drying laundry is perhaps the next biggest user of electricity in many of our homes, and here again, there is a lot of room for reducing carbon emissions. As figure 6.4 shows, the biggest expense in the laundry room may be the cost of heating water. Washing in hot water uses at least *five times* more energy than using cold water. And even a warm-water wash uses approximately double the energy of a cold one. If you regularly wash your clothes in hot or warm water, you can reduce your emissions substantially by simply switching to cold-water washes whenever possible. Cold-water detergents dissolve in the water at lower temperatures and clean clothes just as effectively as in warm or hot water.

Washing machines today are much more energy efficient, using 37 percent less energy (and 50 percent less water) to wash clothes than older standard washers. High-efficiency machines now come in both top-loading and front-loading styles, and they spin the clothes more thoroughly, thereby reducing drying time. That feature is important because spinning dampness out of clothes is more energy efficient than drying them by using heat. Dryers, meanwhile, have not seen any significant improvement in energy efficiency over the past decades; in fact, the federal government doesn't even offer an Energy Star rating for dryers (or for gas stoves or microwaves) because no single model is much more efficient than any other. *Clothes dryers*, as the chart shows, typically cost American households slightly more than $100 in electricity annually. That may not seem like a huge amount, but drying on a clothesline or rack, if that is feasible for your family, can virtually eliminate these costs and related emissions and could be an important contributor to helping you reach the goal of a 20 percent reduction in carbon emissions this year. Using a rack or line to dry even some of the clothes can make a noticeable difference in your energy bill and associated emissions. For those committed to their clothes dryers, some reductions can still be had by drying towels and heavy items separately and by drying loads in quick succession; when the dryer is already hot, it consumes less energy. If your dryer has a moisture sensor, using it to shut off the machine when your clothes are dry can also lower your emissions and costs. A final option for lowering your laundry-related carbon emissions is to replace an electric dryer with a

---

UCS Climate Team *FAST FACT*

Washing clothes in hot water uses at least five times more electricity (if you have an electric water heater) than a cold-water wash does. Even with a gas water heater, switching to cold water can cut your carbon emissions substantially and also save you money.

---

gas-powered model, especially if coal is the predominant source of power for producing electricity in your state. (We'll talk more about where your electricity comes from in a moment.) Gas dryers heat more quickly, dry clothes faster, and, with the national average mix of sources for electricity, cause about 40 percent less carbon emissions per load.

Dishwashers have become significantly more efficient in their water and energy use in recent years. Today's most energy-efficient machines could save you as much as $40 in utility costs each year. According to a recent study at the University of Bonn, Germany, using the newer dishwashers tends to be even more efficient than washing by hand with hot water, provided you run a full load and scrape the dishes off before loading rather than using a lot of hot water to rinse them by hand.

Cooking is another electricity-intensive activity, but in this case the best rule of thumb is to use common sense because the gains won't be as significant as those you can achieve in other areas. In some applications, such as heating small portions, microwave ovens are considerably more energy efficient than conventional ovens. The overall numbers don't add up to large amounts of emissions, however. Plus, microwave ovens' advantage doesn't hold across the board. In fact, in one test, researchers found that boiling one cup of water on an electric stove used slightly *less* electricity than heating it to a boil in a microwave oven. If you are in the market for a new oven, bear in mind that self-cleaning models tend to be better insulated, allowing for faster heating and slightly less energy use; similarly, convection ovens, which circulate heated air, cooking food faster and at a lower temperature, can reduce energy use by 20 percent compared with their conventional counterparts. On the stove top, newer electric ignition gas ranges are about 30 percent more efficient than older models with a continuously burning pilot light. Whatever stove you use, remember to double up on dishes baking in the oven (which can cut emissions per dish in half) and to put lids on the pots and pans you use on the stove top, which can save up to two-thirds of the energy needed to heat the food. Even better is a stove-top pressure cooker, which can reduce cooking time—and hence emissions—by up to 70 percent, according to manufacturers.

Electronics 101

Home electronics make up a growing portion of our home energy use and emissions. Most homes today have at least two snake nests of electric cables. One powers the home's entertainment center, connecting televisions, cable or satellite boxes, DVD and VCR players, video game consoles, and other devices. The second tangle of electricity users can be found in the home office, connecting desktop computers with an array of peripherals, from routers and printers to faxes and scanners.

The most striking thing about these forms of electric usage is the extent to which they are left running around the clock. You may be amazed to see how much you can save just by changing your habits at these two home locations.

Televisions vary, not just in how much electricity they use when running but also in how much they consume when turned off. These days, "off" isn't really off. Studies have shown that some models consume more electricity in 20 hours of being off than they do in 4 hours of being on. Also, today's larger screens and, especially, plasma screen televisions often use more electricity than the older types. If you are in the market for a new television set, consider that LCD sets with "LED backlighting" (especially so-called edge-lit models) reportedly use power more sparingly than LCD sets with fluorescent backlighting or plasma televisions. For the lowest energy costs and associated emissions, choose an LED model or another Energy Star–certified model.

The different models of cable and satellite television set-top boxes and DVD players also vary in terms of electricity usage. According to research conducted by the DOE, playing a DVD on a gaming console can use upward of *20 times* the electricity used by a standard DVD player.

With all these devices, the easiest thing to do is to make sure they are completely shut off when not in use. This simple step will show immediate results on your next electric bill. Perhaps the most foolproof strategy is to plug all these devices into a switched power strip, which is readily available at any hardware store. That way, all of them can be switched off at once when they are not in use.

Home computers should also be shut down completely when not in use. According to one recent report, the energy required to power all the world's computers, data storage, and communications networks is expected to double by 2020. One inexpensive device on the market, the Mini Power Minder, monitors a computer's usage and automatically shuts off power to all peripheral devices plugged into it when the computer goes into sleep mode.

Speaking of sleep mode, taking literally one minute to adjust the power management features on your desktop computer can cut its energy usage in half, allowing you to save some 600 kWh of electricity per year, or more than $60 in annual electricity costs. Depending, of course, on how your electricity is produced, that equates to nearly half a ton of carbon dioxide, or, on average, puts you one-eighth of the way toward your 20 percent first-year emissions reduction goal.

To achieve these savings, all you need to do is turn off your screen saver and let your computer go directly into sleep mode when not in use. Many people don't realize it, but the standby or sleep mode is much more efficient than a screen saver, which is designed to protect the screen from afterimages that can appear when a still image is held for too long. A screen saver has nothing to do with saving energy—in fact, those bouncing geometric shapes use as much energy as an active screen.

For those who aren't sure how to adjust their computers, the DOE's Energy Savers website (www.energysavers.gov) walks users through the process, as does a very easy-to-use online resource available at www .climatesaverscomputing.org. Both resources offer up-to-date informa-

UCS Climate Team *FAST FACT*

Taking a minute to adjust your desktop computer's power management so that the screen saver is turned off and the computer goes right into sleep mode can cut its electricity usage in half and save you $60 per year.

tion on the vast amounts of electricity being saved as these simple steps are adopted on the many millions of computers around the country and around the world.

Here again, the good news is that a number of companies are taking efficiency issues seriously, producing models that use electricity much more frugally. Part of this change is driven by the increased use of mobile devices such as laptops and tablet computers, which have to function more efficiently in order to run effectively on their rechargeable batteries. The average laptop, for example, uses just one-quarter of the electricity used by the average desktop computer to do the same job, making laptops an appealing choice for those seeking to reduce their computing-related emissions.

Phantom Power

As we have already mentioned, many devices around your home use a small amount of power in so-called standby mode even when they are not turned on. Standby power, sometimes called "phantom load" or "vampire power," is used by anything plugged in that can be turned on with a remote, that displays the time, or that has a little red light that glows when it's off—as well as by many devices that give no external sign at all that they are consuming electricity.

Phantom loads don't compare with the large amounts of electricity used for lighting or running the refrigerator. So you might imagine that they are in the "not to worry" category. But this is a case where the sheer scale of the problem means we can achieve fairly big savings, especially if everyone takes action. Plus, there is something particularly galling about items using electricity when we think they are turned off. New data from the Google PowerMeter program has found that as many as 40 percent of

Figure 6.5. Phantom Loads of Selected Household Devices (Measured by Watts)

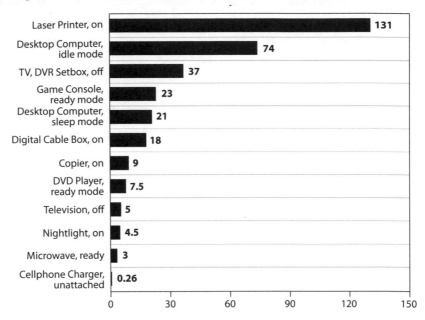

This chart shows the rate of electricity usage (measured in watts) by selected household devices when not in use. Source: Meier, Lawrence Berkeley National Laboratory, 2010.

American homes draw power at the rate of *500 watts or more* even in the middle of the night. Think about it: that's like leaving eight 60-watt incandescent bulbs burning brightly all night long.

The DOE's Lawrence Berkeley National Laboratory (LBNL) has conducted a thorough investigation of phantom loads. According to the researchers, a typical American home has some 40 devices drawing power at all times. Standby power to these devices, they estimate, consumes 5 to 10 percent of the electricity generated in the United States. On a worldwide basis, they suggest, phantom loads may account for *1 percent of total global carbon emissions.*

As the chart shows, computers, printers, television sets, game consoles, and cable boxes are some of the big offenders. The chart displays the wattage of these devices, but as a very rough guide, doing the math shows that using one watt continuously for a year at standard electricity rates is

UCS Climate Team FAST FACT

The typical American home has some 40 devices constantly drawing power—even when they are ostensibly turned off. Standby power from these devices consumes 5 to 10 percent of the electricity generated in the United States; worldwide, it may account for 1 percent of total global carbon emissions.

equal to about $1, so these numbers correspond generally to what many of us will pay for electricity for these devices in standby mode over the course of the year.* As you can see, leaving a laser printer on constantly is quite expensive, costing over $100. Leaving a cell phone charger plugged into the wall when it's not hooked up to a phone, however, draws hardly any measurable electricity; this habit will cost only about 25 cents and a comparably small amount of associated emissions over the course of a year.

Fortunately, some of the newer electronic devices use less standby power than older models; this trend is likely to continue, especially because some state energy efficiency regulations now require reduced standby power loads. Still, the easiest way to reduce your use of standby power is to unplug all electronic devices that are not actively in use. As noted above, plugging multiple items into switched power strips—and then simply shutting the power off at night or when the devices are not being used—is a very easy solution.

After you've uncovered and put a stop to the largest electronic vampires in your home, though, don't drive yourself crazy plugging in and unplugging the microwave. Remember that the big users of household energy and big sources of energy-related emissions involve heating, air-conditioning, lighting, and a few other major appliances. Pay attention to reducing those items and you'll be doing the most to reduce your utility bills—and helping the most to address global warming.

*A device drawing 1 watt of power for all 8,760 hours in a year consumes 8.76 kilowatt-hours (kWh). This would cost $1.01 at 11.51 cents per kWh, the average U.S. price for residential electricity in 2009 (U.S. Energy Information Administration; for more detail, see www.eia.doe.gov/cneaf/electricity/page/sales_revenue.xls).

How Green Is Your Electricity?

The suggestions offered in this chapter can almost certainly save some money on any household's monthly electricity bill. Exactly how much these steps will help reduce global warming emissions, however, depends in part on how your electricity is generated. As we work to make electricity usage more transparent at home, it is also vitally important to try to do so at its source. Just as appliances vary a lot in the amount of electricity they consume, the carbon emitted by producing electricity varies dramatically depending on the source of energy used.

Of course, when utility companies employ renewable sources of energy such as wind power and solar photovoltaics, they produce electricity with no carbon emissions whatsoever. If the electricity you use is produced at least in part by renewable sources, your share of carbon emissions is lower than it would be otherwise. From the standpoint of climate change, if all our electricity caused zero emissions, we could run our hair dryers all day long; it would still cost us money, but we wouldn't be contributing at all to global warming.

If, on the other hand, our electricity is generated predominantly by burning coal, the story is very different. Coal-fired power plants produce nearly half of the nation's electricity but at an enormous cost to the environment: they are responsible for nearly one-third of the nation's *total* global warming emissions (not to mention the mercury emitted, along with a lot of air and water pollution).

Many states, including West Virginia and Indiana, get almost all of their electricity from coal. Other states, such as Maine and Oregon, rely on a mix of more climate-friendly means to generate electricity, including renewable sources. Figure 6.6 gives a breakdown of the amount of coal

---

UCS Climate Team FAST FACT

Coal-fired power plants generate nearly half of the nation's electricity but at an enormous cost to the environment: they produce nearly one-third of the nation's *total* carbon dioxide emissions, as well as mercury emissions and air and water pollution.

---

used in electricity production in each state. As you look at the percentage of your state's electricity that is produced from coal, bear in mind that electricity flows freely across most state borders and that some states export coal, while others import it. So consumers in states such as California, Rhode Island, and Vermont actually get more of their electricity from coal in practice than these production figures suggest.

Where does your household fall on the graph? As you can see, where you live makes a very big difference in the level of carbon emissions from your personal electricity use. If you want to know your share more precisely, the U.S. Energy Information Administration (EIA) offers a so-called carbon coefficient to compute exactly how much carbon dioxide is emitted for each kilowatt-hour of electricity you consume in any state. According to the EIA, the national average is 1.34 pounds of carbon dioxide per kilowatt-hour of energy consumed, but as you can see from the chart, your coefficient will vary depending on where you live. In Oregon, for instance, which uses a large proportion of hydropower (as well as other more sustainable renewable energy sources, such as wind and solar power), the carbon coefficient is 0.14 pound per kilowatt-hour. That's a relatively tiny amount of carbon dioxide for every kilowatt-hour of electricity—at average consumption rates, it's equal to roughly three-quarters of a ton of carbon emissions annually per household. If you live in West Virginia, however, your coefficient is 1.98—you will emit nearly 2 pounds of carbon dioxide for each kilowatt-hour of electricity. This means that an average household in West Virginia is responsible for nearly 11 tons of carbon emissions from the same electricity usage annually.

What can you, as a single residential customer on the electric grid, do about this huge differential? For one thing, if you live in a state that produces electricity predominantly from coal and you care about reducing your carbon emissions, you might consider shifting to natural gas or propane, a less carbon-intensive alternative for appliances such as your furnace, water heater, and stove—or adding your own renewable generating capacity in the form of photovoltaic panels on your roof.

If these options are too expensive, you might consider purchasing "green power." Currently, about half of the nation's utility companies

Figure 6.6. Percentage of Electricity from Coal (State by State)

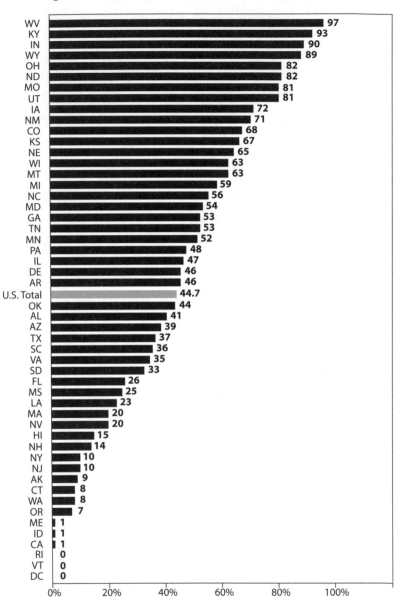

State	Percentage
WV	97
KY	93
IN	90
WY	89
OH	82
ND	82
MO	81
UT	81
IA	72
NM	71
CO	68
KS	67
NE	65
WI	63
MT	63
MI	59
NC	56
MD	54
GA	53
TN	53
MN	52
PA	48
IL	47
DE	46
AR	46
U.S. Total	44.7
OK	44
AL	41
AZ	39
TX	37
SC	36
VA	35
SD	33
FL	26
MS	25
LA	23
MA	20
NV	20
HI	15
NH	14
NY	10
NJ	10
AK	9
CT	8
WA	8
OR	7
ME	1
ID	1
CA	1
RI	0
VT	0
DC	0

This chart shows the percentage of electricity that is generated in each state by power plants that burn coal—the worst fuel in terms of carbon emissions per kilowatt-hour. Electricity flows freely across state lines, however, and some states import and export coal, so the actual amount you consume as a resident of a given state may vary somewhat from the numbers here. Source: Energy Information Administration, 2010.

allow customers to buy green power. It normally costs a few cents more per kilowatt-hour, but it helps move your utility company in the right direction, giving it an incentive to produce more climate-friendly electricity. In many plans, consumers can assign a certain amount of their electricity bill to green power, and the utility company will either purchase or produce green power to fuel their homes or supply the national energy grid.

Even if your utility doesn't offer such an option, anyone can purchase green power with renewable energy credits, or RECs, from a third-party provider. RECs represent the "green" attributes of electricity generated by renewable sources, as distinct from the electricity itself. What you actually pay for is the benefit of adding clean, renewable energy generation to the regional or national electricity grid. The DOE's Green Power Network (available at http://apps3 .eere.energy.gov/greenpower) can help you find out what green power options are available in your area. The website also offers tips on how to support clean energy projects nationwide.

Green power certification programs such as Green-e, which is voluntary, can help ensure that the electricity you're purchasing is coming from renewable energy facilities that meet strict environmental criteria. Voluntary purchases of green energy and certification programs such as Green-e have been important drivers of renewable energy development. In fact, the latest figures from the DOE's National Renewable Energy Laboratory show that voluntary programs accounted for as much renewable energy–generating capacity as that required by various state standards.

Generate Your Own Electricity

As awareness of their global warming impact continues to rise, many homeowners have become interested in generating cleaner electricity on their own. One way to do this is to install *solar electric (photovoltaic) panels*. Solar panels are an increasingly appealing option for environmentally conscious homeowners. Solar power is unquestionably one of the most environmentally benign energy sources available, and its cost, while generally higher than that of other technologies, has dropped by nearly 90 percent over the past two decades. And all indications are that prices will continue to fall in the near and medium terms. A household photovoltaic system can cost anywhere from $16,000 to $45,000, but the energy it generates could potentially meet nearly all of your home's future energy needs, with *no* carbon emissions. A number of incentive programs also help make solar power more affordable, sometimes reducing the overall cost of installation by 50 percent or more.

Such incentives are helping photovoltaic systems become more widespread, especially in California. A state-run program called the California Solar Initiative reports that homeowners in the state have undertaken nearly 80,000 solar projects to date, totaling more than 800 megawatts of electricity-generating capacity. The Database of State Incentives for Renewables and Efficiency (www.dsireusa.org) offers a comprehensive listing of state and local tax rebate programs, as well as incentives offered by specific utilities.

Another possibility, depending on your circumstances, is a residential *wind turbine*. Depending on its size, a small residential wind turbine can generate 5 to 10 kilowatts under optimal conditions, lowering the average home's electricity bill by 50 to 90 percent and avoiding approximately 200 tons of carbon dioxide emissions from conventional power generation over an approximately 20-year lifetime. Such systems are still quite expensive, and they require at least an acre of open property and prevailing winds of 10 miles per hour or more. Wind turbines may also face zoning and permitting hurdles in some locations. But they do offer an attractive and viable zero-carbon option, especially for some rural homes and farms. Larger wind turbines, of course, are quickly becoming commonplace in many parts of the United States as well as in many other countries.

Getting to 20

As we discussed at the beginning of this chapter, electricity use in our homes makes up a significant proportion of our personal global warming emissions. By looking over the strategies in this chapter and ferreting out the electricity hogs in your home, you can make a sizable dent in your global warming emissions. Lighting is a critical category, as are older appliances. You can also zero out electricity emissions by purchasing renewable electricity from your utility—often with very little impact on your electricity bills. While we recommend this step, it is not a substitute for reducing your electricity use at home. Decreasing overall electricity demand means less pressure to build new carbon-intensive fossil fuel power plants.

As we will discuss further in part III, there are many productive ways to get involved in helping to reduce your state's dependence on coal; working to wean our nation off burning coal to produce electricity is one of the most important ways in which we can move collectively toward reducing our global warming emissions.

But for now, by reducing your electricity usage, helping to incentivize renewable energy through green power purchasing, or even generating some zero-carbon electricity, you have made an important start.

CHAPTER 7

A Low-Carbon Diet

The act of putting into your mouth what
the earth has grown is perhaps your most
direct interaction with the earth.

—Frances Moore Lappé

In deciding what to eat each day, most of us consider a variety of factors, from fat and calories to what tastes best. But we don't usually think about the amount of global warming emissions resulting from the food we eat. The fact is, though, if you're trying to reduce your personal share of global warming emissions, your diet can make a big difference.

As the chart on the next page shows, our analysis finds that the food and beverages we each consume account for about 14 percent of our contribution to global warming. Because foods vary widely in the emissions they create, you should be able to significantly reduce your food-related emissions by choosing foods more carefully. Best of all, these choices may be healthier than what you are currently eating and may save you money, too.

Thinking about Your Carbon "Foodprint"

Given the long and diverse paths various foods take to get to the dinner table, it is extremely complicated to calculate precisely how much any particular food contributes to global warming. Many inputs are involved along the way: that tomato in our salad may have been grown in a heated greenhouse; the farmers who grew it may or may not have used a lot of fossil fuel–derived fertilizers or chemical pesticides; and it may have been shipped for thousands of miles to get to us. Global warming emissions are created in all of these steps, but the exact amounts depend on numerous

Figure 7.1. Emissions from Food

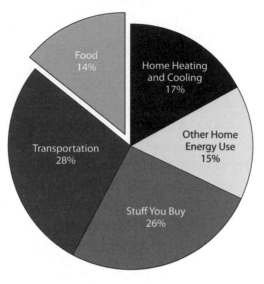

Food makes up roughly 14 percent of your total
global warming emissions—just under 3 tons of
the average American's 21 tons of total emissions.
Source: UCS modeling.

variables, from the extent to which the farm uses sustainable practices to the way the food-processing facility's electricity is produced.

Still, we know enough about the overall picture to make some recommendations for effective climate-friendly choices at the grocery store. We know, for instance, that food's journey to our home most likely involves carbon dioxide emissions from the diesel fuel that runs tractors, combines, and other farm equipment as well as the trucks that transport food; from the fossil fuels used to produce fertilizers and pesticides; and from the electricity, often from coal- or gas-burning plants, used on farms and in food processing. Those emissions are relatively straightforward to quantify.

In most other industries and activities, these kinds of carbon dioxide emissions from the burning of fossil fuels make up most, if not all, of the carbon footprint. In agriculture, however, the story is more complex because it involves emissions of other global warming gases besides car-

---

ASK THE EXPERTS

What Is a Carbon Dioxide Equivalent, or CO_2e?

Most of this book focuses on carbon dioxide (CO_2) because it is by far the main culprit in global warming. As we noted in chapter 3, today's world produces CO_2 in such huge quantities that it tends to dwarf the effects of all the other global warming gases combined. Food and agriculture, however, create other global warming gases that we need to take into account, too. Carbon dioxide—released by everything from driving tractors to processing and packaging food—still makes up the bulk (more than 70 percent) of global food-related emissions. But especially in raising livestock, two other global warming gases—methane and nitrous oxide—play a significant role.

This chapter uses the internationally recognized shorthand term "carbon dioxide equivalent," or CO_2e. This term takes into account the potency of various gases such as methane and nitrous oxide and converts their total global warming impact to an equivalent mass of CO_2, making it easier to discuss and compare overall agricultural emissions.

---

bon dioxide. Among these, methane and nitrous oxide, both potent heat-trapping gases, are created in abundance on farms.

Methane (CH_4) is produced when organic matter (from plants or animals) decomposes without oxygen, as happens naturally in swamps, for instance. But it also happens when cows and other ruminants digest their food. Ruminants—cows, sheep, goats, and buffaloes—have multiple stomachs, allowing them to digest coarse plant material that other animals can't eat. Some of the fiber breaks down in the first stomach in a process known as enteric fermentation, giving off methane, which the animals exhale. And a great deal of methane is generated when manure from farm animals is collected in huge oxygen-poor "manure lagoons," as is done in industrial animal production facilities such as CAFOs (confined animal feeding operations). Wetland rice cultivation also releases methane into the atmosphere because in most rice-growing countries the paddies are flooded, so plant residues rot underwater, emitting methane. (Later in the chapter we discuss the methane generated in landfills as food waste decomposes.)

Even though the amounts of methane emitted in all these activities are

Figure 7.2. Comparison of Global Warming Emissions by Food Type
(by Pound or Pint)

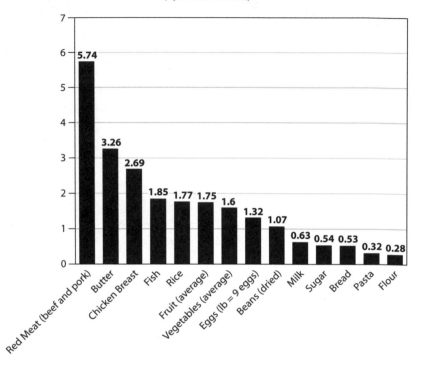

This graph shows global warming emissions (in pounds of emissions per pound or pint) for various foods. Red meat (beef and pork) clearly tops the list, with emissions three times higher than for fish and nearly 18 times higher than for pasta. Source: UCS modeling.

relatively low compared with emissions of carbon dioxide, methane is 25 times more potent as a global warming gas in the atmosphere than is carbon dioxide. As a result, one recent study estimates that methane accounts for about 13 percent of U.S. food-related global warming emissions.

Emissions of nitrous oxide (N_2O) are another significant factor in agriculture. Nitrous oxide comes in part from chemical fertilizers used on crops, and it is also released naturally by soil. Good soil management practices, such as adjusting the amounts and types of fertilizer used, can lower unnecessary emissions of nitrous oxide. Like methane, nitrous oxide is released in tiny quantities compared with carbon dioxide, but

A LOW-CARBON DIET

each pound of N_2O has a global warming impact equivalent to roughly 300 pounds of carbon dioxide. Overall, N_2O is estimated to be responsible for about 15 percent of U.S. food-related global warming emissions.

Not only do agricultural emissions involve gases other than carbon dioxide; farming also differs from other activities in that it offers the potential to sequester carbon in the soil, keeping it out of the atmosphere and thereby offsetting some of the global warming emissions created in food production.

In thinking about your carbon "foodprint," a key point is that the production of different foods results in very different levels of emissions. Our team analyzed the "emissions intensity" of various types of food per pound (or pint). As the chart shows, a pound of red meat (beef or pork) causes nearly *18 times* the emissions of a pound of pasta, for instance.

A number of research teams around the world have conducted similar analyses of food-related emissions, measuring emissions per dollar spent on food or emissions per calorie. The results have differed to some extent on the basis of assumptions built into the models. But no matter how you measure it, one thing stands out in all the data: pound for pound, dollar for dollar, or calorie for calorie, meat—especially beef—contributes the most to global warming.

Eat Less Meat

The single most effective choice you can make to lower the global warming emissions resulting from your diet is to eat less meat, especially beef. Meat causes more global warming emissions than almost any other type of food.

In the United States, according to a recent study by the Union of Concerned Scientists, beef production accounts for more than one-third of all

UCS Climate Team *FAST FACT*

By any measure, the production of meat, especially beef, causes more global warming emissions than almost any other type of food. Eating less meat can be a useful strategy for lowering your carbon footprint.

141

heat-trapping emissions from the nation's agricultural sector. And in parts of the world with lower industrial emissions, livestock-related emissions account for an even greater percentage of global warming emissions. One influential 2006 report by the Food and Agriculture Organization of the United Nations (FAO) analyzed data on livestock globally and determined that production of red meat accounts for about *18 percent* of total global warming emissions and that meat is nearly 50 times more emissions intensive than many other foods. The FAO study, unlike the estimates from the Union of Concerned Scientists, included the emissions caused by deforestation, especially in the Amazon basin, where vast areas of rainforest are cut to make room for raising cattle and growing their feed. This is significant because rainforests are net carbon absorbers, whereas logged forests release carbon dioxide from decaying trees and disturbed soil. While rainforests are cut for ranching, they are also cleared for other agricultural purposes. These include—most notably—soybean and palm oil production for international markets (small-scale farming is no longer a major driver in deforestation). In one analysis, deforestation indirectly related to agriculture was found to account—all by itself—for a whopping 6 percent of total global carbon emissions.

Even without including the effects of deforestation, however, all the signs point to red meat being responsible for more global warming emissions than most other foods. According to our team's analysis, the only food that comes close to the emissions intensity of red meat is cheese. Not only does cheese come from a methane-producing animal, but the production of each single pound of it generally requires about 10 pounds of milk. If you do eat meat, chicken and fish are by far the best choices from a climate standpoint. But by and large, a diet rich in grains, vegetables, and fruits will yield dramatically lower emissions than one heavy in meat.

Why is meat such a large producer of global warming emissions? One reason is simply that it is a resource-intensive food. The land used to produce much of the grain fed to livestock could otherwise grow grain for human consumption. By one estimate, grain-fed cattle must consume some seven pounds of grain to produce a single pound of beef. Of course, cows can be entirely grass fed, and pastures, if properly managed, can

Is There Such a Thing as Sustainable Palm Oil?

Palm oil, a highly saturated fat that is solid at room temperature, is found in thousands of products, from baked goods and ice cream to household cleaning products and shampoo. If you look at the ingredients listed on products you buy at the grocery store, you will frequently see palm oil (or its major component, palmitate). Many food companies have been replacing partially hydrogenated oils with palm oil because it contains no trans fat. Nonetheless, because palm oil contains high levels of saturated fat, it is probably not a particularly healthy alternative. The even bigger problem, however, is the link between palm oil and large-scale deforestation.

Indonesia and Malaysia, which have the largest tropical forests in Asia, are by far the dominant producers of palm oil on the world market today. Their tropical forests are being cleared at a rapid pace to make room for new palm oil plantations. The trees and soils in these forests contain enormous amounts of carbon. When the trees are cut and burned, hundreds of tons of carbon dioxide are emitted into the atmosphere for every acre of forest that is cleared. All told, tropical deforestation accounts for some 15 percent of global warming pollution today.

In response to a worldwide call for action on this issue, a group of palm oil producers, processors, and traders and environmentalists formed the Roundtable on Sustainable Palm Oil (RSPO) in 2004. The group developed criteria for "certified sustainable palm oil," and it offers that certification. However, members of the group are not required to be certified or to use certified sustainable palm oil. Additionally, there are some very serious problems with the current criteria used for certification, which do not take into account heat-trapping emissions from deforestation and changes in land use. Without accounting for those factors, today's so-called sustainable palm oil is likely to continue to drive deforestation and thus global warming while destroying the homes of forest peoples and animals. The RSPO is now working to develop new, improved recommendations on the certification program for sustainable palm oil, but these recommendations are not yet in place. In the meantime, your best bet is to avoid products with palm oil and encourage companies to find more sustainable and healthier alternatives.

sequester substantial amounts of carbon. But the fact is, most cattle in the United States are grown in confined areas and fed corn.

Manure-related emissions (from both cattle and hogs) are concentrated in CAFOs, which cram thousands of animals into small spaces. Globally, the use of CAFOs in livestock production is continuing to rise. In the manure cesspits used by CAFOs, organic matter in the waste most often breaks down anaerobically (that is, without oxygen) and increases methane emissions. Manure in pastures, by contrast, breaks down with oxygen and thus tends to generate carbon dioxide, as opposed to methane.

Because the methane released by animal waste is chemically the same as natural gas, some farmers around the world are attempting to capture some of it as "biogas" to generate electricity. Farmers in the Netherlands, for example, are trying to cook pig manure and use the captured methane to power the local grid. Similar programs are in place at several farms in California and elsewhere in the United States, which use the energy from the captured methane to offset their farms' energy demands. These efforts are laudable from a climate perspective, but to the extent that they promote the use of massive CAFOs, they may not offer the most promising solution to the overall emissions picture from meat production.

Finally, synthetic fertilizers used to grow animal feed also come with a heavy price in emissions, largely because nitrous oxide has a big effect in the atmosphere even in tiny amounts. As we discussed earlier, N_2O is some 300 times more effective at trapping heat than carbon dioxide.

The data are clear that if you are going to make a single change to your diet, lowering your food-related emissions by eating less meat, especially beef, is the most effective choice. This is particularly true for most Americans because the average American diet includes so much meat— roughly 270 pounds of it per year, nearly four times the global average.

Replacing the meat in your diet with grains, vegetables, and fruits can cut your food-related emissions dramatically. It also results in the kind of balanced diet recommended by the U.S. Department of Agriculture and most leading dietitians, nutritionists, and health professionals. You don't need to become a vegetarian or vegan (someone who eats no animal products) to make a significant difference. If a family of four who eat the

---

ASK THE EXPERTS

Should We All Become Vegetarians to Combat Climate Change?

If meat is such a problem for the climate, is it logical to ask whether we should all become vegetarians—or even vegans, who eat no meat, eggs, or dairy products? Our considered answer is no. There is no question that you can reduce your individual emissions significantly by reducing your consumption of meat and dairy. But we do not advocate an agriculture without animals. Healthy, sustainable agricultural practices keep the land productive for future generations by constantly replenishing the soil's fertility. This is efficiently achieved on farming operations that grow both crops and livestock, using manure to build the soil's organic matter and maintain its fertility.

In addition, ruminant animals, which have the unique ability to turn inedible grass into high-quality food, allow for productive use of marginal lands unsuitable for crops. The bottom line: while becoming a vegetarian or vegan would significantly reduce your dietary contribution to global warming and may well be a healthy solution for you, it need not be the goal for everyone.

---

average amount of meat decides to cut their meat consumption in half, they can slash their food-related emissions by three tons or more annually, nearly as much as a half year's worth of driving. Instituting a "meatless Monday" could make a big difference, too.

Minimize Food Packaging and Processing

What else can you do to reduce your food-related emissions? One aspect of a product's carbon footprint that is fairly easy to keep track of is packaging. In general, foods in the United States are accompanied by more layers of packaging than are used practically anywhere else in the world, creating emissions in manufacturing and generating tons of avoidable waste.

Of course, some packaging is necessary: you can't buy tomato sauce by the handful. If packaging reduces spoilage and food waste, as cans do, it may even lower overall emissions in the food chain. But that's no excuse for excessive packaging; many products have unnecessary layers, which are a pure waste.

Supermarkets frequently wrap vegetables such as celery and cucumbers in plastic and Styrofoam, but many offer unwrapped versions as well. While the packaging may be intended to lengthen the life of the vegetables, it's worthwhile asking whether you really need it. Big-box retailers are sometimes the worst offenders. The fact is, you don't have to buy fruits and vegetables encased in plastic clamshells; seek out other options whenever possible. A general rule of thumb is to limit packaging to what is required to reduce food spoilage or get the product home safely.

Foods that come in single-serving containers, such as individually wrapped cheese slices and single-portion bags of chips, are needlessly wasteful. Buying these items in larger sizes or in bulk not only reduces your carbon footprint but also is cheaper if you plan to use all of the product. Nevertheless, while it's wasteful to make a habit of purchasing overpackaged items, don't take yourself (or others) to task for doing so now and then when it is a practical solution. Parents of small children know how much perishable food their kids can waste. If a camping trip requires a few nonperishable juice boxes or an outing to the playground works better with a single serving of applesauce, don't worry about it. Occasional use of single-serving packaging has practically no impact on your individual emissions.

Collectively, however, a prime example of unnecessary packaging is single-use bottled beverages. Approximately 1.3 million tons' worth of plastic PET (polyethylene terephthalate) is used each year in the United States to make single-use water bottles alone, requiring the equivalent of 50 million barrels of oil. More than three-quarters of these bottles end up in landfills. Production of bottled water alone puts the equivalent of 2.5 million tons of carbon dioxide into the atmosphere—and that doesn't include the emissions caused by transporting the bottles around the country. The alternative, drinking tap water, has comparatively few production and transportation emissions, and it costs nothing extra. Switching to tap water is easy and saves both the environment and your pocketbook. Similarly, drinking whatever beverage you choose from a reusable container can make a significant difference.

In fact, largely because of packaging, our analysis shows that beverages such as sodas, sports drinks, and bottled water account for roughly 7 *percent* of the average American's food-related emissions—around three-

---

ASK THE EXPERTS

Is Bottled Water Safer Than Tap Water?

Many people drink bottled water because they are concerned about the safety of their tap water. Their concerns may be justified in some areas, but in most of the United States, tap water may actually be safer to drink than bottled water.

A 2009 report by the U.S. Government Accountability Office showed that the U.S. Food and Drug Administration's safety protections for bottled water are less stringent than the Environmental Protection Agency's guidelines for tap water. The EPA follows strict principles in determining the acceptable levels of hazardous chemicals and minerals in public drinking water. Although companies that produce bottled water are legally obligated to follow similar requirements, the FDA lacks the authority to enforce them. For instance, di(2-ethylhexyl)phthalate, or DEHP, a potentially toxic chemical used to make plastic more flexible, is regulated by the EPA in tap water. Bottled water facilities, however, are not even required to test for DEHP levels.

Bottled water not only adds tons of carbon dioxide to the atmosphere annually and tons of waste to landfills, it offers no clear benefit to your health. If you are concerned about the safety of your tap water, installing a water filter on your faucet or a convenient pitcher is a far better choice for your carbon "foodprint" than drinking bottled water.

---

quarters of a ton of heat-trapping emissions for the average household annually. Although this amount pales in comparison with the carbon emissions resulting from the average American's driving habits, bottled beverages are worth paying attention to because, much like the waste of electricity through "phantom loads" discussed in chapter 6, they present an easy, low- or no-cost way to avoid unnecessary global warming emissions. Reducing your consumption of bottled beverages can thus play a significant role in reducing your food-related emissions that, at least in the case of sodas and sports drinks, will most likely provide health benefits as well.

As with packaging, the extent of food *processing* can make a notable difference in your food-related emissions. Food processing is, of course, a big, generally profitable enterprise. We tend to purchase more and more of our fruits and vegetables in processed form: canned, frozen, dried, or as juice. Remember that each step in processing these foods normally adds to their carbon footprint—from the energy used in freezing, drying, or canning to the added compounds, colorings, and preservatives found in most processed foods.

Finally, be on the lookout for food companies that boast of environmental benefits on their product labels and in advertising while using excessive, carbon-intensive processing or packaging. Companies may emphasize an environmental benefit while still making surprisingly poor choices for global warming in other aspects of their business.

Reduce Your Food Waste

Another significant food-related contribution to global warming emissions is the food that is wasted at each point along the food supply chain, from production to processing and consumption. Wasted food accounts for a surprisingly large amount of emissions because there's so much of it: in the United States in 2009, we wasted more than one-quarter of the food available for consumption—a total of some 33 million tons of food, most of which generates methane gas in municipal landfills instead of being used to create compost, a natural fertilizer.

So, in addition to all the other good reasons for not wasting food, add helping the climate. Of course, it helps if you buy more no more food than you need, especially those foods that will go bad quickly. To aid in this effort, try tracking your use of fresh food more closely, regularly organize your refrigerator, and make creative use of leftovers.

One study analyzed the waste stream of food from production to disposal. The study found that 60 percent of food waste occurred at the consumer level, meaning that individual actions can have a real impact on the total amount wasted. In the United States, the vast majority of food thrown away by consumers ends up in landfills, where it contributes to methane emissions. As we noted above, methane traps 25 times more heat per molecule in the atmosphere than carbon dioxide, and landfills are among the largest contributors of methane to the atmosphere. According to the U.S. Environmental Protection Agency (EPA), food waste is now the largest component of municipal solid waste, representing more than 14 percent of all trash reaching landfills and incinerators.

Figure 7.3. Municpal Solid Waste Discarded (by Material) in 2009

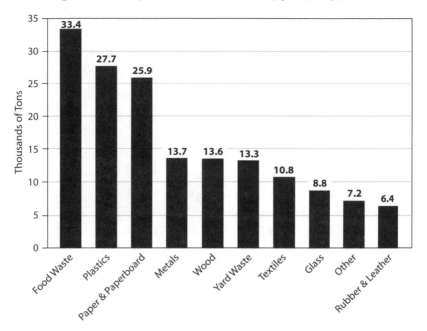

This graph shows the components of municipal solid waste discarded in 2009. Food waste represents the largest component by weight. Source: EPA, "Municipal Solid Waste in the United States: Facts and Figures," 2009.

Composting food waste is a good strategy for keeping it out of landfills. An EPA study demonstrated that every ton of food waste composted saves close to a ton of carbon dioxide equivalent from going into the atmosphere. In addition, the study estimated that applying compost to soils can result in a net storage of carbon. Unlike the anaerobic decomposition in a landfill, composting is an aerobic process; that is, it uses oxygen and doesn't release methane. More information about composting can be found in a report from the Union of Concerned Scientists called "The Climate-Friendly Gardener: A Guide to Combating Global Warming from the Ground Up," available at www.ucsusa.org. It is important to note that you don't have to be a gardener—or even have a garden, for that matter—to compost your food waste; in fact, composting is increasingly catching on in the workplace and on the municipal level.

Outside of curbing food waste at home, consumers can help reduce food waste by participating in food recovery programs. Many organizations collect perishable foods from wholesale and retail sources and the food service industry for distribution to food banks and shelters. By volunteering with a food recovery program, you can reduce the amount of food waste in your community.

What about Organic Food?

You may already buy certified organically grown food to help preserve the long-term productivity of our farmlands and to avoid the often excessive use of fertilizers, herbicides, and pesticides—and associated pollution—in today's industrial agriculture. Does buying organic food reduce your carbon emissions? Unfortunately, the science is not yet definitive in this area.

There are good reasons to believe that organic practices can help the climate. Producing pesticides, and especially chemical fertilizers, requires fossil fuel, and overuse of these chemicals is widespread in conventional farming. So eliminating chemical fertilizers and pesticides and replacing them with organic fertilizers (crop residues, cover crops, compost, and animal manures) and making other changes in farming practices ought to benefit the climate.

Also, organic methods can, theoretically at least, increase the amount of carbon stored in the soil. Using composted manure and planting cover crops can build carbon in the soil just as planting trees does. More carbon in the soil means less in the air, and it also can mean that the soil has better water retention. Because of this, organic farms are known to have higher crop production during droughts than conventional farms—an important benefit, since global warming leads to more frequent droughts in many regions.

In practice, however, agricultural systems are highly complex. Despite the theoretical benefits to the climate of organic farming, some studies have shown that increasing organic carbon in the soil can (but does not always) increase emissions of nitrous oxide and methane, thus reducing or even outweighing the climate benefits of carbon sequestration. Produc-

What Is Carbon Sequestration?

Carbon sequestration is the long-term storage of carbon in the soil. Soil contains about 80 percent of the total carbon on land, so it plays a vital role in the global carbon cycle. Carbon is stored in the soil primarily through "soil organic matter," which is a complex mixture of decomposing animal and plant matter, microbes, and carbon associated with soil minerals.

Although many types of agriculture can sequester carbon, organic farming uses management techniques that maximize carbon sequestration, such as cover crops, longer crop rotation, and the use of composted manure. And the benefits of these techniques go beyond the removal of carbon from the atmosphere: carbon storage in soils enhances soil and water quality, decreases nutrient loss, reduces soil erosion, and increases water conservation.

tivity differences also play into comparisons of organic and conventional animal agriculture. Feedlot cattle often go to slaughter at younger ages than pasture-raised cattle, and as a result conventional systems can have lower global warming emissions per pound of meat than pasture cattle. However, the conventional system's advantages can be offset where pastures are managed to sequester large quantities of carbon.

A study comparing organic dairy farms with conventional ones in Europe, for example, attempted to measure the carbon dioxide, nitrous oxide, and methane emissions from various components of farm operations: the animals themselves, feed (whether pasture or grain), manure storage, and housing, among others. The study got mixed results. Conventional farms tended to have higher emissions per acre than organic farms, but the study also found that conventional farms had lower emissions than their organic counterparts on the basis of the amounts of milk produced. Though the study did not even assess differences in soil carbon sequestration, it amply showed the difficulties involved in assessing the relative climate impacts of organic versus conventional farming.

So what does this information mean for you as you make choices in the grocery store?

All we can say on the basis of the currently available scientific evidence is that buying organic food *might* afford a modest reduction in your carbon footprint. While the Union of Concerned Scientists strongly supports organic farming, the primary reasons to buy organically grown food are to support a more sustainable agricultural system and to improve your health by avoiding pesticides, not to reduce your climate impact.

What about Eating Locally Produced Food?

If the verdict is still out on organic food, what about food produced locally? Can we reduce our carbon emissions by buying local food? Are "food miles"—the miles traveled by our dinner from farm to table—a good measure of global warming impact?

At first glance, it sounds as if local must be better. If the choice is between identical food identically grown nearby or far away, local food is certainly the clear winner because it entails fewer transportation emissions. But suppose the local food is produced on a farm with higher emissions; how does that compare with the savings in transportation? In northern states, for instance, is it better to buy tomatoes grown in local, heated greenhouses or those grown in open-air fields hundreds of miles away?

To answer this question, researchers at Carnegie Mellon University studied food miles and the emissions resulting from U.S. food purchases. They calculated the total transportation requirements—and transportation emissions—of food production, not just delivery of food from farm to retail but also delivery of fertilizer, equipment, and other inputs to the farm.

Their results show that transportation accounts for only 11 percent of the carbon emissions caused by food production. Of that amount, so-

---

UCS Climate Team *FAST FACT*

Emissions from food production account for some 83 percent of a food's global warming footprint; transporting the food from farm to supermarket accounts for *just 4 percent of food-related emissions*. There are lots of good reasons to eat local food, but unless the highly perishable food has traveled by air, reducing global warming is not one of them.

Figure 7.4. Supply Chain Food Miles by Food Group

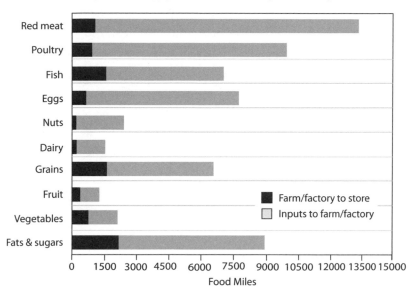

Transporting food from farms to retail stores causes only a small fraction of food emissions from transportation and just a tiny portion of overall food emissions.
Source: Adapted from Kling and Hough, 2010.

called upstream transportation of inputs to the farm (or to farm suppliers) accounts for some 7 percent of overall food-related transportation emissions. Most notably, perhaps, final delivery—the trip from the farm to the supermarket—*accounts for just 4 percent of total food emissions on average.* By comparison, production of the food accounts for 83 percent of the carbon emissions, with warehousing and wholesale and retail operations making up the small remainder.

What does this mean for you? The emissions from producing food are so much greater than those from transporting it that transportation makes up only a tiny part of your carbon "foodprint." Even if local food eliminated *all* the emissions from transportation, long-distance food produced on a farm with 5 percent lower emissions might actually contribute less to global warming. As the chart above shows, this basic fact holds true, with some variations, in all major food categories.

An extreme example of this effect can be seen in farm products shipped to Europe or the United States from New Zealand. Several New Zealand researchers crunched the numbers to show that the carbon emissions from producing and delivering lamb, apples, and dairy products from New Zealand to the United Kingdom were actually lower than the emissions from the same foods produced locally in the United Kingdom. Why? The study no doubt sought to put New Zealand goods in the best possible light, but the numbers are still compelling: as these researchers demonstrated, not only do New Zealand farmers use less chemical fertilizer than their British counterparts, but also more than half of New Zealand's electricity derives from hydropower, which produces no carbon emissions. Those two differences, as it turns out, are enough to offset the emissions from *11,000 miles of ocean shipping*.

However, it is important to note that the mode of transportation does make a difference in this calculation. Mile for mile, as figure 7.5 shows, the volume of emissions from air freight is about four times the emissions caused by truck transport and nearly 50 times more than that of ocean transport. It is certainly well worth trying to be aware of food items transported by air. Examples include fresh seafood from far away, premium cheeses, and highly perishable items such as fruits, berries, vegetables such as asparagus, and cut flowers. If something commands a premium price and is highly perishable, it is very likely air freighted. Similarly, it can be helpful to consider tropical fruit and cut flowers as an occasional treat rather than an everyday necessity. Fruits such as pineapples are typically air freighted, for instance. Bananas and other tropical fruit are shipped, but usually in refrigerated boats and then long-haul trucks. In all these examples, "food miles" make a more significant difference to carbon emissions, so it makes sense to pay special attention to air-freighted items and to encourage your supermarket to publicize information for customers about air-freighted items.

The bottom line when it comes to food miles: as the well-known food author Michael Pollan has noted, there is much to be said for serving food you know "the story behind," which is much easier to accomplish by buying locally. Buying local food is an excellent way to support farmers in

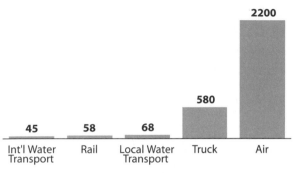

Figure 7.5. Emissions by Mode of Transport
(pounds of CO_2e per 1,000 ton-miles)

Transporting food by air causes nearly 4 times the carbon emissions of transporting by truck and nearly 50 times the emissions of ocean transport. Source: Adapted from Weber and Matthews, 2008.

your area and to ensure freshness and quality. But other strategies are more effective in reducing the global warming emissions resulting from your diet.

Reward "Green" Food Purveyors

We have reviewed some changes we can each make in our diets and some of the choices we have in how our food is grown, processed, packaged, and disposed of—all of which can reduce our impact on global warming. One thing we haven't discussed, however, is eating out. On average, Americans eat meals outside of the home four and one-half times per week, or one in every five meals. As a result, restaurants account for some 24 percent of food-related emissions nationally.

Across the country, more and more restaurants are working to offer appealing and healthy food while also lowering their emissions and finding ways to operate more sustainably. Take, for example, the Mercury Café, a restaurant in Denver, Colorado. This restaurant cooks with all organic food from local farms, and it has worked over the past several years to eliminate as many of its global warming emissions as possible.

Today the restaurant gets all of its electricity from wind turbines and solar panels.

The point, of course, is not simply to laud the work of one Colorado restaurant. There are thousands of restaurants across the country working to lower their global warming emissions. In fact, a trade group called the Green Restaurant Association has, since 1990, offered sustainability ratings for restaurants in the United States and Canada. To become certified as a "green restaurant," an establishment is rated on sustainability in categories from energy use to waste management.

The Green Restaurant Association also honors restaurants that excel in all categories (more information is available at www.dinegreen.com). In 2010, it awarded its highest rating to just one restaurant, the Grey Plume in Omaha, Nebraska. By almost any measure, the Grey Plume sets the standard, operating in a facility built to the highest environmental and energy efficiency standards, employing state-of-the-art recycling techniques, and conserving in all areas, from water usage to the disposal of kitchen grease, which is converted to biodiesel fuel.

Attention to food-related emissions seems to be increasing to some extent. A growing trend in Europe, for instance, is to make climate-friendly options more evident to consumers. In the United Kingdom in 2008, for example, Tesco, one of the largest UK food retailers, began to introduce carbon-footprint labeling on many food items. Similar strategies are currently being developed in France and Sweden. The idea, of course, is that consumers who have readily available information about carbon emissions will make more thoughtful purchasing choices.

Today in the United States, few restaurants or food producers of any kind go to such lengths to inform consumers of the carbon footprint of their products. But as customers interested in lowering our impact on global warming, we can certainly make a statement by patronizing restaurants and food-related firms that are taking steps toward environmental sustainability. By making smart choices in the foods we order and frequenting restaurants working toward environmental sustainability, we can reduce our global warming emissions even when we eat out.

Getting to 20

No matter what kind of diets we have, the food we eat contributes to global warming. We all need to eat, of course, but most of us will be able to shave a few hundred pounds (or maybe even thousands) off our total emissions profile by making conscious choices about our food. With that said, don't count on this category alone to achieve all or most of your 20 percent reduction for this year. Cutting back on meat—particularly beef—is the best way to make gains in this category. If you currently consume a large quantity of meat or cheese, the climate (not to mention your heart) will benefit if you cut back. Other strategies that provide gains without curbing your enjoyment of a wide variety of foods include reducing food waste and avoiding nonessential packaging, with special attention to bottled water and other drinks, such as soda and sports drinks. We don't recommend you worry much about food miles except to be alert to highly perishable items that have traveled by air; those come with a high carbon cost.

CHAPTER 8

The Right Stuff

You can't have everything. I mean,
where would you put it?

—Steven Wright

In the previous four chapters, we have examined our major contributions to global warming. The subjects we have covered so far—transportation, heating and cooling, electric appliances, and food—make up roughly three-quarters of our heat-trapping emissions. The wide variety of goods and services we buy account for the remaining quarter. It is a broad and diverse category, split fairly evenly between tangible items, such as furniture and clothing, and services, such as healthcare and legal advice.

As we will discuss, there are a number of ways to lower emissions in this category, but frankly, it's harder to make a significant dent here than in the other categories. As the chart illustrates, most of the goods and services we buy have a relatively small impact on the climate, and some specific categories lie mainly outside our individual control. See chapter 11 to learn how to have more control in those areas.

On our own, there is not much we can do to reduce the emissions from many of the services we purchase. Emissions related to healthcare, for example, from running hospitals and doctors' offices to supporting health insurance companies and pharmaceutical companies, account for 22 percent of the emissions in this category—some 5.7 percent of the average American's total global warming emissions. Realistically, though, as a healthcare consumer you are not going to choose your doctor, your hospital, or your medications on the basis of their global warming emissions, nor would we recommend that you do. Still, you can make some measur-

Figure 8.1. Emissions from Stuff You Buy

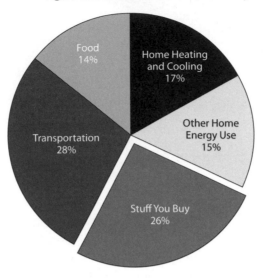

The goods and services you purchase account for more than one-quarter of your emissions, or more than five tons annually for the average American.
Source: UCS modeling.

able reductions in the emissions that result from the goods and services you buy, and in this chapter we offer some suggestions for doing so.

Taken together, the tangible nonfood items we buy—such as clothing, housewares, furniture, and electronics—account for about 10 percent of Americans' total global warming emissions. That translates to more than two tons of emissions for the average American every year. Most of us can reduce our emissions in this category fairly easily by finding smart ways to rein in excessive consumption. This recommendation boils down to two pieces of advice. First, buy less stuff. Second, when you do buy things, try to think about their impact on global warming, namely, how efficiently resources and energy have been used in their design, manufacture, and distribution. Between these two strategies, you may well find you can significantly reduce your carbon footprint with little real sacrifice. We'll talk about each approach separately.

Figure 8.2. Breakdown of Emissions from Stuff You Buy

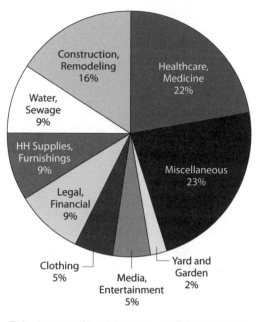

This chart provides a breakdown of the emissions associated with some of the goods and services you purchase. Source: UCS modeling.

Buy Less

Let's face it: most of our homes are filled with items we never really needed—toys our kids played with just a few times; poorly fitting clothes we rarely wear; gimmicky electronics that were popular for a couple of months; ill-considered gizmos bought on impulse. We could each make a real difference in reducing global warming by striving to avoid purchases that are likely to wind up in our attic or garage or in the trash. Buying less stuff has many advantages: it helps simplify and de-clutter our lives, it saves money, and it can lower our carbon emissions.

Many people who have chosen to closely monitor their consumption habits say buying less has other intangible advantages as well. Take the experience of Scott and Béa Johnson in Mill Valley, California, for instance.

When she was younger, Béa worked as a nanny for a family who lost all their possessions in a fire. She says that experience led her to decide to limit her attachment to material goods. Several years ago, she and her husband, Scott, decided to pare down their stuff. They started with small things, such as borrowing books from the library instead of buying them and using cloth dishtowels instead of buying paper towels. As Béa recalls, the first changes they made showed her how much her stuff had psychologically weighed her down. "When we started getting rid of things, it was kind of addictive," she says, adding that, odd as it may sound, "the less I have, the richer I feel."

The Johnsons would be the first to acknowledge that they went considerably further than most families would want to go in the quest to avoid consuming. Today they keep their clothing to a minimum, with about seven changes of clothes for each of them and their two sons. They have turned off virtually all junk mail and buy almost all their food in bulk, even taking their own reusable jars to the store for such items as cheese and shampoo. As a result, when trash day comes, the Johnsons normally have *absolutely no waste or recycling at all*.

But the most striking thing about the Johnsons is that they say they don't feel deprived in any way. They have kept all the things they care most about (photographs and treasured family heirlooms, for example), and they spend the same amount on their kids as they would otherwise—but they're more likely to give them experiences, such as a ski weekend or a certificate for a climbing gym, rather than electronic gadgets. Most of all, the Johnsons say, they just think very carefully before buying any new item.

Most of us won't want to adopt all of the Johnsons' habits. But we could all benefit from adopting some of them. Unfortunately, the environmental literature tends to focus on choosing among items to buy rather than looking for alternatives to purchasing them in the first place. The fact is, cutting down on excess consumption is likely to do more to lower your global warming emissions than worrying about buying one thing versus another.

A good example can be seen in the flurry of recent articles comparing traditional books with electronic readers such as Amazon's Kindle or

Apple's iPad to see which is the "greener" alternative. It is understandable that people would be curious about the subject. But as we will see, the analysis is less useful than it may at first appear.

When analysts crunch the numbers, they estimate that the emissions caused in manufacturing an electronic reader are about the same as those caused in manufacturing 20 to 40 books. So if you are a heavy reader who buys only new books, and if you keep your electronic reader for a number of years, the device might modestly lower your carbon footprint (especially if you replace your print subscriptions to newspapers and magazines with their electronic equivalents). What the debate obscures, however, is that a standard paperback book is responsible for around five and one-half pounds of carbon emissions in its manufacture and transport to your local bookstore. *But we are each responsible for more carbon emissions than that when we drive six miles round-trip alone in a typical car to the bookstore.* The point is this: don't waste time worrying about the carbon footprint of the way you read. Choose the form you enjoy and save your energy for areas where your choices will make a bigger difference—for instance, stopping at the bookstore on the way home from work instead of making an extra trip.

Buy Smarter

When it comes to items such as furniture and clothing, buying less is normally a more effective strategy than buying products that are climate friendly. With that said, when we face a choice between products, an eye to environmental considerations can often make a difference.

The best rule of thumb is to try, whenever possible, to buy products that embody higher resource or energy efficiency than whatever you are replacing. Buying a rake to replace your leaf blower will substantially reduce your emissions for that particular chore. The same goes for buying a fuel-efficient car to replace a gas-guzzler.

In general, buying well-made goods that will last a long time is a good strategy for reducing your emissions. It is also sensible to reward companies that have made progress in addressing global warming. Just make sure that the companies can point to specific efforts they are making rather than

Is Organic Cotton Really Greener?

By most assessments, cotton is one of the most chemical-intensive crops in the world. Although it is grown on just 2 percent of the world's farmland, it accounts for some 10 percent of global pesticide use and roughly 25 percent of global use of insecticides.

At least one analysis from the United Kingdom shows that the chemical load of conventionally grown cotton results in global warming emissions more than double those from organic cotton. All other inputs being equal, even though that organic cotton T-shirt is more expensive than its conventionally grown counterpart, it does represent significantly lower carbon emissions—and is a better option for other environmental reasons as well. So buy organic cotton if you can, but don't go out of your way to do so. Focus instead on the more important steps you can take to reduce your direct transportation and household emissions. Remember: clothing purchases are responsible for only 5 percent of your emissions in this category—or 1.4 percent of your total consumer emissions, as shown in figure 8.2.

merely espousing environmental platitudes to get your business or advertising their products as more environmentally friendly than they really are. That's called "greenwashing," and we discuss it more in chapter 10.

Here's one small example of how to take energy and resource use into consideration. As the box above shows, all other things being equal, organically grown cotton really does cause lower emissions than conventionally grown cotton because growing conventional cotton is an extremely chemical-intensive process, and organic methods remove this component of emissions from the manufacture of cotton fabric.

An equally important strategy to consider is buying used or refurbished items when you can. Such items (unless they are older, inefficient energy users such as used refrigerators or old gas-guzzling cars) virtually always result in fewer emissions than their brand-new counterparts. In other words, consider those garage sales or visits to the thrift shop as helping—however modestly—to combat climate change.

We'll address recycling more directly in a moment. But it also makes sense in general to choose items with reused or recycled content, such as

---

ASK THE EXPERTS

Does Wood Harvested Sustainably Really Make a Difference?

Most of us use wood products every day and purchase more than we realize. Of course, furniture and many of the building materials used to construct our homes and offices are made of wood, as are the paper products we use daily. Unlike fossil fuels and metals, the world's supply of wood is renewable. And, compared with steel, concrete, plastic, and brick, wood is a low-energy and low-emissions material for packaging and building—*but only when it is not the cause of deforestation.*

Worldwide, deforestation is occurring at an alarming rate, with an acre of tropical forest lost *every second*. As a result, emissions from tropical deforestation account for some 15 percent of the world's total carbon emissions—an enormous and largely preventable share. We cannot address global warming effectively if we ignore 15 percent of the problem.

The good news is that more wood products are being reused and recycled today than ever before. Improvements in recycling technology, availability, and financial support continue to help the spread of recycling efforts, which can further reduce pressures on primary forests. Buying recycled wood and paper products is a great way to lessen the demand for virgin timber.

Meanwhile, voluntary certification programs allow timber companies to meet globally approved standards of sustainable management. One of the largest certification programs, by the Forest Stewardship Council (FSC), has a specific set of forest management criteria that are currently being used on 41 million acres of tropical forest. Voluntary certification programs alone are unlikely to solve the problem of deforestation, but they do give consumers the opportunity to influence forestry practices and help prevent deforestation. The next time you are buying wood or wood products, look to see that they are certified as sustainably grown. Buying FSC-certified wood helps fight illegal deforestation by rewarding landowners who are managing their forests sustainably.

refilled toner cartridges for your printer or copy machine and recycled paper products. Some companies offer furniture made from sustainably harvested or reclaimed wood, and homeowners who are remodeling can purchase sustainably harvested lumber. These products in particular can make a substantial difference compared with those made from virgin timber.

What about Recycling?

The strategies we've been discussing can be useful in purchasing new things. But what we do with our stuff when we are through with it also makes a difference. Even though only about 2 percent of total U.S. carbon emissions comes directly from solid waste disposal, that figure doesn't nearly capture the power of recycling in combating global warming, especially considering that the average American creates some 4.3 pounds of trash each day.

Recycling reduces global warming emissions in two principal ways: it reduces the need for virgin materials (and the emissions that result from making or extracting them), and it reduces emissions from waste disposal, particularly methane from landfills. Plus, recycling can save money, especially for those who live in a city or town with high trash disposal costs.

By recovering valuable materials and allowing them to be reused in place of new raw materials, recycling can reduce carbon emissions significantly. This is particularly important because the industries that produce raw materials are often the most carbon intensive in the manufacturing sphere; by comparison, the equivalent recycled materials are produced with low-energy, low-emissions processes.

The impact of recycling depends to some extent on the material. Pound for pound, the biggest emissions reductions come from recycling aluminum. Emissions from aluminum recycling, which is a well-established industry, are a small fraction of those from virgin material production. Making a can from recycled aluminum, for instance, results in just 5 percent of the emissions of producing the same can from virgin materials. Glass and plastics recycling account for smaller overall savings, but they still significantly reduce manufacturing emissions. Aluminum, glass, and plastics, however, represent only a small part of the household waste stream, amounting to less than one-quarter of the volume of material recovered from municipal waste for recycling. (We discussed food waste in chapter 7.) The highest-volume recovered materials are paper and cardboard, which make up half of all the material recycled and composted in the United States.

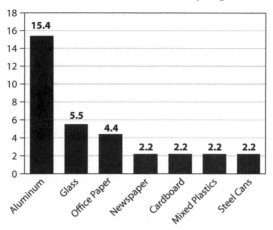

Figure 8.3. Pounds of CO_2e Emissions
Saved Per Pound of Recycling

Each pound of waste you recycle keeps more than twice its weight in CO_2e emissions out of the atmosphere. This graph shows the emissions saved by recycling one pound of material, as considered from a life cycle perspective, including reductions in the need for virgin materials and avoidance of potential methane emissions from disposal in a landfill.
Source: www.epa.gov/warm.

Americans currently recycle more than half of all the paper and cardboard they use, providing an important source of fiber to the paper industry. Today some recycled paper is even exported—usually to the paper industries of countries with limited forest resources. The mechanisms for recycling paper in the United States have become so strong that in some years they have come close to producing a glut in the paper market. The solution to that problem is simply to make sure to buy recycled paper products whenever possible.

Making paper from recycled material results in slightly fewer emissions than making it from virgin wood. But the most important benefit of paper recycling for global warming, according to estimates by the U.S. Environmental Protection Agency, is that it greatly reduces the need to cut down more trees. This in turn leads to more carbon sequestration in forests. Paper recycling, in other words, can mean more living trees absorbing and retaining carbon, keeping it out of the atmosphere.

In addition to its value in lessening the need for new materials, recycling lowers global warming emissions by reducing the amount of trash, which, no matter how it is handled, creates global warming emissions. This clearly holds true with incineration because burning organic waste gives rise to carbon dioxide and other air pollution. Incinerators are common only in the Northeast and in a few other states; Connecticut and Hawaii are the only states that burn roughly half of their trash. Some facilities capture energy from the incinerated trash, which offsets their emissions, but the number of such facilities is still quite small. Across the country, roughly 80 percent of our solid waste is currently deposited in landfills. And the problem for global warming is that landfills emit methane.

Waste is packed so densely in landfills that no air circulates in them except very near the surface. Just as with the farm emissions we discussed in chapter 7, this means that landfilled organic waste decomposes without oxygen, giving rise to methane gas, which, as we've discussed, is some 25 times more potent than carbon dioxide as a contributor to global warming. Landfill methane emissions are now a little lower than they were in the 1990s because of the expansion of paper recycling and the growing use of methane capture, which is now required in many locations. Burning the methane in such efforts does yield carbon dioxide emissions, but the methane captured and burned is often used to generate electricity, reducing the need for electricity from other sources, such as coal.

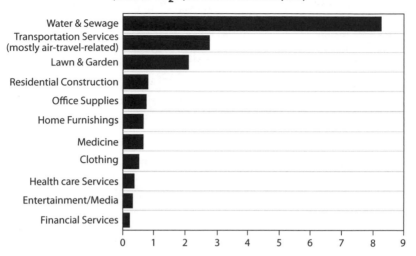

Figure 8.4. Emissions per Dollar Spent—Selected Categories
(Tons of CO_2e per Million Dollars Spent)

This graph shows global warming emissions created per dollar spent in various categories. Ranked in this way, water and sewage together make up our most carbon-intensive expenditure. Source: UCS modeling.

Carbon Intensity

As we have seen, one of recycling's main benefits is reducing the need for some carbon-intensive extraction of new source material. Different activities vary significantly in their carbon intensity, which can be determined by measuring the amount of carbon dioxide equivalent (CO_2e) emitted in the activity per dollar spent on it. The most carbon-intensive activities are not necessarily the largest overall contributors to global warming emissions, but looking at the most intensive activities can help us find ways to reduce emissions.

In keeping with this book's aim to systematically approach the emissions we are each responsible for, let's take a moment to look at the most emissions-intensive categories of our expenditures. The chart ranks emissions per dollar spent, excluding transportation, home energy use, and food consumption. It shows which of our expenditures contribute most, dollar for dollar, to global warming. In the rest of this chapter, we will focus on what you can do about some of these particularly carbon-intensive purchases and activities.

Water and Sewage

As the chart shows, a basic service we all take for granted—our water supply and sewage disposal—turns out to be by far the most carbon-intensive item among those listed. When we turn on the faucet, many of us imagine the water moving naturally from a reservoir to our home, much the way the current flows in a river. But the truth is, getting municipal water to our house or apartment normally involves huge pumps that require a surprisingly large amount of electricity. If you've ever carried several gallons of water, you know how heavy it is. When you think about it that way, it is easier to understand why pumping it up to that faucet in your high-rise apartment takes so much energy. All told, the electricity consumed to move and treat the water we use represents slightly more than 2 percent of total household emissions.

That may not sound like a lot, but the electrical costs associated with your water supply make it a surprisingly energy-intensive service, undoubtedly one of the most carbon-intensive purchases you make. As the chart shows, moving and treating water produces some 8.2 pounds of carbon dioxide for every dollar spent—more than three times the carbon intensity of most other sectors.

Of course, the situation is considerably more extreme in some drier parts of the country, where communities must pump their water from distant rivers, lakes, or reservoirs. In California, for example, 19 percent of the state's electricity is used to provide water-related services, including water pumping and wastewater treatment. Water from northern California is pumped hundreds of miles, over 2,000-foot mountains, to reach consumers in southern California. The energy used to deliver water to a household in southern California is actually equal to *one-third of the total electricity consumed by an average household.*

The state of Arizona faces an equally extreme situation, pumping some 500 billion gallons of water per year through an aqueduct that

UCS Climate Team *FAST FACT*

Water and sewage services are among the most carbon-intensive purchases you make. Water-related services account for a full 19 percent of California's electricity usage annually, for instance. That state uses one-third as much energy to deliver water to an average home in southern California as the average home there spends on electricity.

stretches 336 miles and climbs 2,800 feet to get from the Colorado River to Phoenix and Tucson. This endeavor, called the Central Arizona Project, is the largest user of electricity in the state, consuming one-fourth of the output of a major coal plant just to move water over mountain ranges and across the desert.

Worse yet, the costs of transporting water over great distances in places such as California and Arizona are likely to rise even higher in the coming years as some water sources are depleted and local water becomes scarcer. One anticipated effect of global warming, in fact, is that the Southwest will become even drier. Population pressures and current climate realities make it likely that municipalities will increasingly turn to even more energy-intensive technologies, such as desalination, to provide clean water to consumers. And as explained in the box on the next page, increased use of desalination will further raise the already high level of global warming emissions caused by the delivery and treatment of water.

What does the carbon-intensive nature of water-related services mean for you as a consumer? Quite simply, it means that using less water can help reduce your global warming emissions. Aside from the energy you use to heat your household water, you can save energy and reduce emissions by simply conserving water. Yes, you can take shorter showers and water your garden sparingly, but also consider onetime fixes that will make a difference for years to come: installing low-flow showerheads and toilets; investing in front-loading, low-water (and low-energy) washing machines; repairing leaking faucets and pipes; and using rain barrels to catch and store water. Taking these and other measures to lower your

---

Can't Desalination Solve the Problem of Water Shortages?

What happens when the well, lake, or reservoir runs dry? When freshwater supplies are oversubscribed or exhausted, the only alternative in many areas is to use either ocean water or the brackish (moderately salty) groundwater that often results from saltwater infiltrating underground aquifers. In either case, salt must be removed before the water can be used for drinking or cooking. Desalination uses large amounts of electricity, creating correspondingly large emissions if fossil fuel is the energy source. One study estimated that if a typical southern California city switched to desalination of brackish groundwater, it would create 50 percent more carbon emissions than result from the current long-distance transport of water. Relying on desalination of ocean water, the study found, would more than double today's already sizable water-related emissions.

Around the world, more than 13,000 desalination plants currently remove the salt from some 12 billion gallons of water each day. While most of these plants are in oil-rich Middle East nations, they are becoming more common in many locales, despite their high economic and energy costs. One major ocean desalination plant is operating in the Tampa Bay region of Florida, which has experienced water shortages due to rapid residential and commercial development and agricultural demands for water. An even bigger ocean desalination plant is planned in Carlsbad, near San Diego in southern California.

Even using the most energy-efficient means currently available, these desalination plants emit about a ton of global warming emissions for every 132,000 gallons of usable water they produce. This means that current desalination efforts worldwide already account for at least 33 million tons of carbon dioxide per year—a number that makes water conservation an even more important priority in these areas to forestall global warming.

---

water use will also reduce the energy needed to purify the water, pump it to you, and treat what goes down the drain. You'll see the savings on your water bill for years to come—and you'll be reducing the sizable unseen emissions caused by generating the electricity that keeps your water flowing.

Yard and Garden

Even though lawn and garden activities account for less than 1 percent of an average American's global warming emissions, yard work ranks among the most carbon-intensive activities we engage in. If you have a big yard and, especially, a large lawn, your emissions may well be above average in this category. If so, this could be an area ripe for making adjustments.

A life cycle analysis of lawn and garden care in Seattle found that the leading source of global warming impacts in this sector is the use of fertilizers and pesticides. As discussed in chapter 7, these chemicals are one cause of high emissions in agriculture. Many Americans use the same products on their lawns at rates (per acre) similar to those of farms. The biggest global warming impacts from lawn and garden care are the upstream industrial emissions in the production of these chemicals. However, as in agriculture, the potent heat-trapping gas nitrous oxide (N_2O) is released in small amounts directly from lawns after nitrogen fertilizer is applied. Reducing or eliminating fertilizers and pesticides can cut lawn-related emissions in half. Of course, carbon emissions are just one problem with lawn chemicals; some of them are quite damaging to the environment and well worth avoiding for that reason as well.

The second most important source of lawn and garden emissions, the Seattle study found, is weekly lawn mowing with a gasoline-powered mower. Switching to an electric mower or, even better, a classic push mower, the study found, could significantly reduce or eliminate these emissions. Using less water can also result in further indirect savings.

Composting yard waste may provide a climate benefit, depending on how the compost is used. It is most beneficial when it replaces or reduces the need for chemical fertilizer, thus eliminating the emissions from producing and using a carbon-intensive product. Compost can also help by increasing the retention of water and carbon in the soil. For more ambitious composters, food waste composting, as discussed in chapter 7, also offers a way to reduce landfill methane emissions.

In addition to adopting more climate-friendly lawn-care practices,

> **UCS Climate Team** *FAST FACT*
>
> The biggest global warming impacts from lawn and garden care are the upstream impacts from the production of chemical fertilizers and pesticides. Reducing or eliminating your use of them can cut your lawn-related emissions in half.

those who are interested can convert their yards from a net global warming problem to a net gain in the fight against a warming planet. This strategy, however, means at least cutting back on the lawn, if not replacing it altogether.

The fact is, a uniform expanse of green grass is a monoculture, an unnatural phenomenon maintained only by waging constant war against nature, with water, fertilizer, and herbicides. The ideal American lawn began as an imitation of lawns and meadows found on estates in England and France. But the grasses native to those countries—including Kentucky bluegrass, which was originally imported from England—are easy to grow only in certain parts of the United States, mainly in the Northeast and Midwest. In other parts of the country, you can save water and lower your use of lawn chemicals, as well as your carbon emissions, by cultivating plants native to your area. Planting a natural lawn of indigenous local plants, which will look more like a wild meadow than a golf course, can complement your house in a climate-friendly way.

Even better for global warming, you can plant trees or shrubs to lower your overall carbon profile. Trees and shrubs sequester more carbon than a lawn does and are a significant improvement for your carbon footprint over a chemically treated lawn. Plus, strategically placed trees can shade your home from hot summer sun and shield it from winter winds, further lowering your carbon emissions from heating and cooling.

Construction and Remodeling

Just as you can turn carbon liabilities into assets by changing what you grow in your yard, you can achieve similar results with many of your expenditures. Let's look briefly at one last sector that is both sizable in terms of overall emissions and relatively carbon intensive: construction and remodeling. Construction of new homes and remodeling of old ones account for about 4.4 percent of the average American's total global warming emissions. If you are that average American, you and your spouse or partner will buy a newly built house—or build one yourselves—once in your lifetime. If you already own a home, you may find yourself working almost continuously on renovation or remodeling projects, large and small.

Most residential construction emissions result from that once-in-a-lifetime purchase of a new house. But homeowners' ongoing renovations also add up. For the purpose of discussion, we've lumped new construction and remodeling together because they involve such similar activities. If you are building a house or putting on a major addition, your choices about building materials will obviously affect your emissions. For houses with the same heating and cooling requirements, those built with more wood and less steel or concrete will have lower emissions related to construction (taking into account the industries that supply the materials). And, as we have discussed, wood harvested sustainably can lower your emissions further.

When considering the global warming impacts of construction and remodeling, the first rule is the simplest one: buy or build no more house than you need; a larger house means more carbon emissions. One study found that even a poorly insulated house of 1,500 square feet uses less heating and cooling energy than a well-insulated house of 3,000 square feet—although the best of all for reducing your carbon footprint, of course, is a well-insulated small house.

Beyond that, however, as we discussed in chapter 5, keep in mind that construction choices determine our future needs for heating, cooling, and other uses of energy in our homes *for decades to come*. That's why construction and remodeling offer great examples of how we can turn a global warming problem (the emissions caused by home construction) into part of its solution (the energy savings we can lock in for the lifetime of the house).

When designing a new house or remodeling an existing one, consider all the alternatives discussed in chapters 5 and 6 for lowering your heating, cooling, and lighting emissions. It is more effective, and cheaper in the long run, to design a house with high-efficiency heating and cooling systems, ample insulation, maximum use of natural light, and other energy-saving features than to make these changes later. One big obstacle to progress in energy-efficient construction is that real estate developers tend to leave out such features in order to keep house prices low—even though the additional costs of constructing a high-efficiency house will pay for themselves many times over in lower energy bills.

As we will discuss further in chapter 10, interest in green building is spreading rapidly. More and more contractors are learning about and adopting green techniques, for commercial and government buildings as well as for residences. This area presents great opportunities for the nation to reduce its overall carbon emissions. Build or remodel with greatly increased energy efficiency and you will make up many times over for whatever emissions you create in the construction process with reductions in future emissions from energy usage.

A Word about Voluntary Carbon Offsets

No discussion of the emissions associated with the goods and services we buy would be complete without mentioning voluntary carbon offsets. The idea is to pay an organization to engage in some carbon-reducing activity, such as building renewable energy capacity or planting trees, to compensate for—or offset—the emissions created in a given activity. As we discussed in chapter 4, if you are flying a long distance, you can purchase carbon offsets equal to the emissions caused by the flight. Carbon offsetting is increasingly used by corporations and nonprofit organizations to compensate for the fact that many staff members need to fly to meetings and hearings as part of their jobs or cause global warming emissions in other unavoidable ways.

While the idea of—and the market for—carbon offsets is now well established, and it's easy to find a reputable organization that sells offsets, it is worth remembering that offsets cannot replace the good you do by reducing your own emissions. It's fine to support renewable energy and tree planting, but, however worthwhile such efforts are, they don't alter the fact that a megawatt of energy not used is the surest carbon reduction strategy of all.

Still, it can be argued that carbon offsetting will help us make the transition to a more sustainable future. For those interested in purchasing carbon offsets, the best bet is to start with a reputable nonprofit agency that offers, rates, or certifies offsetting options. Among the possibilities are the Verified Carbon Standard (www.v-c-s.org), based in Washington, DC; the Climate Action Reserve (www.climateactionreserve.org), based in Los Angeles; Green-e (www.green-e.org), based in San Francisco; and the Gold Standard (www.cdmgoldstandard.org), based in Switzerland.

Getting to 20

As noted at the beginning of this chapter, the goods and services we buy do add up to a sizable proportion of our emissions profile. Unfortunately, however, about half of these emissions are outside our immediate control, and the other half are spread across so many categories that it is hard to make many deep reductions in this area. Still, all of us can shave a few percentage points off our total emissions profile by cutting back on overall purchases of new products and recycling what we use. We can also pay particular attention to our purchases and behavior in some of the most emissions-intensive activities, such as water use, construction and remodeling, and yard care. A good rule of thumb in this category is to try, whenever possible, to think about long-term returns and environmental benefits from your purchases. When there are highly efficient options for appliances, equipment, and vehicles, for instance, it almost always makes sense to junk energy hogs in favor of the most efficient models you can afford.

The Bigger Picture

We're at the end of the story of how our individual choices and purchases affect global warming. In this and the preceding chapters, we have covered the largest slices of our consumer spending, described the most carbon-intensive things we do and buy, and suggested alternatives wherever possible. With this information, you should be able to relatively easily reduce your global warming emissions by at least 20 percent in your first year and probably by a lot more in the years to come.

By cutting your emissions by 20 percent or more, you've done several positive things. You've demonstrated that significant reductions are well within everyone's grasp, that each of us can make better personal choices without disrupting our daily lives. Because you're sensible, you've shown that this change can be made cost-effectively and can even save you money. But perhaps most important, you have taken a personal step that the entire nation must take within the next several years if we are to preserve a healthy climate for our children.

Bravo.

You're not off the hook yet, though. Our personal choices and purchases matter a great deal, but the truth is, we can't shop our way to a stable climate. And, as important as our individual choices are, none of us can stop global warming alone. So at this point, rather than exploring the impacts of ever-smaller consumption choices, let's turn to the bigger questions about how our society as a whole responds to the issue of global warming and where you fit into that picture.

PART III

RESCUING THE FUTURE

CHAPTER 9

Step Up, Connect, Transform

Setting an example is not the main means
of influencing others; it is the only means.

—Albert Einstein

Now that you have followed the steps in the previous chapters to lower
your personal share of global warming emissions by 20 percent or more,
what else can you do? You may be inspired to go further toward carbon
neutrality. If so, we salute your efforts. But one of the most important contributions you can make is also to step up, connect with others, and share the
knowledge and experience you've gained. After all, your efforts are vitally
needed. You now have the tools to help others make more effective climate
choices, too. Only by passing along the know-how and working with others
in our communities can Americans make the really substantial and necessary reductions in emissions to forestall the worst of global warming.

Start with Family and Friends

Because you're reading this book, it's very likely you are concerned about
global warming and want to do something about it. Chances are some of
your friends and relatives also recognize that global warming is a problem
but are simply less engaged and motivated than you. Talking to friends
and family members is the best way to start widening your impact. Tell
them about the results you have achieved and encourage them to follow
your lead. The idea, of course, is not to criticize others' lifestyles. Instead,
approach the subject in ways you think they'll find appealing.

The best way to engage people is to meet them where they are, to
tap into their present concerns and values. Their concerns may be dif-

What's the Best Way to Motivate Friends and Family to Reduce Their Carbon Emissions?

Now that you have lowered your own carbon emissions, here are some ideas for motivating others. Start with friends and family members. Try to put yourself in their shoes, and approach the issue in the way you think will be most effective with them. For example, you might talk about how the changes you made

- Saved hundreds of dollars at the gas pump and in annual heating, cooling, and electricity costs
- Were surprisingly easy to accomplish
- Will help the country become less dependent on foreign oil
- Make you feel better about the world you are passing on to future generations
- Are helping reduce health problems related to air pollution, such as asthma
- Are part of your faith's teachings to care for God's creation and help those who are most vulnerable
- Are an important way to teach your children to value efficiency and chipping in
- Are interesting because they showcase some fascinating new (and cleaner) technologies

ferent from yours, but they are no less valid. If you know that particular friends or relatives care as much about global warming as you do, you could explain how you reduced your carbon emissions by *four tons* and are inspired to help others to do the same. You could pass along this book or offer to come to their house and point out some ways to reduce their carbon footprint. With people who seem less concerned about environmental issues, you could explain that you've just saved hundreds of dollars in annual energy costs and were surprised how easy it was—and you'd like to let them know about it, too.

This is hardly an exhaustive list, but you get the picture. After all, who doesn't like saving money? What parents don't want to teach their children responsibility? When you figure out what motivates your particular audience, you'll find they are much more willing to have conversations and engage.

Inspire, Don't Frighten

Those of us who read the scientific literature about the current rate of global warming and its expected consequences are likely to conclude that this is an extremely urgent problem and that everyone on the planet should be worried—very worried. Well-meaning people often want to pass on that sense of urgency about global warming, contending that citizens would be motivated to act if they only knew more of the details. It seems as if that should be the case, but deluging people with facts and figures rarely changes their opinions or motivates them. In fact, some research shows that scaring people can have the opposite effect.

In one study in 2010, for instance, researchers at the University of California, Berkeley, found that people who were given articles about global warming that contained dire messages about the future were considerably more likely to express skepticism about the science of global warming than were people who had been given almost identical articles that presented potential solutions.

What *does* work to motivate people? Researchers have found that people feel most inclined to work to address climate change when they understand three things:

1. *The basic mechanism behind global warming*: that we are overloading the atmosphere with carbon dioxide when we burn fossil fuels and cut down forests and that this gas is blanketing Earth and trapping more and more heat.

2. *The prospects for achieving practical solutions*: that we have plenty of technology and know-how today to meet the challenge.

3. *The economic benefits of energy efficiency and renewable energy*: that making the transition to low-carbon sources of energy will help ensure that our future is prosperous and healthy.

These points are straightforward and true. And because they focus on practical approaches and existing solutions, they are also hopeful and motivating. This doesn't mean you ought to downplay the severity of global warming, sugarcoat its consequences, or imply that solving such a big global challenge is simple. Effectively addressing global warming will take concerted action by citizens, corporations, and governments over the course of a generation or more. But for people to take the first steps, they need to have a compelling vision of what we have to do and to understand clearly that we can do this.

Can a low-carbon future really be clean and prosperous?

The answer is yes. In fact, many leading economists contend that doing nothing about climate change is the far more costly option. Elinor Ostrom, the first woman to win a Nobel Prize in economics, makes the case succinctly: "In the economic emergency we are experiencing [in 2010], some people think that we cannot afford to address the problem of climate change. It's the other way around: If we don't act now we will run into even greater economic problems in the future." A number of high-profile economic analyses have reached the same conclusion. The 2006 Stern Report, for example, finds that while aggressive climate action could cost 1 percent of the global gross domestic product (GDP), inaction could end up costing 5 to 20 times as much.

To explore the economic feasibility of driving down U.S. emissions, the Union of Concerned Scientists analyzed what would happen to our economy between 2010 and 2030 if the government acts aggressively to reduce global warming emissions. Our researchers, using a computer model developed by the U.S. Energy Information Administration, analyzed a scenario in which the United States fast-tracked the deployment of clean energy sources by 2030 to reduce the nation's carbon emissions to more than 50 percent below 2005 levels.

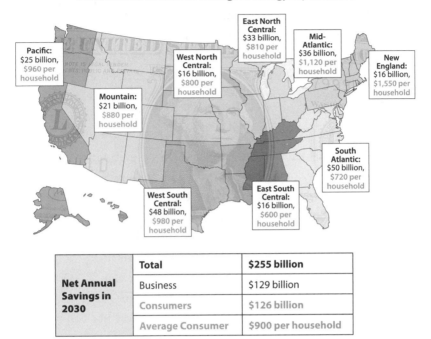

Figure 9.1. A Clean-Energy Future by 2030:
Business and Consumer Savings of Energy Expenditures

	Total	$255 billion
Net Annual Savings in 2030	Business	$129 billion
	Consumers	$126 billion
	Average Consumer	$900 per household

As detailed in the Union of Concerned Scientists' report "Climate 2030: A National Blueprint for a Clean Energy Economy," savings on energy bills (largely from greater efficiency) can more than make up for the cost of vehicle and building efficiency improvements and implementation of new renewable energy technologies. Businesses saved some $255 billion in energy costs; consumers nationwide saved about $900 per household on average. Note: Values may not sum properly because of rounding. Source: Union of Concerned Scientists, "Climate 2030: A National Blueprint for a Clean Energy Economy," 2009.

The results of the analysis were compelling. The detailed report, called "Climate 2030: A National Blueprint for a Clean Energy Economy," is available at www.ucsusa.org. As the chart shows, the key finding was that the savings on energy bills (largely from greater efficiency) more than made up for the cost of implementing new renewable energy technologies. Businesses saved some $255 billion in energy costs; consumers nationwide saved about $900 per household on average.

Equally important, the study showed that this transition to a clean energy economy can be consistent with growing economic prosperity. The model showed virtually identical economic growth under both the current path of fossil fuel dependence and the clean energy scenario—without even taking into account the higher costs of climate change if we remain on the fossil fuel path. The clean energy approach not only resulted in huge savings by 2030; it showed that deep cuts to emissions are both feasible and economically achievable along the way.

Step Up in Your Community

While a low-carbon future makes economic sense, it won't happen without the efforts of many people working together. Now that you've encouraged your family and friends to reduce their emissions, you've probably found that spreading the word and motivating others was easier than you thought it would be. Now it's time to expand your impact even further. Each of us is well equipped to help reduce emissions at the neighborhood and community levels through our networks of local affiliations.

There are as many ways to engage as there are days in a year. You just need to find the right fit for you. Lift your head out of this book for a minute and think about the best ways you could help drive down emissions in your community. Consider what you do every day: maybe you are involved in town or city government or your children's school or religious or civic organizations. Maybe you go bowling with buddies or belong to a reading group. Any of these are great places to share what you've learned and to extend your efforts beyond your day-to-day life.

The key thing to remember is that every one of us has a stake in our future health and prosperity. To tackle global warming, we need all kinds of people to get involved. Veterans' groups have taken on the issue from the perspective of reducing our reliance on oil and thus reducing our need to fight wars overseas. Hunters and anglers have a deep connection to the land and see firsthand the early impacts of global warming—whether it be the drying of wetlands critical for migrating waterfowl or low stream flow and rising water temperatures affecting trout and other fish species—which often motivate them to take action to try to fight global warming.

Local business groups have also been active on climate and energy issues. If you belong to such an organization, look for ways to engage your group in a positive conversation about the issue, and think about what steps you might take. You may meet with opposition in some quarters, so be prepared and listen carefully as others raise their concerns. As a member with a stake in your organization's mission, you are in a unique position to educate, inform, and find common ground.

If you attend a church, synagogue, or mosque, consider encouraging others in your parish or congregation to join your efforts to reduce carbon emissions. An important tenet of many religions is stewardship of God's creation, as well as care for the poorest and most vulnerable among us. The consequences of global warming will very likely have an outsized impact on the world's poorest people because the expected droughts can be ruinous to subsistence farming and make drinking water scarce and expensive. And extreme weather can be especially damaging to the homes and livelihoods of people with few resources. So there are good reasons for your religious community to discuss climate change.

Those comfortable with public speaking might offer to lead a study group or suggest global warming as a topic for an upcoming discussion or sermon. Learning about climate change and its connection to energy use can be an excellent service-learning project for a youth group. If you offer to lead the kids, you'll greatly increase the odds that they will eagerly embrace efforts to lower emissions. A service-learning project might focus on the energy usage of the church's facility, while a more ambitious effort could seek to involve and educate the families within your religious community. The kids could audit energy use, develop energy reduction goals, make some low-cost changes, and explain to members and their families why taking these steps is so important. A service project could even reach out into the larger community. For example, the kids (and perhaps some adults) could learn basic weatherization techniques and then offer to weatherize the homes of elderly members, or they could partner with an elder service organization.

A number of faith-based organizations are already working on climate change, including Interfaith Power and Light, the National Religious Partnership for the Environment, and the Evangelical Environmental Network. These groups may have further ideas to help your religious institution work on these issues.

Create Your Own Work Group or "Eco-Team"

In addition to working with established local, school, civic, or religious groups, another powerful method to expand your reach is to start your own group or adapt a social group that gathers regularly to take on some efforts to reduce emissions. No elaborate preparations are required, and passing around this book can be a good way to break the ice. During one of your group's next get-togethers, you might simply pitch the idea for everyone there to get a free utility-sponsored energy audit and then suggest that the group come together regularly to help one another implement the easily achievable recommendations, such as installing programmable thermostats, weather stripping, and caulking or adding insulation. To turn this useful chore into a social event, consider having a potluck after-party for each get-together.

Erika Spanger-Siegfried, a senior analyst in the Union of Concerned Scientists' Climate and Energy Program, launched just such a local eco-team several years ago. As she recalls it, her book club got motivated to take action after watching documentaries on environmental and energy issues. Soon they organized a meeting with a few additional friends to share their concerns, and the eco-team was born. As Spanger-Siegfried explains, the group helped its members make changes—and stick to them—by having people available to lean on for advice and encouragement. As she puts it, "Even though I have been trying to make environmentally conscious choices for years, I learned that joining with others in this effort, and having fun doing so, can actually deepen your commitment."

Over the next several years, Spanger-Siegfried's group focused on waste reduction and started a community-supported agriculture (CSA) program, in which participating families provided a local farm with financial support at the beginning of the growing season and then took turns picking up a share of the farm's produce each week during the summer and fall. The group also took up household energy efficiency projects, with members helping one another reduce their carbon emissions.

CASE STUDY

Energy Efficiency Meets Reality TV

A competition called *Energy Smackdown* offered an ambitious twist on the concept of community work groups. Envisioned initially as a local cable television show building on the idea of NBC's reality-TV show *The Biggest Loser*, in which contestants work to lose weight, *Energy Smackdown* challenged teams in three Boston-area cities to see which team could achieve the biggest reductions in their carbon emissions. The teams were made up of approximately 100 households in Arlington, Cambridge, and Medford, Massachusetts. Each participating household received a free professional energy audit; these audits gave the teams a baseline of energy usage and helped the participants identify some energy-saving ideas.

Over the course of a year, the households took on many of the energy-saving changes we have discussed in this book: replacing incandescent lightbulbs with compact fluorescents, caulking and weather-stripping their homes, changing their diets and driving habits. The efforts were filmed for the local television show. Executive Director Donald Kelley said, "We call this a competition, but it's really a fun way to help people make important changes."

The results were dramatic: not only did the winning household in the program reduce its emissions by some 54 percent, but participants also reduced their average annual carbon emissions by 20 percent. More than half of them sealed and insulated their homes; some 38 percent replaced at least one major appliance with an Energy Star model; and one enterprising household managed to lower its electricity use by a whopping 73 percent.

Of course, groups vary widely in size and scope, but the successful ones tend to share common traits. Here are some tips for your eco-team or work group:

- *Set a group goal.* Identify the group's top priorities and determine the roles each member can play to address those priorities.
- *Start small.* Tackling a modest project first can help your group become comfortable working together and give everyone the confidence to tackle larger tasks.
- *Create some structure—but not too much.* Recognizing that everyone's life is busy, try to find an agreed-upon meeting schedule that

works for all members of the group and keeps projects moving forward.

- *Keep it fun.* Perhaps the most important ingredient in your group's success is to allow time to socialize while you work toward lowering your carbon emissions.

If you live in a tight-knit neighborhood, especially one with lots of kids, you might consider initiating a neighborhood-wide challenge. Kids love a good contest, and parents might welcome the opportunity to teach kids the value of conserving energy. Start by listing the totals of each household's utility bills. Whoever reduces their energy use by the largest percentage (or the largest amount per person) wins the challenge. Be creative and make it fun. Let the group define the challenge; you can even offer the winner a prize, such as a gift certificate to a local restaurant. As the case study indicates, the idea of a competition can be a powerful motivator.

An even higher impact could be achieved by organizing neighborhood-wide energy efficiency "barn raisings," as has been done in communities across the country. Most such efforts arrange for volunteers to spend a few hours on a weekend weatherizing one home. The homeowner usually pays for materials, though many groups also raise funds to cover costs for low-income owners. You might find it easier than you would guess to start a "barn-raising" effort in your area.

In fact, the idea has been catching on all around the world. On October 10, 2010, for instance, the group 350.org organized global warming work parties in almost every corner of the globe. Groups installed solar panels at a homeless shelter in Cape Town, South Africa; planted trees in

---

UCS Climate Team *FAST FACT*

Work groups or "eco-teams" can be a great way to engage people to reduce carbon emissions. On one day in 2010, the climate group 350.org organized some 7,000 global warming work parties in 188 countries, undertaking a wide variety of projects, from planting trees to retrofitting buildings and installing solar panels.

Sri Lanka; painted roofs white in New York City's Harlem neighborhood; and retrofitted buildings in Amsterdam, Holland. All told, this world-wide effort sponsored more than 7,000 events in 188 countries—a truly impressive undertaking to reduce emissions on a global scale.

All Emissions Are Local

It's called global warming and it is, of course, occurring on a global scale. But as they say about politics, all emissions are local. Until our local leaders and elected officials hear that our communities want action on global warming, they are unlikely to push aggressively for the range of solutions we need. We will talk about state and federal approaches to addressing climate change in chapter 11. But the exciting news is that thanks to a phenomenal amount of grassroots action, cities and towns across the nation now stand at the forefront of action on climate change.

Consider, for instance, that more than 600 city and town governments in the United States have signed on with ICLEI—Local Governments for Sustainability, a network started by the United Nations, to take specific climate protection actions in their communities. Meanwhile, more than 1,000 mayors of cities and towns in all 50 states have signed a Climate Protection Agreement under the auspices of the U.S. Conference of Mayors, all of them committing to reduce their city's emissions to 1990 levels.

But even these impressive numbers underestimate the prairie fire of climate action taking place at the local level. Eighteen of the 20 largest U.S. cities have made commitments to significantly reduce their global warming emissions. For example, Chicago, the nation's third-largest city, is implementing a plan to reduce its emissions to 25 percent below 1990 lev-

---

UCS Climate Team FAST FACT

Local efforts to reduce emissions are catching on fast across the United States. More than 1,000 mayors of cities and towns in all 50 states, for instance, have signed on to a Climate Protection Agreement under the auspices of the U.S. Conference of Mayors; the agreement commits each of them to reducing their city's emissions to at least 1990 levels.

els by 2020. City planners there are helping residents and businesses save money by instituting more efficient energy practices, providing better transit options, and making the city a healthier and cleaner place to live.

Not surprisingly, this nationwide movement includes cities such as San Francisco, California, and Portland, Oregon, which have long been in the forefront of efforts toward environmental consciousness and sustainable living. Over the past several years, for instance, San Francisco has adopted energy efficiency measures that have already kept more than 60,000 tons of carbon emissions out of the atmosphere. The city retrofitted municipal buildings, including San Francisco General Hospital and Trauma Center and the Moscone Center convention facility; was among the first cities to install LED traffic signals citywide; and adopted mandatory green building standards for municipal construction as early as 1999. Thanks to its array of energy efficiency measures, San Francisco has already reduced its emissions to 5 percent below their 1990 levels; over the next several years the city plans to reduce emissions further, to 20 percent below 1990 levels.

Like San Francisco, Portland is frequently ranked among the country's greenest cities and has put in place an aggressive plan to reduce emissions. The city has especially excelled at reducing transportation emissions, building a heavily used light-rail and streetcar system and some 445 miles of bike paths. In fact, in 1996 the city ruled that all employers must reduce single-occupancy vehicle trips to their work sites by 10 percent to reduce pollution and combat global warming. As a result of its efforts, Portland has seen car use decrease substantially. According to a recent study, less than half of the city's commuters now drive to work, and more than 5,000 Portlanders commute by bicycle each day. For those who still need to drive cars, the city boasts a large network of locations for ready-to-go rental Zipcars.

But it is not just large cities or those famous for being environmentally conscious that are participating in the dramatic changes underway. Forward-thinking programs are on display in even the smallest towns. Greenburg, Kansas—population 1,389—decided to turn disaster into opportunity after more than 90 percent of its buildings were devastated by a tornado in 2007. This rural community in southwestern Kansas set a goal of building "a prosperous future through sustainable community design." The town is well on the way to implementing a plan that show-cases an array of sustainable low-carbon choices. Taking advantage of its abundant wind resources, it has come up with an ambitious plan to pro-vide the entire town with 100 percent clean, renewable electricity. Green-burg's efforts have already been recognized internationally: in 2010 the town was listed as a United Nations Global Green City.

Farsighted projects such as Greenburg's plans for wind turbines and solar arrays can help ensure a clean and prosperous future. Still, siting such projects is sometimes controversial; surprisingly vocal opposition can spring up against even the cleanest and best-thought-out projects. The box offers some perspective on that problem.

One good way to deal with siting issues for renewable energy projects is to build the projects on less desirable parcels of land, such as former landfills. These areas of open space work well because they are usually accessible and cannot readily be put to other uses. Towns around the country are successfully implementing this strategy. In Massachusetts, for example, some 28 municipalities already have plans to build solar panel arrays on capped landfills. Other communities have looked at former landfills, such as the giant Freshkills site on Staten Island, New York City, as locations for new wind turbines.

Wherever they are sited, and despite local objections about new renewable energy projects, the main point is that municipal efforts to reduce global warming emissions are springing up almost everywhere across the country. Here are just a few selected examples:

- In Babcock Ranch, Florida, near Fort Myers, a private developer has partnered with the electric utility, Florida Power & Light Company. Together they plan to build the world's largest solar photovoltaic power plant and to create the world's first city that generates more electricity from solar power than it consumes.

- The municipal utility department in Fort Collins, Colorado, has instituted a program called ZILCH (Zero Interest Loans for Con-

What If My Community Doesn't Want
a Wind Turbine or Solar Array?

In the abstract, at least, Americans don't just like clean energy; they love it. Poll after poll shows that a large majority—more than 80 percent—favor using more renewable energy sources, such as wind, solar, and geothermal power. In order to meet the clean energy challenge, lots of renewable energy—and the transmission lines to carry that power to your home—will have to be installed in the coming decades. When it comes to siting and building sources of renewable energy, however, projects are often met with fierce local opposition, and sometimes from surprising quarters.

The key is not to hold clean energy projects to a higher standard than fossil fuel or nuclear power plants. When siting a new energy-generating plant, the choice is never between renewable energy and no energy at all: given the urgency of climate change, we badly need to build new sources of clean energy. Because of this, we should try to support their development unless rigorous review of a project shows environmental impacts that outweigh the project's benefits and that cannot be truly resolved.

Practically speaking, turning down well-sited renewable energy facilities means accepting the problems associated with fossil fuel or nuclear power. Nuclear power has no direct global warming emissions, but it is expensive and carries the risks of catastrophic accident, radioactive waste, enormous water requirements for cooling, and the considerable hazards associated with mining uranium ore. Fossil fuels not only contribute to global warming when they release carbon into the air; they also have negative impacts on our health and well-being—from mountaintop-destroying mining practices to toxic water and polluted air. Fossil fuel and nuclear plants also often use large amounts of water for cooling, which is particularly problematic in the Southeast, West, and Midwest.

When renewable energy projects are proposed in your community, get involved. Insist that the siting review process be thorough, and if the project's benefits are strong, get behind it. Seek out resources that can help educate the community. For example, the Union of Concerned Scientists helped found the American Wind Wildlife Institute to facilitate timely and responsible development of wind energy while protecting wildlife and wildlife habitat. By becoming involved, you can help urge your community to say yes to new sources of renewable energy.

servation Help) to provide interest-free financing for home energy improvements and upgrades.

- Holyoke, Massachusetts, recently announced a new $20 million project to build a 4.5-megawatt solar array at two city locations, to include some 18,400 American-made solar panels. Making reliable green power available is part of the city's plan to attract business and light industry.

- San Diego, California, has kept more than 700,000 tons of carbon dioxide equivalent (CO_2e) emissions out of the atmosphere each year by capturing methane gas from the landfill.

- Burlington, Vermont, has started an outreach program to help residents lower their carbon emissions. Already the program has achieved an estimated annual reduction of some 1,500 tons of carbon dioxide emissions in the residential sector alone.

Some school districts are taking action on lowering emissions. An excellent pioneering example of cost-effective low-carbon planning is the work done by Spirit Lake Elementary School in Spirit Lake, Iowa. Using a combination of grants and loans, the school district installed a wind turbine behind the elementary school playground back in 1993. This single turbine was able to completely offset the school's electric bills. On the basis of that success, the school district built a second, larger turbine in 2001. Now, having paid back their construction costs in energy savings, the turbines generate enough electricity to power all the district's school buildings, generating some $120,000 worth of free electricity each year

---

UCS Climate Team _FAST FACT_

Even some school districts are working to significantly lower emissions. Back in 1993, the Spirit Lake Elementary School in Iowa, for instance, used a combination of grants and loans to install a wind turbine, which was so successful it zeroed out the school's electric bills. Since then, at least 250 similar projects have sprung up at schools throughout the country.

---

and even producing surplus power, which the school district sells, providing badly needed revenue for instructional programs.

Since the success of Spirit Lake Elementary School's initial wind turbine project, scores of schools and municipalities have implemented similar strategies. In fact, the U.S. Department of Energy's Energy Efficiency and Renewable Energy program lists some 250 wind turbine projects operating or planned at secondary schools and colleges in almost every state.

As you can see, whether you work with friends and family, your religious group, the local community, or your school district, your efforts to fight global warming are part of a much greater whole. There is a wealth of information and know-how available around the country, but your efforts are sorely needed to meet the tremendous scope of the problem. Check your town or city website to find out what kinds of climate and energy efficiency initiatives are going on in your community. You can use some of the tools suggested in this chapter to get your town to be even more active. Think about your community's next big project—building a new school or library, perhaps, or upgrading old streetlights or rehabilitating aging municipal buildings. These are excellent opportunities to incorporate greater energy efficiency and low-carbon technology to reduce global warming emissions and save (or even make) money in the long run. By engaging your family and friends and by getting involved in your community, you can lead the way to a prosperous and sustainable future.

CHAPTER 10

Stepping Up at Work

There are no passengers on Spaceship Earth.
We are all crew.

—Marshall McLuhan

Jobs in the United States are as diverse as the nation's people: some of us work in offices, others in stores, factories, restaurants, or hospitals. Some are employed by large corporations, and others are sole proprietors of small businesses or consultancies. But no matter what your job is or where you do it, you can help reduce emissions at work. Small changes can make a big difference when they are widely adopted. Our workplaces offer a powerful venue to magnify the impact of the effective climate choices we make as individuals.

From manufacturing to retail, companies large and small are waking up to the issue of global warming and sometimes taking meaningful steps to address it. To be sure, some companies are too shortsighted to invest in improving their energy efficiency even when doing so would yield savings within months. Others would rather boast about how "green" they are than make substantive changes. But many firms are realizing how much goodwill they can generate—and how much money they can save—by finding ways to lower their carbon emissions. Wherever you work, you can play a part in encouraging your employer and coworkers along this path.

Scaling Up Reductions

By helping your workplace make effective climate choices, you can take your know-how to a bigger stage. When a large corporation or organization institutes company-wide changes, it can make a huge difference in driving down overall emissions as well as leading the way for other businesses. Take, for instance, the chemical manufacturing company DuPont. Inspired by scientific consensus on the urgency and magnitude of the threat from global warming—and undoubtedly motivated to turn energy savings into shareholder profits—DuPont decided to invest in more energy-efficient processes and equipment, renewable energy, and other emissions-reducing approaches. Between 1990 and 2006, the company managed to cut its worldwide heat-trapping emissions to 72 percent below 1990 levels, reducing its energy use by 7 percent even while production expanded by 30 percent. As a result of its efforts, DuPont saved *roughly $2 billion in energy costs.*

The power of scale is evident in some of the climate choices made over the past several years by the retail giant Walmart. One of the largest corporations in the world, Walmart consumes more electricity annually than any other private user in the United States. So when the company pledged in 2007 to reduce its electricity usage by 20 percent by 2013, that meant lowering its usage by *some 3.5 million megawatt-hours.* That's nearly enough to permanently shutter an entire midsized coal-fired power plant and keep close to 4 million tons of carbon dioxide emissions out of the atmosphere annually.

In her useful book *The Green Workplace,* Leigh Stringer recounts the story of an employee at Google who decided to take action when he realized that all of the kitchens and break rooms at the company's campus in Mountain View, California, were stocked with bottled water. Recognizing the practice as environmentally wasteful, in part because of the carbon emissions caused by transporting the water, the Google worker started an employee petition to urge the company to offer tap water instead. Within a week, he had collected over 2,000 signatures. At its headquarters alone, it turned out, Google was buying roughly 13,000 bottles of water per day and spending over $1 million annually. As a result of the petition drive, this single worker—with the help of his petition-signing colleagues—was able to get Google to stop buying bottled water for all of its North American offices.

UCS Climate Team *FAST FACT*

Corporate decisions can have huge impacts. Walmart's pledge to cut its electricity usage by 20 percent by 2013 meant reducing annual energy usage by some 3.5 million megawatt-hours. That's nearly enough to permanently shutter a midsized coal-fired power plant and keep close to 4 million tons of CO_2 emissions out of the atmosphere annually.

You don't have to work at a giant corporation to make effective—and significant—climate choices at work. Tom Bowman, the owner and proprietor of the Bowman Design Group, a small California-based company that designs exhibits for corporations and museums, offers a good case in point. After designing an exhibit on climate change for the Marian Koshland Science Museum of the National Academy of Sciences in Washington, DC, Bowman decided he wanted to address global warming in his own work life. He realized, though, that he didn't know the most effective steps to take. He thought about installing solar panels but found them too expensive for his budget and their payoff period too long.

After getting an energy audit, Bowman made the following changes. He redid the office lighting, saving some $300 annually on the firm's electric bill. He bought power strips to turn equipment off at night and avoid phantom loads. He traded in the company's SUV for a hybrid Prius. He bought energy-efficient equipment, including the most efficient air conditioner he could afford. The results of Bowman's actions were dramatic: he cut his firm's gasoline use by 63 percent, cut landfill waste by 45 percent, and reduced electricity costs by 40 percent. Altogether, he reduced his firm's carbon emissions by 65 percent.

Bowman's changes also saved about $9,000 annually, an amount he hopes to apply to making further energy efficiency upgrades. He recognizes that his firm's 13-ton reduction in emissions may seem insignificant compared with the scale of emissions at large corporations, but he says the comparison misses the point. "In the end," Bowman says, "these reductions were absurdly easy to achieve, and they pay dividends. Duplicating

---

UCS Climate Team *FAST FACT*

The proprietor of one small California-based design firm found that by making some simple changes he was able to cut his firm's emissions by 65 percent, its gasoline use by 63 percent, its landfill waste by 45 percent, and its costs for electricity by 40 percent. The changes, which he calls "absurdly easy," saved the firm some $9,000 annually.

---

them across the nation's 29.6 million small businesses would yield significant gains."

Reductions at Work Start with You

Even if you're not at the top of a major corporation or a small company, you can still make a difference at your workplace. Not only can you help reduce your organization's global warming emissions; you are also likely to improve its bottom line. Many people mistakenly believe that organizations and companies have to choose between economic and environmental considerations. But in fact, the opposite is more often true: making effective and sustainable climate choices often means doing more with less— exactly the kind of thinking that helps businesses maximize their profits.

The information offered in this book can help you suggest a number of changes that could help your workplace save money while reducing emissions. Approaching the issue from a cost-savings perspective can pave the way for other kinds of emissions reductions, too, such as commuting programs, which have less effect on the company's bottom line.

A good way to start is by learning about any environmental efforts already being made at your workplace. Ask your boss or human resources representative whether your organization has an energy or sustainability task force. If so, find out how you can join its efforts. If not, see if you can be a catalyst for starting a "green team" at work. You'll probably find it easier than you might think to get others to join in. Ask around or send an e-mail to find other workers who are concerned about climate or energy issues. Then set up a time at lunch or after work to get everyone together to brainstorm about what projects might make the most sense for your organization.

Figure 10.1. Thinking Through Your Organization's Environmental Practices

R&D	Can you use resources more efficiently?
Marketing	Can you reduce packaging? Can you reward bulk purchases?
Operations/ Logistics/ Purchasing	Can you reduce transportation emissions from product shipping and staff travel? Can you minimize packaging, storage, or waste? Can you reuse, recycle, compost waste? Can you purchase recycled paper? Or promote measures to reduce paper use (such as setting printers for 2-sided printing)?
Real Estate/Facilities	Can you improve energy efficiency in lighting, or heating and cooling? Can you invest in green building improvements?
Human Resources	Can you improve employee incentives for behavior changes such as telecommuting, ridesharing, mass transit use?
IT	Can you adopt Energy Star requirements for purchasing computers and electronic equipment? Can you improve practices for disposal/recycling of outdated computers and electronic equipment?

One useful approach is to think about the tasks you perform each day at work. As you think over each one, ask yourself whether you might be able to do more with less energy or resources.

Next, apply the same set of questions to the tasks performed by your immediate work group or department and expand out from there to the organization as a whole. Of course, the particulars will vary a lot, depending on the type of work you do, but the table offers some suggestions about the kinds of questions to ask. You won't have all the answers right away; at this point, what's most important is to start asking useful questions to identify opportunities for emissions reductions in all the work processes throughout your organization.

Measure Current Usage

Once you and your coworkers have identified some areas or processes that are ripe for improvements in efficiency, you'll need information on how much your organization currently spends on energy. That information will allow you to build a strong case for reducing energy usage and give you a baseline to judge how effective your suggestions ultimately are. Something as simple as getting permission to have the local utility company conduct an energy audit of your office or business, for example, can reveal a number of low- or no-cost options that can save money and reduce emissions.

Such measurements often yield a lot of useful information. When the software maker Adobe installed digital smart meters to monitor electricity use at its California facilities, the information yielded results right away. It turned out that the utility charged for electricity on the basis of Adobe's peak usage during the day, so all the company needed to do to lower costs was stagger the times when office systems were turned on each day to avoid a spike in usage. Implementing that one change more than repaid the company's modest investment to install the smart meters. Shifting electricity demand to a different time of day doesn't reduce overall usage, but it can lower costs somewhat. And from an environmental point of view, it can avoid the utility's use of dirtier plants that are turned on only for high peaks.

Educate Your Coworkers

Getting your coworkers on board will help immeasurably as you work to change environmental practices at your workplace. People are usually open to adopting more energy-efficient practices—many just haven't thought much about the issue. Everyone is busy, of course, and few people have taken the time to learn the details of complex topics such as global warming and energy efficiency.

There are lots of ways to help educate coworkers and get them more involved. If it is an accepted practice at your workplace, try bringing in a lunchtime speaker to talk about the link between energy use and the environment. Solicit ideas from your coworkers or connect with community groups working on climate change, and build bridges between your organizations. You might try partnering with a group on an Earth Day activity; if your employer encourages employee fitness, you might organize a Bike to Work or Carpool Month or some other low-key project to get the conversation started.

Use Incentives and Competition

As you and your green team begin to suggest ways to reduce the company's carbon footprint, remember that the most successful strategies are often those that seem more like fun than work. The last thing our coworkers need is to feel that we are adding to their workload. Look into possible incentives for the kinds of changes you are trying to encourage. Some companies, for instance, give the best parking spots to the most efficient cars, such as hybrids. Others offer gift cards or small cash rewards to employees who take public transportation to work or suggest improvements the company can make in its environmental practices. Perhaps your organization can offer perks to encourage employees to make effective climate choices.

In addition to incentives, competition can be a very effective strategy. Try organizing a race between departments or work groups to see which one can achieve the biggest reductions in emissions. One innovative website, www.carbonrally.com, will even help your organization launch such a competition, turning the act of lowering emissions into a game in which teams take on challenges, ranging from pledging to reduce paper use by 25 percent to leaving their cars at home for a week. Organizations as disparate as the Sharp Corporation, the Massachusetts Bar Association, and the staff of *Seventeen* magazine have participated in Carbonrally challenges.

Reward Results

Whenever possible, urge your employer to reward ideas offered for more sustainable practices. After all, companies are increasingly find-

---

UCS Climate Team *FAST FACT*

Companies are increasingly finding that employee-generated ideas about sustain-ability can pay off. Xerox recognizes employees' best sustainability ideas with its coveted annual Earth Award. In 2010, employees' suggestions reduced the com-pany's carbon emissions and eliminated some 2.6 million pounds of waste, saving roughly $10 million.

---

ing that employee involvement in sustainability issues pays off. Xerox, for instance, has a program to solicit its employees' green ideas, offer-ing highly prized Earth Awards to recognize the best sustainability ideas each year. In 2010, Xerox lauded the work of a team at its Oregon facil-ity that designed a more sustainable package—made from 100 percent postconsumer recycled material—for one of the company's lines of col-ored ink. Xerox also recognized a team at a factory in upstate New York that devised a more efficient process for handling wastewater, cutting the plant's waste by 60 percent and saving some $80,000 annually. All told, in 2010 alone Xerox implemented employee suggestions that reduced carbon emissions and eliminated some 2.6 million pounds of waste, saving the company roughly $10 million.

Greening Healthcare

One sector that is starting to reduce its sizable carbon footprint is health-care. The fact is, the nation's nearly 6,000 hospitals are among its most energy-intensive commercial sector buildings, using twice as much total energy per square foot as most other commercial buildings. Taken together, the nation's hospitals also generate upward of 7,000 tons of waste per day.

Across the country, healthcare providers are finding themselves at the center of a movement to embrace sustainable practices in the workplace. Part of this involvement stems from their mission as health profession-als. According to estimates by the U.S. Environmental Protection Agency (EPA), for instance, the U.S. health sector's 73 billion kilowatt-hours of electricity usage (more than enough to provide electricity to all the residents of two cities the size of Houston) is responsible for additional cases of asthma, respiratory illness, and hospital emergency room visits totaling some $600 million per year in increased health costs.

The healthcare industry is so large—accounting for some 16 percent of the U.S. gross domestic product—that any changes made in this sector can reap big rewards. If you work in this field (as one in nine Americans currently does), you probably know that hospital administrators and other healthcare professionals are quite aware of the billions of dollars they could collectively save by reducing energy use, not to mention the huge potential reduction in global warming emissions. Many hospitals are starting to actively pursue sustainable strategies across all aspects of their operations, ranging from energy efficiency and recycling to newer trends such as maximizing daylight in new buildings.

Interdisciplinary green teams, comprising physicians, nurses, and other staff, are being set up at many hospitals to brainstorm ideas for new initiatives. And a growing number of hospitals have hired sustainability coordinators to monitor inputs and waste and to oversee green projects.

Thanks to these kinds of efforts, a wealth of information is starting to emerge, much of which can be helpful for other workplaces as well. The World Health Organization, for example, produced an influential report outlining the "seven elements of a climate-friendly hospital," with recommendations on energy efficiency, green building design, alternative energy, transportation, food, waste, and water supplies.

In the United States, the organization Practice Greenhealth offers a wide array of information on sustainability issues particularly geared to the healthcare field. Among its offerings is the *Green Guide for Health Care* (available for download at www.gghc.org), which gives detailed recommendations on best practices in hospital design, operations, waste management, purchasing, and other areas.

The effects of this kind of work are evident already. The Cleveland Clinic, a large Ohio-based hospital, for example, has won multiple environmental awards for dramatically increasing its recycling and achieving a 20 percent reduction in its energy usage over the past three years alone.

Other hospitals are opting to purchase renewable energy to power their operations. York Hospital, in York, Maine, for example, gets 90 percent of its energy from carbon-free sources, including wind power and hydropower. As a result, despite enlarging its operations, the hospital cut carbon emissions by more than one-quarter over the past several years, keeping more than 300 tons of emissions out of the atmosphere.

Green Building

As is true in our homes, an organization can make some of the most significant emissions reductions through green building—either in retrofitting an existing facility or in building a new one. Nationwide, some 40 percent of all emissions come from our buildings, including residences and public and commercial buildings. If your company or organization is building a new facility or renovating an older one, try to get involved during the very early planning stages to encourage the inclusion of energy-efficient features. Remember that any decisions about a new or upgraded facility will lock in its energy usage—and emissions—for years, if not decades, to come.

One of the most important considerations in any building project is construction cost. So it's notable that a widely recognized 2007 study by the international construction consulting firm Davis Langdon found no significant difference between average construction costs for green buildings and those built conventionally. Meanwhile, many studies have shown that the lower operating costs and higher market advantage of a green facility enhance its value substantially. In other words, it costs little or no more to build in energy efficiency, and doing so will pay dividends to your organization for the life of the building.

The EPA's Energy Star program offers a rating system for buildings

---

What Is a LEED-Certified Building?

LEED, or Leadership in Energy and Environmental Design, is a widely adopted certification program begun in 1998 to encourage builders, architects, and home buyers to adopt environmentally sustainable building practices.

LEED operates on a credit and point system. The system is divided into 13 sustainability categories, such as water efficiency and indoor environmental quality, each of which carries a certain number of credits; each credit earns one or more points, for a possible total of 100 points. LEED recognizes four rating levels, depending on the number of points earned: certified, silver, gold, and platinum. In this way the program takes a complex, multifaceted problem and incentivizes a variety of sustainable features.

The ratings that builders and architects can earn are recognized by the real estate market, offering a mark of prestige similar to the certification of the Energy Star program for appliances. And LEED has raised awareness of the environmental implications of construction practices, instigating enormous activity in green real estate around the country. More information about LEED is available from the non-profit U.S. Green Building Council (www.usgbc.org).

---

along with a detailed *Building Upgrade Manual,* available at the agency's website (www.energystar.gov). Residential and commercial buildings that are judged by a third party to be 15 percent more energy efficient than average can qualify to receive the agency's Energy Star rating.

An even more detailed guide to making sustainable design choices is a certification program called LEED, or Leadership in Energy and Environmental Design, overseen by the nonprofit U.S. Green Building Council. Begun in 1998, the LEED program is designed to encourage builders, architects, and home buyers to adopt environmentally sustainable building practices. With more than 21,000 buildings around the world currently certified by LEED and another 88,000, including some 31,000 commercial buildings, now working their way through the certification process, the program is clearly spurring advances in green building techniques; each successive version of the program has greatly improved its system of credits and sophistication.

Awareness of green construction practices and of the environmental impact of buildings is on the rise, and research indicates that LEED certification is already a highly desirable attribute in the real estate market. While the results are still preliminary, some studies of the commercial real estate market have shown that LEED-certified buildings are selling for more, commanding higher rents, and showing higher occupancy rates than their less efficient counterparts.

In addition to saving money and reducing emissions, a green building project can make a powerful public statement about your organization's commitment to sustainability. Examples of the positive influence of green building abound, including many at colleges and universities, where flagship environmental buildings set an important example for students, faculty, and the public. When Oberlin College in Ohio built a new facility for its Environmental Sciences Program in 2000, the school decided to make the building a showcase for the kind of sustainable thinking featured in the environmental science classes. The award-winning Adam Joseph Lewis Center for Environmental Studies has been recognized as one of the most advanced examples of sustainable architecture in the United States. The building includes solar photovoltaic panels, geothermal heating and cooling, and even a "living machine" greenhouse system to recycle the building's wastewater. Some 150 monitoring systems provide information to a real-time display in the lobby, showing visitors that the building often produces more energy than it consumes.

Buildings such as the one at Oberlin, which was begun before the LEED certification system was established, no doubt inspire and encourage others to follow suit. Today, some 678 colleges have signed an agreement pledging to make all future buildings at their schools sustainable at the LEED Silver level of certification or better and to work toward reaching carbon neutrality at their campuses.

Of course, showcase facilities have been built for commercial enterprises as well. A grocery store built by Whole Foods Market in Dedham, Massachusetts, offers one such example. The facility demonstrates the company's forward-thinking energy and sustainability practices to customers, employees, and investors, as well as the local community. The

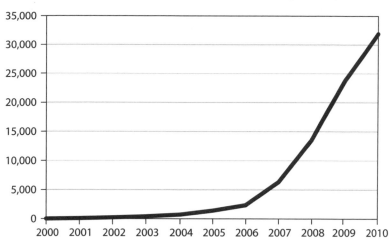

Figure 10.2. Total Number of Registered LEED Buildings, 2000–2010

As of 2010, some 31,454 commercial buildings were working toward LEED certification worldwide. Source: U.S. Green Building Council, 2011.

store was constructed from recycled steel and many other recycled materials, incorporates a "cool roof" for energy efficiency, meets 90 percent of the store's energy needs with a fuel cell and photovoltaic solar panels, and recycles or reuses some 80 percent of its waste. The Dedham store—one of the company's 10 LEED-certified stores—demonstrates a broader commitment by the firm, which now stands among the largest corporate users of renewable energy, having purchased renewable energy credits for wind energy to cover 100 percent of the company's electricity needs.

Companies and organizations that take prominent steps to lower their emissions and build sustainable facilities should feel justified in communicating their accomplishments to their customers. Unfortunately, however, some companies have recognized that espousing green rhetoric in advertisements can be an effective marketing strategy even when they have little to show for their claims.

Take, for instance, the coal industry's branding of its latest technology as "clean coal," which is anything but a clean energy source. Or the advertising over the past several years by the oil company BP stressing its com-

How Do I Know If a Company's Claims Are Just Greenwashing?

"Greenwashing," the environmental equivalent of whitewashing, refers to an all-too-common practice by a company or organization: presenting misleading information about its environmental policies or the environmental benefits of its products or services. Because environmentally sustainable products and practices are popular, companies may be tempted to tout themselves as "green" even if their actions don't live up to the image they portray. Watch out for companies that

- tout tiny "eco-friendly" projects (like planting a few trees) while most of their business is environmentally destructive or carbon intensive;
- make claims that aren't substantiated by a reliable source or third-party certification;
- advertise "green" commitments while lobbying against environmental laws and regulations;
- make claims so broad or vague as to have no real meaning;
- exaggerate their environmental achievements to cover up for bad behavior or public relations problems in other areas.

When it comes to company-sponsored statements about sustainable practices, it's smart to study them with a healthy dose of skepticism. Seek out third-party verification if possible, and look for solid evidence that companies are actually living up to the environmental values they espouse. It's not always easy to separate fact from corporate hype, but organizations such as the Union of Concerned Scientists can help you stay informed about this kind of corporate hypocrisy. Every other year, for instance, the organization publishes an "Automaker Rankings" report, highlighting which companies "walk the walk" when it comes to the environmental performance of their vehicles. Two websites—www.sourcewatch.org and www.stopgreen wash.org—also have useful information about greenwashing.

mitment to renewable energy with the tagline "Beyond Petroleum," even though the company's investments in renewable energy are very small relative to their investments in oil and gas. Examples of "greenwashing" are common among consumer products as well. Kimberly-Clark famously touts a line of disposable diapers as Pure & Natural Huggies, advertising the use of organic cotton even though the diapers, almost identical to regular Huggies, include only a small amount of cotton on the outside. The Pure & Natural line also boasts of packaging made with "20 percent recycled content," whereas many manufacturers of consumer products today routinely use 100 percent recycled packaging without even mentioning it. Other forms of greenwashing are more subtle. Clairol prominently advertises its Herbal Essence shampoo as "a truly *organic* experience," even though it is made almost entirely of the same chemical ingredients as most other shampoos.

You may well have spotted examples like these yourself. While discerning consumers can often tell the difference, this kind of greenwashing has become fairly pervasive. As the box suggests, we can each help make sure our organizations—and the companies we patronize—actually engage in substantive efforts to reduce emissions, not just talk about them.

Transparency and Accountability

One way to avoid concerns about greenwashing is to institute greater transparency and accountability. As with all the work that must be done at home and in our communities to reduce global warming emissions, an important step is to measure current emissions. Several nongovernmental organizations around the world have launched programs to encourage companies to measure and publicly report their emissions data. Consider urging your firm to join one of these projects if it hasn't already.

Some of the work on getting companies to report emissions was begun decades ago by Ceres, a nonprofit organization founded by a small group of investors in 1989 in response to the *Exxon Valdez* oil spill. Ceres continues as a national coalition of investors, environmental organizations, and other public interest groups that works with companies to address sustainability challenges such as global warming emissions. It runs the Global Reporting Initiative, a voluntary registry in which companies disclose data about their use of materials and water as well as the associated waste and emissions they create.

Perhaps the largest such reporting program geared specifically to

global warming is the UK-based Carbon Disclosure Project, which publishes emissions data for some 3,000 of the world's major businesses. Of
the 500 largest companies in the world, 409 volunteered emissions data in
2010, the most in any year so far. The Carbon Disclosure Project is making an important contribution by publishing a good deal of data that have
never before been publicly available. It is, however, a voluntary program,
and the data are based on companies' self-reporting in response to the
project's detailed survey.

Other projects seek to publish more verifiable data. One in North
America, the Climate Registry (www.theclimateregistry.org), began in
2009 and is sponsored by various agencies and nonprofit organizations,
including the EPA and the Center for Climate and Energy Solutions
(C2ES), formerly the Pew Center on Global Climate Change. The registry requires that the emissions data it publishes be verified by an accred-
ited third party. Already the registry has more than 200 founding members, including corporations, utilities, and nonprofit organizations. Other
such reporting programs include the Greenhouse Gas Protocol initiative
(www.ghgprotocol.org); the UK-based Carbon Trust (www.carbontrust.
co.uk); the Climate Savers Program, administered by the World Wildlife
Fund (information at www.worldwildlife.org); and the Climate-Safe Business Network, run by the World Resources Institute. In addition, a growing number of private consulting groups offer to help companies develop
carbon reduction and other sustainable development programs.

These programs offer companies the chance to establish public benchmarks as they work to operate more sustainably. As the programs have

---

UCS Climate Team FAST FACT

A number of voluntary reporting projects, such as the UK-based Carbon Disclosure Project (www.cdproject.net), ask companies to disclose their global warming
emissions, setting public benchmarks to encourage improvements in their performance. Even though the reporting is voluntary and mostly unverified, more than
3,000 organizations worldwide now submit emissions data to the Carbon Disclosure Project, including 409 of the world's 500 largest companies, as of 2010.

evolved, they have brought unprecedented transparency to the entire supply chain, allowing companies to know more about their suppliers' climate-related practices. Because many large corporations manufacture products in developing nations, where emissions are rising rapidly, this information should help reduce emissions all along the supply chain.

One company that has led in tracking emissions throughout its supply chain is the computer maker Dell, which currently receives information about global warming emissions from all of its primary suppliers. As part of its effort, Dell has set clear goals for its suppliers, asking them to publicly establish targets for carbon reductions and to incorporate their own suppliers into the program as well.

Walmart is another large and influential corporation that focuses on reducing emissions throughout its supply chain. Walmart asks suppliers to assess their carbon footprints in each of four categories: energy and climate, material efficiency, nature and resources, and people and community. The company then scores suppliers to determine whether they have reached targets it has set in each category. While not mandatory, this program has increased carbon consciousness in many suppliers since it was put in place. Given the sheer number of Walmart's suppliers—some 60,000—such a supply chain effort can have sizable consequences.

Putting It All Together

Once you have helped spur your workplace to reduce emissions and encouraged it to report its progress and, perhaps, track the emissions of its suppliers, your organization will no doubt realize the benefits of operating more efficiently. Companies and organizations around the world are doing more than ever before to reduce their carbon footprints and operate sustainably.

We still have a long way to go, however. It's time to think big. Now we need to figure out how to fully close the loop on our activities by designing for reuse, recycling, and "remanufacturing" and by operating in the most sustainable ways possible.

That might sound like pie in the sky, but to a remarkable extent this larger vision is starting to be realized in a variety of industries. Some countries, such as Germany and Japan, are far ahead of the United States in this regard, with laws requiring that products such as automobiles, household appliances, and office equipment be designed for easy disassembly and recycling.

Some U.S. corporations are already doing it. Patagonia, a retailer of outdoor gear and an environmental leader, has launched a clothing recycling program for its polyester fleece garments, for example. The company now recycles not only its own polyester garments but also those sold by its competitors. Because a fleece garment made from recycled polyester is indistinguishable from one that contains virgin polyester, made from petroleum, Patagonia has recognized that it can make garments from recycled fleece with less than one-quarter of the energy needed to make new fabric.

The Atlanta-based carpet manufacturer Interface offers another example. Using an innovative design process, Interface lowered its carbon emissions by some 35 percent from its 1996 baseline and decreased the energy consumed per square yard of carpeting by 45 percent. This achievement is part of a broader vision for sustainability that the company's founder, the late Ray Anderson, and his team parlayed into a global leadership position in the carpet tile industry, with a pledge to become a carbon-neutral company by 2020.

Farsighted efforts such as these point the way toward the prospect of greatly reduced emissions. As promising as these efforts are, however, the truth is that voluntary projects by a handful of individual companies will not drive down emissions as quickly or as far as we need them to go. Government incentives and standards for better practices as well as limits on pollution are the final, and critical, piece of the emissions puzzle. That's what we will explore in the next chapter, including what you can do to spur the government to implement the policies we need now to combat global warming.

CHAPTER 11

Making Government
Work for Us

Alone we can do so little; together
we can do so much.

—Helen Keller

You have made a number of effective climate choices in your own life. You've spread the word to friends, family members, and coworkers. Now it's time to make sure your elected officials hear your voice, too. From our cities or towns to state and federal government, officials are making decisions on our behalf and with our tax dollars. Put simply, these funds can be spent to improve our energy future or to impoverish it. Along the way, especially in Washington, DC, lobbyists help protect companies that benefit from continued reliance on coal, oil, and gas, regardless of its long-term impact on the environment or the U.S. economy, blocking renewable energy and delaying energy efficiency measures and other efforts to limit carbon emissions.

Listening to the rhetoric of oil, coal, and gas company executives, one might think they were champions of limited government and the free market. But in truth, fossil fuel companies are heavily subsidized. Their enormous profits would shrink considerably without federal support. According to a study by the Environmental Law Institute, the U.S. government provided the industry with $72 billion between 2002 and 2008, mostly in the form of permanent tax credits for producers of oil, coal, and natural gas. That's twice the total of direct subsidies and tax breaks that renewable energy received in the same period. If we hope to reduce carbon emissions, we need to reverse these priorities right away and devote our resources to developing clean energy instead of subsidizing emissions as usual.

Government has long played an active role in shaping our energy and transportation systems—from building enormous dams to creating the interstate highway system. Government funding for research and development on the jet engine even led directly to the technology for today's gas-fired power plants. Government also plays an important role in creating market incentives by taxing or subsidizing goods and activities, hopefully in keeping with the wishes of its citizens. And government has had to step in and require automakers and power plants to clean up their act and cut emissions that cause asthma, lung disease, and cancer. With a problem of the magnitude of global warming, it makes sense for government to take a hands-on role in implementing solutions, along with citizens and businesses. Action at the state and national levels is a crucial component of any successful effort to drive down emissions.

As engaged citizens, we each have a vital role to play in spurring this government action along.

It has become popular in some quarters to attack government inefficiency and inaction, and, to be sure, there are plenty of discouraging examples of foot-dragging or worse on climate solutions and other environmental issues. The lack of a truly comprehensive binding international agreement on global warming is a disheartening setback. Closer to home, the inability of the U.S. Congress to pass a limit on global warming emissions, and the ongoing efforts by some in Congress to hamper the ability of the U.S. Environmental Protection Agency (EPA) to regulate carbon emissions, point up the intense ideological divide and capitulation to corporate interests in Washington that too often keep our elected officials from safeguarding our future. Ultimately, any complete solution to the

UCS Climate Team FAST FACT

According to a study by the Environmental Law Institute, the U.S. government awarded subsidies to the fossil fuel industry totaling $72 billion between 2002 and 2008, mostly in the form of permanent tax credits for oil, coal, and natural gas producers—twice the amount of direct subsidies and tax breaks received for renewable energy in the same period.

global warming problem will require us to get past gridlock to achieve a sensible national energy policy.

But despite inaction in Congress, the picture is more heartening than it might first appear. A variety of state and national policies—such as energy efficiency standards for appliances, buildings, and vehicles, and standards requiring the sale of renewable electricity and low-carbon fuels—are already resulting in emissions reductions. And, as we will discuss in more detail, you can help to strengthen and broaden these standards.

Equally important, state and local governments play a key role in shaping where our energy comes from and how it is used, issuing permits for new energy-generating facilities and making decisions about things such as building codes, zoning laws, regional access to transit, and regulation of electric utilities. State and local governments also serve as a critical proving ground for new ideas and approaches that could be scaled up. Promising programs are underway around the country, and your involvement can foster more of them. The key point, of course, is this: a single state or federal provision can lock in enormous reductions in emissions, far beyond what any of us could hope to accomplish individually. By getting involved in the formulation and implementation of government policies related to energy use and global warming, you can increase your impact many thousands of times over.

And when you do become more actively engaged in climate-related policies at the local, state, and national levels, you'll be in good company. Many of the country's best and most creative minds are working to address global warming. Scientists, engineers, technical experts, business executives, faith leaders, military planners, policy makers, and active citizens are working right now to reduce our emissions through a host of innovative strategies that can strengthen our economy and improve our health.

What Government Can Do

How can our government help move us toward a low-carbon future? Think of the basic tools as carrots, sticks, and seeds. "Carrots," or incentives, aim to encourage climate-friendly actions. "Sticks," or rules with penalties to ensure compliance, prohibit actions that are outmoded, inefficient, or harmful. "Seeds," or funding for research, development, and pilot projects, help spark and incubate innovative new technologies and techniques. When it comes to climate change, there are many potentially effective government options, but most fall into one of four major categories, all of which use carrots, sticks, and seeds:

1. *Augment energy efficiency* in our buildings, appliances, equipment, industries, and vehicles.

2. *Build renewable energy capacity* to ensure that an increasing portion of our electricity comes from clean, renewable sources.

3. *Limit permissible levels of emissions* by, for example, setting carbon standards for vehicles, fuels, power plants, refineries, and other major emitters, or by implementing a price on carbon.

4. *Invest in research and development* to foster new technologies that can help reduce emissions in the future.

To better understand how these strategies work in practice, let's look briefly at some specific government programs in each category.

EFFICIENCY STANDARDS

As we've discussed in previous chapters, improving our energy efficiency is typically the fastest and easiest way to reduce carbon emissions. Energy efficiency programs are particularly appealing because they can yield significant reductions in emissions quickly *and* save money for consumers and businesses. An analysis by the Union of Concerned Scientists has shown in detail how efficiency measures using existing technology could cut total U.S. energy consumption by 29 percent by 2030. Previous chapters have shown how smart consumer decisions are an essential component of this process. But individual choices alone cannot work quickly enough to achieve the high level of energy efficiency and renewable energy use we need, especially if companies are not making those products and resources available to consumers. Government policies and programs are essential for overcoming the entrenched market barriers that currently impede our progress in combating global warming.

Appliances and Equipment. Government efficiency standards for appliances and equipment save energy by requiring that various new products achieve minimum levels of efficiency by a specific date. As more energy-efficient products enter the market, they replace older, less efficient models while still offering consumers a full range of options.

Efficiency standards have been one of the federal government's most successful strategies for reducing energy consumption in homes and businesses since their inception more than two decades ago. By one estimate, the government's efficiency standards in place by 2006 had already saved some 1.3 percent of the total energy that the nation would otherwise have used that year—equivalent to the total energy usage of some 6.6 million households.

As we have also discussed in earlier chapters, the federal government has established minimum efficiency standards for many residential and commercial products, such as washing machines, refrigerators, dishwashers, and air conditioners. Several states—including Arizona, Connecticut, Maryland, New Jersey, and Washington—have augmented these standards with additional ones for products not covered by federal standards. Not only do each of us as consumers benefit from these standards, but we can also speak up and encourage our state to do more. State efficiency standards are reviewed regularly. By looking into what other states have done and urging our elected officials to strengthen our state's standards and adopt new ones, we can help bring about even greater efficiency.

Remember that most manufacturers are fully capable of making their products a lot more energy efficient. But changes in their processes might incur modest costs—and the benefits will accrue only to consumers. So government has to prod manufacturers (as in those "sticks" above) to offer more efficient products; they will comply because they know that their competitors must abide by the same rules.

In addition to efficiency standards, many states have implemented a variety of "carrots" in the form of incentive programs, including rebates and tax exemptions for energy-efficient appliances and equipment. Make sure your elected state and federal officials know that you want to see more of these incentives to help lock in more efficiency for consumers and greater reductions in carbon emissions.

Energy Efficiency Codes for Buildings. Energy codes require all new residential and commercial construction to meet a set of minimum criteria for energy efficiency. Today, the most stringent codes are the 2009 International Energy Conservation Code (IECC) and Standard 90.1-2010 of the American Society of Heating, Refrigerating, and Air-Conditioning Engineers (ASHRAE). These model codes are updated every three years, and states should require automatic review of the updates to ensure that their codes reflect the latest standards. Adopting more stringent energy efficiency codes over time ensures that builders deploy the most cost-effective technologies and best practices in all new construction.

If you care about green building, a good way to get involved is to learn about your state's current building codes and urge your elected officials to aggressively implement the strictest and most up-to-date ones, so that new and remodeled buildings will be as energy efficient as possible. You can also encourage your state to go beyond building codes by promoting standards that set the bar even higher for energy efficiency, such as the U.S. Green Building Council's Leadership in Energy and Environmental Design (LEED) rating system and the EPA's Energy Star program for new homes. These programs, often called above-code standards, provide guidance and incentive for builders to be even more vigilant about energy efficiency than they might be otherwise.

The key point is that government has many ways to require or encourage more efficient uses of energy, and these can achieve enormous reductions in carbon emissions over time. Each area offers opportunities to get involved and maximize our impact on global warming. Let's discuss a few other important efficiency programs before moving on.

Energy Efficiency Resource Standards. Some 26 states have enacted programs, called energy efficiency resource standards, that require utilities to save energy according to a specified schedule. To meet the state's requirements, utilities can choose either to undertake a program to get consumers to adopt energy-efficient technology or to integrate more efficient technology into their own mix of power generation. Either way, these standards reduce emissions by mandating that utilities use (or generate) power more efficiently.

Find out from your elected officials whether your state has strong energy efficiency resource standards. If not, make sure they know that this issue is important to you. You can pursue this issue at the federal level as well. Already a number of other countries, including France, Italy, and the United Kingdom, have adopted national energy efficiency resource standards; the United States should adopt a national standard, too. Such a national standard would require electricity and natural gas providers to meet targets for reducing their customers' energy use, spurring utilities to increase their investments in efficiency. Your vocal support, and the active engagement of others like you, is needed to help persuade Congress to enact such a national standard.

Transportation Efficiency. More than 30 years ago, in response to a crippling oil embargo, the federal government created a set of fuel efficiency standards for cars and light trucks called the Corporate Average Fuel Economy (CAFE) standards. If car makers did not meet the standards, they were subject to a fine (those "sticks" again). By any measure, the standards have been a remarkable success. Without them, today's consumers would be stuck with the same fuel economy choices available in the 1970s, when vehicles averaged around 15 miles per gallon on government tests, with disastrous costs to the economy and environment.

Although fuel economy standards are still saving consumers money, they stagnated for nearly 20 years until 2007, when Congress began to toughen them by requiring that America's cars and trucks average at least 35 miles per gallon by 2020. According to an analysis by the Union of Concerned Scientists, if Congress hadn't delayed the adoption of tougher standards between 1998 and 2011, U.S. consumers could have consumed 130 billion fewer gallons of gasoline during that period, sparing the planet *nearly 1.65 billion tons* of global warming emissions from vehicles. That's equivalent to the total emissions from all U.S. automobiles in 2010.

Today, the government is finalizing the next generation of standards for fuel efficiency and global warming pollution, covering new cars and trucks from 2017 through the 2025 model year, with measures requiring automakers to move annually toward fuel economy standards of about 50 miles per gallon and per-mile carbon reductions of about 50 percent below today's levels by 2025.* Analysis by the Union of Concerned Scientists estimates that the combination of these new standards with ones covering new vehicles through 2016 will cut U.S. oil consumption by nearly 4 million barrels per day in 2030—about as much as we currently import from the Persian Gulf and Africa combined. In 2030, the two sets of standards will ultimately combine to prevent some 770 million tons of emissions from being released into our atmosphere—the equivalent of shutting down more than 160 coal-fired power plants.

GENERATING ELECTRICITY FROM CLEAN, RENEWABLE SOURCES

In addition to fostering greater energy efficiency, government has a vital role to play in determining where our energy comes from. Along these lines, one of the most powerful arrows in the government's quiver is the renewable electricity standard (sometimes called the renewable portfolio standard, as in a utility's energy mix, or "portfolio"). As described below, this market-friendly standard can be one of the most powerful tools we've discussed yet to hasten our shift toward clean, renewable energy.

Renewable Electricity Standards. Renewable electricity standards require utilities to generate a certain percentage of their electricity from renewable power sources by a specific date. Since the late 1990s, national and local clean energy groups have worked with state legislators around the country to pass these standards, and today 29 states have mandatory programs. These programs work by allowing multiple renewable energy technologies to compete with one another in the marketplace so that utilities can choose the most cost-effective options first. By requiring a clear and firm target date, the laws offer certainty to investors and

*In real life, this standard would translate to a combined city and highway gas mileage of around 36 miles per gallon, as listed on the window sticker in the new car showroom.

Figure 11.1. Renewable Electricity Standards
29 States and DC

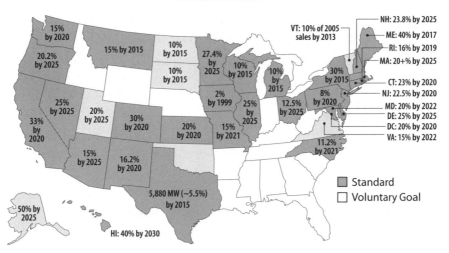

Twenty-nine states and the District of Columbia have adopted renewable electricity standards, requiring electric service providers to produce a certain percentage of their power from clean, renewable sources by a specific target date. Source: Union of Concerned Scientists, 2011.

developers of renewables while helping utilities move away from older, carbon-intensive sources of energy.

More than two-thirds of the states that have enacted mandatory standards have already raised or accelerated their requirements. Existing renewable standards now lock in the use of enough clean power by 2025 to meet the electricity needs of some 47 million typical homes and reduce annual carbon dioxide emissions by an amount equivalent to taking more than 30 million cars off the road.

As the map shows, 29 states and the District of Columbia have established mandatory renewable electricity standards, while seven states have adopted voluntary renewable energy goals. If your state has no such standard or one that is weak or voluntary, your input could make an important difference in passing a stronger measure. Inform your state officials about the positive difference the laws have made elsewhere and how successful they have been in spurring the development of clean, renewable sources of energy. We'll look more closely at California's new renewable electricity standard—the toughest in the nation—in a moment.

The success of renewable electricity standards in states as diverse as Texas, Minnesota, California, Pennsylvania, and North Carolina also makes a compelling argument for Congress to pass a national standard—another effort where your voice can make an important difference in prompting needed government action.

Federal Renewable Energy Tax Incentives. Although the United States has thus far failed to adopt a national renewable electricity standard, federal tax incentives have been important "carrots" driving renewable energy development over the past decade, especially in wind power. Production and investment tax credits help defray the upfront costs of installing renewable energy technologies and help level the playing field with fossil fuel and nuclear technologies, which historically have received much greater tax subsidies.

Unfortunately, while the subsidies to the fossil fuel and nuclear industries are mostly permanent, federal renewable energy tax credits have suffered from on-again, off-again extensions, resulting in a boom-and-bust cycle that injects needless uncertainty into the financing and construction of planned projects and raises their costs. For example, federal tax credits for solar power are currently in place through 2016, but those for wind power and other technologies are set to expire at the end of 2012. Here again, you have an important opportunity to pitch in. Call and write to your congressperson and senators and urge them to support permanent, aggressive tax incentives to speed the development of more renewable generating capacity.

What else can the government do? The following sections are for those looking for additional pressure points in current government energy policies.

LOW-CARBON FUEL STANDARDS

While some oil companies are making token investments in biofuels and hydrogen, they have yet to provide significant quantities of low-carbon fuel choices at the pump. Federal and state governments can do something about that by requiring the carbon content of fuels sold to drop over time and by fining companies if they fail to get better choices on the market.

California already has regulations on the books requiring a 10 percent reduction in the carbon content of gasoline by 2020—either directly or by running cars on low-carbon biofuels, natural gas, hydrogen, or electricity. Meanwhile, states in the Northeast are considering a clean fuel standard that would deliver similar benefits. The federal government does have a requirement called the Renewable Fuel Standard, but so far the requirements for truly low-carbon biofuels have been effectively waived every year. More states need to follow California's lead, with an ultimate goal of federal adoption and implementation.

NET METERING

If generation of renewable electricity from rooftop solar photovoltaic panels and other small-scale technologies is ever to become truly viable, it will require what is known in the energy field as "net metering," which allows customers to sell electricity back to the grid. For those who have solar panels on their house, for instance, net metering lets the excess electricity they generate flow into the grid, making their electric meters run backward and thereby lowering their electricity bills. Forty-five states have at least one utility that permits customers to sell electricity back to the grid, but only 18 states require all their utilities to offer net metering. Here again, a government policy can mandate a straightforward change that would make technologies such as small-scale photovoltaic systems much more desirable and feasible in the short term. If your state doesn't require net metering, tell your elected officials how effectively it is working elsewhere and urge them to follow suit.

FEED-IN TARIFFS

One change in state electricity regulations, known as a "feed-in tariff," could also greatly aid the spread of clean energy by guaranteeing that those who install solar panels on their roof or a wind turbine in their backyard will be paid a fixed rate for the electricity they generate over a set number of years. A multiyear guarantee, at a rate above the current price for electricity, ensures that homeowners, businesses, and other institutions can safely invest in small-scale renewable energy and speedily recoup their initial costs. Only a handful of states and utilities have adopted such price guarantees in this country, but the policy has been successfully adopted elsewhere in the world and has helped countries such as Germany and Spain become leaders in solar energy.

EMISSIONS REDUCTION TARGETS AND LIMITS

We've talked about programs to require or encourage efficiency and programs to augment renewable generating capacity. Many states, individually or in concert with their neighbors, are also implementing emissions reduction targets and limits. Let's briefly review how some of these efforts work. Some 23 states have adopted statewide emissions reduction goals for utilities and industry. The programs vary in their strictness and timetables, but having enforceable statewide limits will help ensure that states meet global warming emissions goals.

Oregon and Washington, for instance, have passed laws requiring that new power plants either reduce carbon emissions on their own or offset a certain portion of their anticipated emissions by paying a fee to an independent organization, which will then select and fund offset projects such as the development of renewable energy or the planting of trees. These states and others, including California, now deny long-term contracts for energy produced by power plants that emit more than a certain amount of carbon per unit of electricity, thus giving the utilities an incentive to reduce emissions.

Some states are also banding together to limit emissions. The leading effort in this regard is called the Regional Greenhouse Gas Initiative. RGGI (pronounced "Reggie") is a collaborative effort of 10 northeastern and mid-Atlantic states to limit emissions from power plants in those states, reducing emissions by 10 percent below 2009 levels by 2018. Sales of emissions permits under RGGI have generated more than $880 million since the program's launch in 2009, most of which the states have invested in energy efficiency projects, to great effect. Another major program, the California cap-and-trade program (often referred to as AB 32), is set to begin in 2012. AB 32's overall goal is to reduce the state's emissions to 1990 levels by 2020.

EMISSIONS STANDARDS

In 2011, the U.S. Supreme Court confirmed that the EPA is empowered, under the Clean Air Act, to regulate global warming emissions from major sources in order to protect public health from the dangers of unchecked climate change. As of this writing, the EPA's authority to regulate these emissions has come under strong attack in Congress. Despite this, 2010 saw the first-ever national global warming emissions standards finalized for new cars and trucks sold from 2012 through 2016, with even stricter standards through 2025 expected by the summer of 2012. And as of 2011, the EPA has pledged to issue carbon performance standards for power plants and refineries to ensure that these facilities limit their emissions and that we begin the transition to cleaner energy sources.

OTHER PROGRAMS

Here are a few other government programs with important implications for combating global warming.

Public Benefit Funds. Almost half of U.S. states have funds, often called public benefit funds, dedicated to supporting energy efficiency and renewable energy projects by collecting a small charge on the bill of every electric customer. With this steady stream of funding, states can provide money for projects such as energy assistance for low-income households, weatherization programs, investment in renewable energy technologies, and subsidies for efficient appliances.

Targeted Research and Development Funding. Government funding for research and development (R&D) in clean energy technologies can foster innovation, help lower the costs of renewable technologies, and acceler- ate their use (as in those "seeds" discussed earlier). For years, research grants and incubator programs for clean energy startup companies have advanced the performance of emerging renewable energy and energy efficiency technologies and have lowered their costs. Such programs have, in most cases, proven to be a sound investment of taxpayer dollars, with lifetime economic benefits typically far exceeding their initial cost, particularly in energy efficiency technologies. Encourage your elected officials to support greater funding of R&D in clean energy at both the federal and state levels.

Putting It All Together

Most of the government programs and standards we have reviewed so far address specific aspects of energy efficiency and renewable energy. But some government efforts seek to tackle the problem of global warming more broadly.

CLIMATE ACTION PLANS

Many states that have implemented programs to reduce their global warming emissions have benefited from adopting climate action plans, which lay out goals and targets. These plans help state decision makers identify cost-effective and appropriate ways to reduce global warming emissions. To date, 36 states have completed comprehensive climate action plans or are in the process of revising or developing them. In addition, more than half of all U.S. states have set up advisory boards or commissions to develop and implement climate action plans.

Find out if your state has a climate action plan, and if it does, review an online copy of it to identify upcoming issues on which you can work to keep your state on track. If your state has yet to make such a plan, encour-

---

UCS Climate Team *FAST FACT*

To date, 36 U.S. states have completed comprehensive climate action plans, setting forth goals and targets for reducing global warming emissions. If your state has a climate action plan, get a copy of it to help you identify key issues where your input can help keep your state on track. If your state has yet to make a climate action plan, encourage your elected officials to do so.

age your elected officials to create one, drawing on the wealth of good ideas in existing plans around the country.

PRICING CARBON

All of the innovative policies outlined above share one key attribute: they reduce carbon emissions to help forestall the worst consequences of global warming. All of them can make a big difference as we make the transition as quickly as possible to a more efficient energy system run largely on renewable sources. Even with these initiatives, though, the fact is, the time is long overdue for the federal government to set stringent limits on carbon emissions. Currently, it doesn't cost a dime for anyone—a homeowner, a driver, a power plant, or a concrete factory—to dump unlimited amounts of carbon into the atmosphere, even though there is overwhelming evidence that these emissions are harmful to the health of life on our planet. One way or another, that has got to stop.

There are two major approaches for limiting carbon emissions. One approach, a *carbon tax*, makes companies pay on the basis of the volume of emissions they generate, with the tax providing an incentive to reduce emissions. A *carbon cap*, on the other hand, sets a limit on emissions and typically requires that companies buy permits for their emissions. Set up as a *cap-and-trade system*, these permits can be traded between companies, although the overall amount of permits remains fixed. Companies that find ways to curb their emissions more cheaply are rewarded and can trade with those that find it more costly and thus have to pay higher permit fees. The price on carbon is also an incentive for entrepreneurs to invent and commercialize new low-carbon technologies. The revenues generated under either a tax approach or a cap-and-trade approach can be used for public purposes. For example, they could be used to fund efficiency and renewable energy programs or to help lower-income families cope with rising energy prices, or they could be returned to the public in the form of a dividend.

To be successful, any carbon-pricing approach must be well designed. Loopholes must be minimized so that the planned reductions in emissions actually happen. The program's reduction goals must be strong, and they must be reviewed and updated regularly to ensure that the reductions achieved successfully avoid the serious risks identified by the latest science.

No matter what technique is ultimately adopted, the core idea is this: carbon emissions have a cost and should have a price. Given the grave threats posed to our health and livelihoods, people (and companies) should not be allowed to freely emit unlimited amounts of carbon into the atmosphere.

What Can You Do?

We've reviewed a smorgasbord of government policies that can help fight global warming by reducing carbon emissions. All of them play an important role. If you want to know what you can do to influence your government's climate policies, the answer is simple: *make your voice heard.* More than anything, what is needed now is a concerted effort from the ground up to communicate that, for the benefit of our children and grandchildren, we need our elected officials to address global warming now and put in place sensible policies to hasten our transition to a low-carbon future.

Whenever possible, the best option is to establish one-on-one contact with our elected leaders, letting our city, state, and federal officials know how strongly we feel about the need to combat global warming through firm government action. Only if they receive this information from many quarters will they be pushed to take the necessary steps. This is not to suggest that you deluge your legislators with letters and phone calls throughout the year. Rather, now that you have learned more about the issues involved, try to contact them strategically—in relation to relevant community events or pending votes—and encourage others to do the same.

A personal e-mail may be the easiest way to get your message across, but individual telephone calls and letters have even more impact. And attending legislators' office hours, in-district meetings, or town hall–type events are great ways to let them know how much you care about climate action.

When you contact federal legislators, remember that printed letters can now take four to six weeks to reach their offices because of security procedures for mail handling. Phone calls are the best method of communication when an issue is urgent, such as a pending vote on a climate- or energy-related topic. Just a couple of phone calls to an office over a short period of time can bring an issue to the attention of your legislator and have a surprisingly large impact. Staff members on Capitol Hill routinely report that legislators pay close attention to—and are sometimes even swayed to change their vote by—the number of constituent calls they receive on an issue. Here are some tips to consider when you do call your legislator.

Call congressional offices directly or through the switchboard. If you do not have the direct number, you can reach U.S. representatives by calling 202-225-3121, and you can reach U.S. senators by calling 202-224-3121. Ask the operator to connect you to a particular legislator's office. Phone numbers for most federal, state, and local officials—as well as valuable information about their positions on issues and their staff members—are available on their websites.

Ask to speak to the aide who handles energy and climate issues. Your call will be more influential if you speak to the correct staff member. But don't be discouraged if you can't reach him or her directly; congressional aides are frequently very busy. Just leave your message with the receptionist or on the aide's voicemail, stating your views. Remember, polite persistence is always the most effective strategy for voicing your views.

Plan your call: know your facts, note your expertise, and be brief. Make sure to let the legislator know you are a constituent. Prepare and practice your main message in advance to be sure you'll cover everything you want to say.

Be timely—call when a vote is imminent. National and local advocacy groups such as the Union of Concerned Scientists work continually on climate and energy issues. These organizations can be a great help in letting you know when a vote is coming up on a specific piece of legislation or when your input can be particularly helpful. You will find a wealth of information at www.ucsusa.org, and you can join an e-mail list to be kept up-to-date on the latest developments.

UCS Climate Team *FAST FACT*

Action alerts from the Union of Concerned Scientists can help you stay involved in key state and federal initiatives to reduce global warming emissions. To find out more, visit www.ucsusa.org.

Let them know what you think after a vote, too. Legislative offices take particular note of constituents' responses to votes. A vocal reaction from a number of voters sends a strong signal about whether the legislator's stance on climate and energy issues is politically viable or risky. This makes it equally important to express your thanks for a positive vote on an energy issue as well as your displeasure about one that is negative.

COMMUNICATE EFFECTIVELY

As you become more involved in climate action at the local, state, and federal levels, it is worth noting that there has never been an easier time to spread the word. Websites, e-mail, blogs, Facebook, Google, Twitter, texting, YouTube, podcasts, and more—today each one of us has tools to communicate quickly and continually with people we know and to reach out to others.

There is no limit to the ways in which you can use these technological tools in the fight for a low-carbon future. You can keep close track of government initiatives and find out where you can pitch in. You can share your personal experiences—both successes and challenges—as you work to reduce your personal emissions. You can organize events and engage others in political action. As we have seen in the Middle East, the latest communication and social networking tools have even helped people rise up against oppressive regimes. If these tools can work for those ends, they can certainly aid in the effort to reduce global warming emissions.

With the myriad of online tools, though, it's important not to forget traditional media. Remember that all means of communication, from public conversations to press coverage, can help you engage with others to put pressure on elected officials.

Writing a letter to the editor of your local newspaper, for instance, is still one of the most effective and efficient ways to reach a large audience both online and off. Letters are printed on the editorial page, which is always one of the most-read pages. Not only will you reach daily newspaper readers; community leaders and congressional staffers also keep a close eye on local papers to see what issues are important to their constituents. To increase the likelihood that your letter will be printed, follow these simple rules:

- Respond to a specific article.
- Be timely (write within a day or two).
- Refer by name to the legislator or corporation you are trying to influence.
- Write briefly and clearly.
- Make your letter a call to action.
- Mention your relevant professional expertise.
- Follow the publication's guidelines closely, including contact information and word count—typically under 200 words.

To increase a letter's impact after it is published, clip it out of the paper and mail it to specific decision makers along with a short cover note.

Turning your community actions on reducing emissions into "news" is another way to publicize the importance of this issue. Getting local media to cover your story or come to an event isn't really difficult. Let's say you are organizing an energy efficiency "barn raising" or planning a local petition drive that you'd like the local paper to cover. All you need is a media advisory and some time to make a few phone calls. Your advisory should be a short, one-page notice about the event or initiative explaining what it is and where and when it will take place. Be sure to include your name and contact information so the reporter can call or e-mail you for more details. It's important to send your media advisory out at least a week in advance to give reporters time to add your event to their busy schedules.

Whatever methods you use, the key thing is to engage with your elected officials as actively as you can and to publicly lend your voice to the expanding efforts to reduce emissions and build a more sustainable future.

The Case of California

We end this chapter with a case study that shows both the power of an engaged citizenry and the great difference those bureaucratic-sounding government standards can actually make.

California won an important climate victory in April 2011, when it enacted a landmark renewable electricity standard requiring the state's utilities to provide *at least one-third of their electricity from clean and safe renewable sources, such as the wind and the sun, by the year 2020.* The new standard creates the most aggressive renewable energy requirement in the country and positions California as a national leader in clean energy investment. In fact, according to an estimate by the Union of Concerned Scientists, with the new law in place, California, given its size, will very likely produce *more than one-quarter of all the required renewable energy generation in the nation by 2020.* That is, unless other states follow its laudable example in the meantime.

In short, California's new standard represents an enormous victory as the nation moves toward a clean-energy economy that will reduce the heat-trapping emissions that cause global warming while reducing our dependence on fossil fuels.

Of course, California has often led all the other states on climate change and environmental issues. The state's carbon emissions per capita—including the emissions from coal-fired electricity imported from

---

UCS Climate Team *FAST FACT*

California's 2011 renewable electricity standard, one of the most aggressive laws in the country regarding renewable energy, requires utilities to derive at least one-third of their electricity from clean and safe renewable sources, such as wind and solar power, by the year 2020. The standard gives investors and developers the certainty they need to develop plans and make investments. The law provides an important model for the nation.

other states—are already about 40 percent below the U.S. average. In part, no doubt, the state's mostly mild climate is responsible for this outstanding performance. But climate alone cannot account for such a significant disparity: a lot of the credit goes to the state's energy and environmental policies—and to the citizens and organizations that have worked hard over the years to implement them.

As it turns out, citizen involvement was crucial to the passage of California's new renewable electricity standard, and the Union of Concerned Scientists was the lead group advocating for an aggressive standard. Laura Wisland, an energy analyst in the California office of the Union of Concerned Scientists, explains that early in 2011, the organization helped mobilize members to call their elected officials and urge them to take up the issue in the legislature that spring. Before the legislators could become bogged down in other matters, the organization's members and staff called and met in person with leaders in both houses to demonstrate the popular sense of urgency about the issue.

Shortly after this initial citizen-led push, the California State Assembly Committee on Utilities and Commerce (the first committee to handle the energy bill) held a special hearing to place the issue firmly on the legislative agenda. With help from technical experts at the Union of Concerned Scientists, citizens successfully built support for a tough new standard from a broad range of stakeholders, meeting regularly with leading elected officials and engaging the media to report on the issue.

It took lots of hard work, but the payoff from this citizen involvement will be enormous. By generating one-third of its electricity from renewable sources, California will help lead the way to a lower-carbon future for all Americans.

With a concerted effort, you can help make similar changes in your state's approach to climate change. In fact, as you begin to engage with your elected officials and make your voice heard at the local, state, and federal levels, you'll be amazed at the difference your involvement can make.

CHAPTER 12

Welcome to Our Low-Carbon Future

There is no high-carbon future.

—Lord Peter Mandelson, former secretary of state for business,
enterprise, and regulatory reform, United Kingdom

Outside Madison Square Garden in the heart of New York City, visitors are dwarfed by a seven-story sign designed by scientists at the Massachusetts Institute of Technology and paid for by Deutsche Bank. With a whir of numbers in a vast digital readout, the sign—the world's largest "carbon counter"—offers a real-time running total of the cumulative number of metric tons of carbon dioxide in the atmosphere worldwide. As of this writing, the count stands at 3.69 trillion metric tons, the highest level of atmospheric carbon in 800,000 years. Worse yet, the numbers whirring on the counter show that carbon dioxide is being added to Earth's atmosphere at the rate of *800 tons per second.*

The giant carbon counter is, of course, a public relations effort designed to raise awareness of global warming. It is certainly frightening to consider the pace at which carbon is building up, and the sign effectively conveys the feeling of a ticking time bomb for the planet.

Unfortunately, although the numbers are scientifically accurate, the huge carbon counter's effect is ultimately a lot like that of many media accounts of global warming: at once frightening and disempowering. Dwarfed by the gargantuan sign, visitors standing idly by it on the sidewalk seem to epitomize the feelings of impotence so many of us have about global warming. With carbon accumulating at such an unimaginably fast rate, it seems as if we are helpless to change the situation.

As this book has attempted to show, however, nothing could be further from the truth. By taking some of the steps outlined in these pages—in our own lives, in our communities, and as citizens—each of us *can* make a significant difference. In fact, we already are.

Across the country and around the world, people are mobilizing to use energy more efficiently and to generate it from clean, renewable sources. To be sure, the fight against global warming is a steep uphill battle. As the sign shows, carbon continues to build up in the atmosphere at a rapid rate. And temperature increases in the next few decades will be determined largely by our past emissions of heat-trapping gases. So we are going to experience some additional warming no matter what steps we take today. Global population growth and rapid increases in development in countries such as India and China mean higher global energy demands, many of which continue to be met by burning fossil fuels.

What is striking to note, though, is the rate at which investments in and development of renewable energy are growing. Big changes are underway, and their pace is accelerating.

What we need next to New York's carbon counter is another readout, one that depicts the cumulative effect of people's emissions *reductions* around the world to help us better chart the extent to which we are bending the curve, starting to slow the pace at which carbon is building up in the atmosphere. This sign would document the explosion in green building that is locking in energy efficiency for decades to come in homes, offices, and factories worldwide. It would capture the benefits from automobile emissions standards now in place in the United States and Europe and fuel efficiency standards working to cut vehicle fuel use in China, Japan, and South Korea. And, equally important, the sign would chart the growth of clean, renewable sources of energy. It would show that in 2009 alone the world added some *80 gigawatts—80 million kilowatts*—of zero-carbon, renewable electricity capacity. To put that in perspective, U.S. coal plants have a collective capacity of around 335 gigawatts. Even though wind and solar facilities are more variable in their energy output than coal plants, *in this one year alone* the world built enough new renewable generating capacity to replace nearly one in every 10 of the United States' polluting coal-fired power plants. And the pace of growth of renewable sources of energy continues to accelerate.

Not counting hydroelectric dams, renewable energy sources now produce just 3 percent of the world's electricity. Clearly, much more needs to be done. China, for instance, continues build new coal-fired plants and to rely on coal for at least three-quarters of its electricity. The good news, though, is how quickly the share of nonhydropower renewables is growing. Solar photovoltaics connected to the electric grid still make up a small piece of the overall picture, but the trajectory of their growth is particularly dramatic, with generating capacity increasing by roughly 60 percent per year. In fact, worldwide photovoltaic generating capacity *has risen 100-fold since 2000*. Wind energy, too, is expanding at a rapid rate, with cumulative capacity doubling in the past three years alone.

In other words, while we still have far to go, a huge global transition has begun—one of the biggest ever—and each of us can play a role in ensuring that the momentum continues to build.

The task is undoubtedly urgent; there is no time to spare. Given the climate effects already underway, most assessments consider the coming decade to be crucial for dramatically lowering our carbon emissions to avoid the most destabilizing effects to our climate. Worse yet, there are many forces—especially those who profit most from business as usual—trying to slow down or stop the changes we need to make for a healthy and prosperous future.

Still, while the stakes are undeniably high and timetable is tight, don't bet against humanity's capacity to mobilize and change. History is filled

---

UCS Climate Team *FAST FACT*

Not counting hydropower, renewable energy sources now produce just 3 percent of the world's electricity, but the share is growing fast. Solar photovoltaics connected to the electric grid still make up a small piece of the overall picture, but their growth is particularly dramatic, increasing in generating capacity at roughly 60 percent per year. In fact, worldwide photovoltaic generating capacity has increased 100-fold since 2000.

with examples of large and often swift changes, even in the energy field. You don't have to look any further than the story of whale oil.

Whaling was once an enormous multinational enterprise. From the 1700s through the mid-1800s, the blubber of hundreds of thousands of whales was boiled down into oil to be burned in the lamps that lighted much of the Western world. Whaling grew to be the fifth-largest industry in the United States. At its height in 1846, the U.S. whaling fleet included more than 700 ships; in that era some 8,000 whales were slaughtered annually, producing upward of 18 million gallons of whale oil.

In its day, whaling spawned dazzling fortunes. Coastal New England is still dotted with opulent captains' houses that amply illustrate the riches the industry brought to a few. Like the oil industry today, whaling was an entrenched and seemingly permanent source of energy in its time. And then, in the second half of the 1800s, whale oil was quickly displaced by kerosene and soon thereafter by the electric light.

The point, of course, is that the sources of the energy we depend on have changed rapidly before, and they can—and will—change again. While it is often hard to see around the technological corner, there is almost no doubt that we are at the start of a dramatic shift in the way we produce and use energy. The only remaining question is whether we can make this transition quickly enough to avoid some of the worst consequences of climate change. It won't be easy; the challenge we face is enormous. But we have ample evidence that with a concerted effort we can make great changes. And, to at least some extent, how much and how fast we can bend the curve depends on you.

Glimpsing the Future

What will our daily lives look like several decades from now if we tackle global warming today? As we have noted earlier, you don't need to imagine some high-tech sci-fi scenario. Very likely, the landscape will seem remarkably familiar. Our houses and offices will look largely the same, but they will be retrofitted for greater energy efficiency. Our home appliances will do much the same jobs they do today but will use far less electricity. The goods we buy will be produced much more efficiently, using many more reused and recycled components.

The biggest piece of the transformation will happen behind the scenes, in the ways our energy is produced. Most of it will come from clean, renewable sources. Many homes and commercial buildings will be heated and cooled by geothermal systems buried beneath the ground, or by solar collectors mounted on roofs, or wind turbines dotting rural landscapes or sited offshore.

Our communities will be retrofitted, too. More of us will live in urban centers, but even in densely populated areas, green spaces will be designed into courtyards, urban pedestrian ways, and rooftops to help combat the "heat island" effects of city living and contend with runoff from the heavier storms expected in a warmer world. Many of our suburbs will be transformed into walkable, bikeable mixed-use communities with parks, shops, schools, and other local services more closely integrated into residential areas.

We will still drive cars, but the close-knit structure of our communities, along with a robust and efficient mass transit system, will reduce our dependence on them, allowing us to spend less time stuck in traffic and more time with our family and friends. When we do drive, our cars, most likely electric, will be far more energy efficient and will deliver or even improve upon the performance and safety we've grown to expect. And for longer-distance travel, energy-efficient high-speed rail will link major cities, minimizing the need for most short and intermediate-length airplane flights.

Here's the most amazing thing about this scenario: the future it describes is within our reach today. We already have many of the tools we need to make it happen. And if we invest wisely in R&D, we will surely develop new, cleaner and more efficient technological tools that can speed us to a low-carbon future even more quickly. As this book has shown, the first steps we take toward this future will often *save* us money, and the next steps will not cost a lot.

Continuing to ignore global warming, however, will cost us dearly.

We simply can't wait any longer for someone else to fix the problem for us. If we take the necessary steps now, we can give our grandchildren a strong foundation upon which to build further solutions.

In fact, if we are successful, our grandchildren will think very differently about the many ways we wasted energy and the carbon emissions we tolerated. Burning fossil fuel in our basements to heat our homes or at big plants to power our hair dryers may seem about as antiquated to them as the notion of lighting homes with whale oil sounds to us today.

Making It Happen

Can we accomplish the transition to a low-carbon society? Of course we can. The world is experiencing some of the effects of global warming already, so we need to move fast. But to a surprising extent, in some parts of the world, the changes are already well underway. Take Denmark, for instance.

In 1973, Denmark relied on oil for 80 percent of its electricity. That year OPEC (the Organization of the Petroleum Exporting Countries) put an embargo on oil exports, creating debilitating shortages and skyrocketing prices. Like much of the rest of the world, Denmark began to invest in energy efficiency and alternative sources of energy to reduce its reliance on oil. But in the 1980s, oil prices dropped and most countries went back to their old ways. Denmark, however, stayed the course. Today, the primary power plant serving Copenhagen is almost three times as efficient as the typical U.S. coal plant, and nonhydropower renewables alone supply 29 percent of Denmark's electricity.

As a result, during the past 25 years, while the Danish economy has grown by roughly 75 percent, *the country has still cut its carbon emissions in half.* Much of that reduction has been accomplished through aggressive energy efficiency efforts and the installation of wind turbines, which now provide a clean, local zero-carbon source for roughly 20 percent of the country's electricity.

Denmark is not alone. Sweden now gets some 56 percent of its electricity from carbon-free sources. China has doubled its existing wind power capacity *in each of the past five years.* Many proponents of the status quo try to portray renewable sources of energy as some kind of fringe "alternative," but more and more, these sources are becoming the backbone of the world's electricity-generating system. Consider that if we include hydropower and biomass sources, renewable energy worldwide constituted one-quarter of global power capacity in 2009, delivering 18 percent of the planet's electricity. That's more electricity than was generated in that year by many well-established sources of electricity—such as by all the world's nuclear power plants combined. In some countries, the change is even more pronounced. In Germany, for example, which has been a leader in the renewable energy field for a decade, more than 300,000 people are currently employed in renewables industries, almost as many as in Germany's largest sector, the automotive industry.

The current growth of wind power is one of the clearest signs of the change now underway. In both Europe and the United States, wind power accounted for 39 percent of all new electricity-generating capacity in 2009—more than any other generating technology—for the second year in a row. To give just one of many surprising examples, the state of Iowa now generates more than 15 percent of its electricity from wind. A quick look at the graph gives a sense of the gale force of new wind power installations over the past decade. There is no doubt that the rapid pace of global warming means we need to move quickly to achieve a clean energy future. And while renewables are growing, they have yet to make enough inroads in avoiding the planet's heavy dependence on fossil fuels. But the good news is that with this kind of wind at our backs, we are already on the way. And the steps you take to reduce your energy usage—including the effort to make that initial 20 percent reduction in emissions this year—can move us along even faster.

UCS Climate Team FAST FACT

Denmark, which relied on oil for almost all of its electricity as recently as 1973, now gets some 29 percent from wind and other clean, renewable sources. Denmark is not alone: Sweden already gets some 56 percent of its electricity from carbon-free sources, and many other countries are on track to meet aggressive targets for installing new renewable capacity over the next decade.

Figure 12.1. Wind Power, Existing World Capacity, 1996–2009

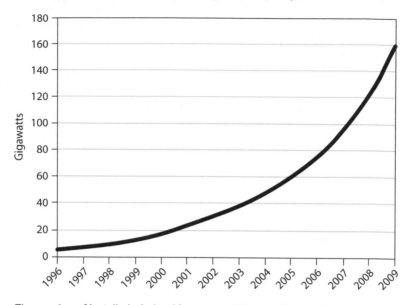

The number of installed wind turbines around the world is growing at an exponential rate. Worldwide generating capacity from wind power doubled in the past three years, as represented on this graph. Source: REN21, 2010.

The point to remember is that these kinds of changes don't just happen by themselves. Important steps toward a low-carbon future are made up of decisions by government officials at the national, state, and local levels and by investors, community leaders, and—most important of all—by actively engaged citizens working together.

As we have discussed for each of the sectors we've reviewed— from transportation to the stuff we buy—success in reducing emissions requires a three-part strategy:

1. *Saving energy* by using less of it and using it more efficiently, these being the simplest and most cost-effective ways to reduce our reliance on fossil fuels, especially coal and oil

2. *Building new renewable energy capacity* by installing zero-carbon technologies such as wind turbines, photovoltaic solar panels, and geothermal heat pumps

3. *Investing in research and development* to create the technological innovations that will lead us to even cleaner and more efficient energy and transportation solutions

You have an important role to play in each of these steps: first by making some smarter climate choices at home and then by sharing your vision with others in widening circles of influence. With more and more citizens getting involved, a massive shift has already begun, and its effects are starting to be felt in communities across the United States and around the world. You can get started right now with our individualized online tool at www.coolersmarter.org.

As citizens in a democratic society, we *can* break our addiction to fossil fuels, stave off the worst of global warming, and take our country in a different direction. Working together, we can step back from the brink of ecological disaster and move toward a more sustainable balance between the natural world and human civilization, ensuring a healthier planet for our children and grandchildren.

To succeed, we need to work from the top down *and* from the bottom up. We won't finish the work this year or this decade, but with your concerted efforts, we can work toward a low-carbon future and greatly reduce the consequences of global warming. It is inspiring, hopeful, and urgent work.

Welcome aboard.

ACKNOWLEDGMENTS

Any book with seven authors that covers so much technical information is going to have a lot of moving parts. We certainly have many people to thank for helping it all fit together. First of all, this book was made possible in part by the generous support of The 11th Hour Project and the Ayrshire Foundation. We also owe a huge debt of gratitude to Warren Leon and Michael Brower, who conceived of and wrote *The Consumer's Guide to Effective Environmental Choices: Practical Advice from the Union of Concerned Scientists* more than a decade ago, laying the groundwork for this effort.

In addition to the wealth of specialized knowledge and inspiration on the author team, we drew heavily upon the research and expertise of our colleagues at the Union of Concerned Scientists, including Doug Boucher, Rachel Cleetus, Steve Clemmer, Nancy Cole, Peter Frumhoff, Doug Gurian-Sherman, Noel Gurwick, Jim Kliesch, Jeremy Martin, Alden Meyer, Alan Nogee, Karen Perry Stillerman, Heather Tuttle, Laura Wisland, and Katy Zoot. We also deeply appreciate the advice and counsel we received from Kevin Knobloch, Kathy Rest, and David Whalen. A special thank-you also to Rich Hayes, who lent his sound judgment throughout the project.

We deeply appreciate the thoughtful reviews provided by a number of leading experts, including Michael Brower (AWS Truepower), Karen Ehrhardt-Martinez (University of Colorado), Peter Frumhoff (Union of Concerned Scientists), Deborah Gordon (independent transportation policy consultant), Chuck Kutscher (National Renewables Energy Laboratory), Warren Leon (Clean Energy States Alliance), James J. McCarthy

(Harvard University), Roni Neff (Johns Hopkins Bloomberg School of Public Health), Richard Pirog (Michigan State University), Daniel Sperling (University of California, Davis), and Helene York (Bon Appétit Management Company Foundation). Of course, any errors remaining in this book are the sole responsibility of the authors.

We were ably aided in our research by our intrepid research assistants Brady and Walker Powell. Special thanks to both of them and to Laura Reed for valuable feedback and invaluable encouragement.

We are grateful to the Stockholm Environment Institute research team (Frank Ackerman, Ramón Bueno, and Elizabeth A. Stanton) for conducting the modeling research, and we offer a special thank-you to Frank Ackerman for a wealth of ideas that appear in this book.

We'd also like to thank Marshall Goldberg of MRG & Associates for additional modeling assistance.

Our agent, Faith Hamlin of Sanford J. Greenburger Associates, deserves special recognition for her steadfast support and assistance in developing this project, as does Peg Anderson for her meticulous editing on a tight timeline despite the very real and charming distraction of her brand-new granddaughter. We'd also like to thank our longtime partners in design, David Gerratt and Amanda Wait of DG Communications, for producing the graphics for this book. And finally, we are grateful to Emily Davis and the entire team at Island Press for ably guiding the book through the publication process.

Resources

Global Warming Science and Impacts

UNION OF CONCERNED SCIENTISTS

www.ucsusa.org

The website of the Union of Concerned Scientists has extensive information about climate science and impacts. The organization also offers an individualized online tool to help you reduce your emissions at www .coolersmarter.org.

NOAA CLIMATE SERVICES

www.climate.gov

This website by the National Oceanic and Atmospheric Administration provides many government resources on climate change and the impact it is having across the country (and around the world).

REALCLIMATE

www.realclimate.org

RealClimate provides information about climate science by well-respected climate scientists currently working in the field. It was developed as a resource for the interested public and journalists to provide scientific context often missing from mainstream commentary on climate science.

SKEPTICAL SCIENCE

www.skepticalscience.com

This website provides a helpful iPhone app to debunk common contrarian claims about climate change. It draws its material from the peer-reviewed scientific literature.

Carbon Calculators

COOLCLIMATE NETWORK'S CARBON FOOTPRINT CALCULATOR

http://coolclimate.berkeley.edu

This tool, developed by the Lawrence Berkeley National Laboratory, calculates household emissions accounting for car, air, and public transportation, household energy use, and shopping habits, and enables you to compare your emissions with the emissions of those with similar incomes. For greatest accuracy, you'll need energy bills, car mileage, and your checkbook to use this tool.

HOUSEHOLD EMISSIONS CALCULATOR

www.epa.gov/climatechange/emissions/ind_calculator.html

This tool from the U.S. Environmental Protection Agency calculates household emissions based on your energy bills, car travel, and recycling habits.

Car Choices

HYBRID SCORECARD

www.hybridcenter.org

All hybrid cars are not created equal. This scorecard looks at the environmental value provided by U.S. hybrid makes and models.

GREEN VEHICLE GUIDE

www.epa.gov/greenvehicles

This tool from the U.S. Environmental Protection Agency allows users to compare the emissions and gas mileage of cars by make, model, and year.

FUELECONOMY.GOV

www.fueleconomy.gov

This website, run jointly by the U.S. Department of Energy and the U.S. Environmental Protection Agency, provides a range of information to help consumers improve the gas mileage of current vehicles. It also provides a tool similar to the Green Vehicle Guide that allows users to compare mileage per gallon, annual fuel costs, global warming emissions, and air pollutants by make, model, and year.

ACEEE'S GREEN BOOK
www.greenercars.org

This online database, offered by the American Council for an Energy-Efficient Economy for a small subscription fee, scores the environmental impacts of cars and trucks.

Other Travel Choices

THE CAR SHARING NETWORK
www.carsharing.net

This nonprofit website lists car-sharing programs in the United States.

AMERICAN PUBLIC TRANSPORTATION ASSOCIATION
www.publictransportation.org

This website provides a comprehensive database of public transportation options in communities across the United States.

ERIDESHARE.COM
http://erideshare.com

This free online resource connects people for ride sharing, from commuters to cross-country travelers.

Energy Audits

EFFICIENCY VERMONT
www.efficiencyvermont.com/stella/filelib/HowEnergyEfficientIs YourHome_Final.pdf

Efficiency Vermont offers a simple printable form for calculating your home energy use.

HOME ENERGY SAVER

www.hes.lbl.gov/consumer

Developed by the Lawrence Berkeley National Laboratory, this online tool allows you to input precise information about your home, from energy prices and insulation R-value to window sizes and appliance year, to determine where you can find the largest energy savings.

Home Energy

ENERGY STAR PROGRAM

www.energystar.gov

This voluntary labeling program is designed to identify and promote energy-efficient products to reduce greenhouse gas emissions. Run jointly by the U.S. Environmental Protection Agency and the U.S. Department of Energy, it provides energy use information and ratings on more than sixty product categories (and thousands of models) of common household and business appliances and equipment.

AMERICAN COUNCIL FOR AN ENERGY-EFFICIENT ECONOMY

www.aceee.org/consumer

The ACEEE's *Consumer Guide to Home Energy Savings* provides comprehensive information about appliances and home improvements that save energy.

ENERGY SAVERS

www.energysavers.gov

This website is a comprehensive resource for household (and business) energy efficiency and renewable energy information from the U.S. Department of Energy. Includes information about tax rebates and incentives.

NATIONAL RENEWABLE ENERGY LABORATORY

www.nrel.gov/learning/homeowners.html

The NREL's website provides references for a range of renewable energy technologies appropriate for heating or powering new or existing homes.

Green Power Purchasing and Offsets

GREEN-E

www.green-e.org

Best known as a certifier of green power, this nonprofit consumer protection program also certifies carbon offset programs.

GREEN POWER NETWORK

http://apps3.eere.energy.gov/greenpower

The U.S. Department of Energy lists green power options by state.

THE GOLD STANDARD

www.cdmgoldstandard.org

This is a nonprofit agency based in Switzerland that certifies and rates different offsetting options.

DATABASE OF STATE INCENTIVES FOR RENEWABLES AND EFFICIENCY

www.dsireusa.org

Here, the U.S. Department of Energy sponsors comprehensive information on state, local, federal, and utility incentives for renewable energy and energy efficiency.

U.S. GREEN BUILDING COUNCIL

www.usgbc.org

Among other resources, this website provides a directory of certified green builders and architects by sector.

Food

CLIMATE-FRIENDLY GARDENER

www.ucsusa.org/assets/gardenguide

This 12-page booklet provides guidance for home gardeners interested in climate-friendly practices.

LOW CARBON DIET CALCULATOR

www.eatlowcarbon.org

This consumer-friendly tool developed by the Bon Appétit Management Company Foundation provides a visual drag-and-drop menu of common foods and meals that allows users to see the carbon intensity of their meals. The tool was developed using life cycle emissions of various foods gleaned from the peer-reviewed scientific literature.

FOOD CARBON EMISSIONS CALCULATOR

www.foodemissions.com

*Clean*Metrics, a private consulting group, has set up a simple food emissions calculator based on its proprietary database of food carbon emissions using life cycle analysis.

LEOPOLD CENTER FOR SUSTAINABLE AGRICULTURE

www.leopold.iastate.edu

This website provides many resources about the interconnectedness of food and climate change.

Groups Working on Climate Change

The following is a sample of the broad range of groups with diverse interests working on climate change.

U.S. CLIMATE ACTION NETWORK

www.usclimatenetwork.org

USCAN is the largest U.S. network of organizations working on climate change and is a helpful resource for finding local, state, and national groups working on climate change. Member organizations include a diverse array of groups, from 350.org, Clean Air-Cool Planet, Environment America, the National Wildlife Federation, the Natural Resources Defense Council, and the Sierra Club to the National Audubon Society, Oxfam America, and the National Association for the Advancement of Colored People (NAACP).

BLUEGREEN ALLIANCE

www.bluegreenalliance.org

The BlueGreen Alliance is a partnership between labor unions and environmental organizations dedicated to expanding the number and quality of jobs in the green economy.

ICLEI—LOCAL GOVERNMENTS FOR SUSTAINABILITY USA

www.icleiusa.org

The ICLEI is a membership organization of cities and towns working to reduce global warming.

INTERFAITH POWER & LIGHT

www.interfaithpowerandlight.org

Interfaith Power & Light mobilizes a religious response to global warming in congregations through the promotion of renewable energy, energy efficiency, and conservation.

EVANGELICAL ENVIRONMENTAL NETWORK

www.creationcare.org

The EEN is an organization dedicated to equip, inspire, disciple, and mobilize people in their effort to care for Earth as God's creation. The EEN publishes and develops material for churches, families, and individuals to address climate change and other environmental challenges as they seek to explore and express their faith more fully.

NATIONAL RELIGIOUS PARTNERSHIP FOR THE ENVIRONMENT

www.nrpe.org

The National Religious Partnership for the Environment is an association of independent faith groups, including the U.S. Conference of Catholic Bishops, the National Council of Churches of Christ, the Coalition on the Environment and Jewish Life, and the Evangelical Environmental Network, that seek to offer resources of religious life and moral vision to a universal effort to protect humankind's common home and well-being on Earth.

OPERATION FREE

www.operationfree.net

Operation Free is a group of veterans and national security organizations calling for action on climate change and clean energy.

UNITED STATES CLIMATE ACTION PARTNERSHIP

www.us-cap.org

USCAP is an alliance of major corporations—from Dow Chemical to General Electric—and environmental organizations calling for federal legislation to reduce global warming emissions.

CLIMATEANDINSURANCE.ORG

www.climateandinsurance.org

The National Association of Mutual Insurance Companies created this website as a resource for industry professionals to learn more about climate change and its possible implications for the property-casualty industry.

Our Paths to 20

Team Member Statements about Reducing Our Own Carbon Footprints

JEFF DEYETTE

Senior Energy Analyst, Climate and Energy Program

When my wife and I bought our first home in 2009, I was excited to finally put into practice some of the energy-saving techniques I had long studied and endorsed at work. We had done what we could to reduce energy consumption in our old apartment—such as installing a programmable thermostat, insulating the water heater, using compact fluorescent lightbulbs, and buying an Energy Star–certified air conditioner for our bedroom—but as renters we were not able to do much more.

After moving in, our first order of business (after installing the CFLs and programmable thermostat) was insulation. First, we insulated all the hot water and steam radiator pipes in the basement. The difference was like night and day: in cold weather, our basement was no longer warmer than our living room! We also found reflective insulation to place behind our recessed wall radiators to help bring more heat into our living space. To tackle the larger spaces—the attic and exterior walls—we took advantage of state and federal tax incentives to bring down the costs of insulating, installing it ourselves in the attic and hiring a contractor to blow insulation into the walls. These improvements made a huge difference. Last winter, we used more than 100 fewer gallons of heating oil than we had the first winter in our house. Tax credits also allowed us to replace the house's old and inefficient kitchen appliances with Energy Star–rated versions for even more reductions in our carbon emissions.

BRENDA EKWURZEL

Climate Scientist, Climate and Energy Program

Perhaps the most important change I have made is my decision to live within walking distance of work, allowing me to abandon my former practice of making a long daily commute by car. I now walk three blocks to the Capital Bikeshare kiosk (in Washington, DC), put on my helmet, and ride most of the way to my office, dropping the bike off at a conveniently located kiosk near work. Because the trip takes less than one-half hour, the bike ride is free (aside from my annual membership fee). And it normally gets me from home to work in about 15 minutes.

At home, I also replaced windows and doors in my condominium. Unfortunately, I wasn't eligible for a tax credit, but I still bought the most energy-efficient windows I could find. Now, in cold weather, when I put my hand on the window, it is actually warmer than the nearby wall. I buy green power from my utility for a small additional cost. And, for those few occasions in winter when I want to make a fire in my traditional fireplace, I have found logs made from used coffee grounds that burn well, with far fewer emissions and no unpleasant odor. And, yes, when my fireplace is not in use, I make sure the damper is closed tightly to prevent unwanted heat loss!

DAVID FRIEDMAN

Deputy Director and Senior Engineer, Clean Vehicles Program

Ten years ago, when I first came to work for the Union of Concerned Scientists, I bought my first new car. Coming to work for a nonprofit, I couldn't afford a hybrid. So I did my homework and purchased a Honda Civic HX, a relatively rare model of gasoline car with the highest fuel economy of any car sold at the time. (Honda made only about 500–600 of these lean-burning engines that year.) The car is still running well and has dramatically reduced my carbon emissions.

More recently, the biggest decision my wife and I have made to reduce our carbon footprint was to buy a house just two miles from work in Florida, where we live. Before our son was born, we both bicycled to work. Today, we are keeping it up with one of us continuing to bike either to or from work each day while the other drives to drop our son off at day care. Despite the Florida heat, we keep our house at 80 degrees Fahrenheit. We have switched our lightbulbs to compact fluorescents and use power strips to turn off our electronic equipment. At some point, I'll be in the market for a new car again. If I had to buy one today, it would certainly be a hybrid, but I'm keeping a close look at the coming generation of electric-drive vehicles, which could help reduce my emissions even further.

MARGARET MELLON

Senior Scientist, Food and Environment Program

I commute to work on the metro and have owned a gas-electric hybrid Prius for three years, both of which have dramatically lowered my emissions. For decades, my diet has included fish and dairy (often organic) but very little pork, beef, or poultry. The meat I do eat usually comes from local or organic producers. Buying local and organic meat may not help much from the climate standpoint, but it matters a great deal to me to know that the animals were raised humanely and not fed antibiotics. Over the years, my partner has moved in my direction on eating less meat while I've moved in his direction on using more aggressive thermostat settings and being better about turning off lights every time I leave a room, as he prefers to do.

At home, we have replaced most of our incandescent bulbs with more efficient compact fluorescent bulbs. We have a programmable thermostat and have bought energy-efficient appliances, including a dishwasher with two separate drawers that allows us to efficiently wash a smaller load when we need to. We compost our food waste, and last year we purchased an in-home seltzer maker, which has allowed us to stop buying bottled water almost entirely. The magnitude of this purchase on our carbon footprint may not be that great, but it certainly feels good to no longer be discarding so many plastic bottles.

JOHN ROGERS

Senior Energy Analyst, Climate and Energy Program

The lens for much of my work on climate issues and climate solutions is my children and the kind of world they're growing up in. I've offset some of the environmental impact of adding to the world's population by preparing my two boys to be the environmental leaders of tomorrow; at ages seven and eight, they are fully attuned to the value of compact fluorescent and LED lighting, hybrid cars, and turning off the television at the power strip. Still, expanding our household has meant having to work harder on our carbon footprint. We've taken important steps toward bringing our old house onto the necessary carbon path. My first line of attack was the lighting. I was an early adopter of compact fluorescents, and I was inspired a decade ago to swap out virtually every bulb. We've since replaced our old, inefficient furnaces and an air conditioner with top-efficiency models, ditched an inefficient water heater in favor of solar water heating and an on-demand heater, and buttoned up the house with a new door, improved windows, air sealing, and more and more insulation. One measure of the effectiveness of those efforts is the fact that, despite building an addition that increased the square footage of our home by 10 percent, our electricity and gas bills have shrunk to pre-kid levels and are staying put.

But we continue to look for ways to do more. We're getting professional help to seal our house much more effectively, while ensuring we still get fresh air, and insulating the basement correctly. We're looking into more efficient car options for when my early model hybrid or my wife's station wagon needs replacing. We're continuing to buy green power but still trying to figure out how we might be able to make a solar array work despite shading. When our utilities show us how we stack up against our neighbors, we want to be the ones to beat.

SUZANNE SHAW

Director of Communications

Having grown up in the Los Angeles area, with its infamous sprawl and congestion, I feel fortunate now to live in a city with great public transportation, which allows me to avoid the frustration of sitting in traffic. Since we are a one-car family and don't use the car for commuting, when I wanted to reduce my global warming emissions, the first place I looked was at my home's heating and cooling. My house came with an ancient oil furnace, which I replaced with a high-efficiency natural gas furnace. While this was an investment of several thousand dollars, the old furnace had been so inefficient that the new one paid for itself within several years. The house also had zero insulation except for newspaper (from World War II, no less!) stuffed into a few cracks. So I blew insulation into the walls and put a layer in the attic. This project wasn't very expensive and made a huge difference in the comfort level of the house.

I installed a programmable thermostat (which came with a rebate coupon allowing me to recoup the entire cost of the unit) and swapped out most of our home's incandescent lightbulbs with compact fluorescents. (I do keep a few dimmable incandescent bulbs in the kitchen, as the current generation of dimmable CFLs still has room for improvement.) My family is committed to buying the most efficient Energy Star models we can when the time comes to replace our appliances. And we wash our clothes in cold water without noticing any difference. Over the years, these changes have greatly reduced my energy bills, so that I now pay about half of the average amount of similar homes in my zip code. I have also begun to buy green power from my utility, which, given fluctuations in electricity prices over the past several months, seems to have caused no noticeable increase in my electricity bill.

SETH SHULMAN

Senior Staff Writer

While I have long been relatively conscious about my energy usage, working on this book gave me some new impetus to review my family's carbon emissions and some useful information that helped me make significant additional reductions. Because I commute to work by car and the time was right to replace an old Volvo wagon, I made the most substantial reductions by buying a car that nearly doubles my fuel efficiency, slashing some 3 tons of carbon emissions annually. Last fall, I added more insulation to my attic and more aggressively programmed my thermostat, lowering the temperature further at night and while my family was away at work or school during the day; I saw the results in energy savings right away.

My family has long had a mostly vegetarian diet, so I couldn't find additional reductions there. But I did break one longstanding bad habit by buying two power strips and shutting off power to the television and home office equipment when not in use. I had always tended to leave my office laser printer on, assuming that it went into "sleep" mode. I had no idea that habit alone was costing me roughly $130 in electricity annually! I'm happy to report that even though I live in a big, old house, when our electric utility company began a program comparing our electricity usage with that of our neighbors, the recommendations in the book helped me to move surprisingly easily from average electricity usage into the greenest quadrant of similar homes in my neighborhood.

An Explanation of Our Research and Analysis Methodology

Precisely calculating the global warming emissions associated with house-hold consumption in the United States is a complex process.* Direct emissions from a car's tailpipe or a lawnmower's motor are relatively obvious and easy to quantify, but these direct "tailpipe" assessments fail to account for what are often called "upstream" or "indirect" impacts, which can be considerable. In the case of the lawnmower, for instance, upstream impacts include emissions resulting from manufacturing, emissions resulting from the retail process (including from the wholesaler who sells the mower to the retailer), and emissions resulting from shipping raw materials to the manufacturer and transporting the finished product to the wholesaler and then to the retailer. A similar pattern exists for all consumer goods.

Quantifying emissions that result from purchasing a service, such as an appointment with the dentist, or from consuming food is even more difficult. To do it effectively, one has to incorporate a fairly detailed understanding of emissions from electricity use and production, as well as the emissions that result every step of the way from purchases of materials and parts and from fuel use, transportation, and a host of other potential sources.

To accomplish this task in a detailed and comprehensive manner, we worked with a team of modelers at the Stockholm Environment Institute's U.S. Center, including Frank Ackerman, Elizabeth A. Stanton, and Ramón Bueno.

*The terms "household consumption," "consumer expenditures," and "consumer or household demand" are all used in this report and refer to the same activities.

The team began by gathering and analyzing a significant amount of scientific data (primarily source emissions estimates) as well as detailed economic information on consumer and industry spending patterns.

The team analyzed emissions from all sources in 2006, the most recent year available when we initiated the project. We found that 7,075 million metric tons of carbon dioxide equivalent (CO_2e)* had been emitted that year in the United States, of which 5,418 million metric tons were attributed to specific types of consumer expenditures and uses and included in our industry analysis.[†] Although we reviewed and analyzed numerous sources, we relied on sources including the U.S. Department of Energy's *Emissions of Greenhouse Gases in the United States 2006*[‡] and "Official Energy Statistics from the U.S. Government: Households, Buildings, Industry, and Vehicles, 2001"[§] and the U.S. Department of Transportation's "U.S. Government Energy Consumption by Agency and Source (Trillion Btu)."[**] All emissions data were entered into a spreadsheet model

---

*Carbon dioxide equivalent (CO_2e) is a measure used to incorporate the contribution of a variety of greenhouse gas emissions on the basis of their global warming potential relative to carbon dioxide.

[†]Please note that these raw data have subsequently been converted to conventional pounds and tons (2,000 pounds per ton) in the examples and tables throughout the book. Initial data are from U.S. Department of Energy, Energy Information Administration (EIA), "Distribution of Total U.S. Greenhouse Gas Emissions by End-Use Sector, 2006," p. 5 in *Emissions of Greenhouse Gases in the United States 2006*, DOE/EIA-0573 (Washington, DC: EIA, November 2007). Approximately 24 percent of the total reported gases (mostly from industrial sources) were excluded from the analysis, either because they were far removed from consumer activity or to avoid double counting in the model.

[‡]Ibid.

[§]U.S. Department of Energy, Energy Information Administration (EIA), "Official Energy Statistics from the U.S. Government: Households, Buildings, Industry, and Vehicles, 2001."

[**]U.S. Department of Transportation, Research and Innovative Technology Administration, Bureau of Transportation Statistics, "U.S. Government Energy Consumption by Agency and Source (Trillion Btu)," table 4-19 in "National Transportation Statistics 2008." Available at http://www.bts.gov/publications/national _transportation_statistics. Although most of the data incorporated in the analysis are from 2006, the results of this study also reflect emissions coefficients based in part on data from 2002 and 2003 for the transportation sector.

to derive national industry shares of consumption-based emissions and industry emissions coefficients for use in the analysis.*

To make this economic information fit together, the team needed to include analysis of industry output and consumer demand by industry sector for 2006, as well as to incorporate an understanding of the inter-industry linkages to determine upstream impacts. For these we relied on an economic modeling tool called IMPLAN, using information from the IMPLAN 2006 U.S. Data File.[†]

IMPLAN was originally developed in the 1970s by the USDA Forest Service to assist in land and resource management and planning. In the early 1990s, a group working on IMPLAN databases at the University of Minnesota formed the Minnesota IMPLAN Group (MIG) to privatize the development of IMPLAN data and software to make it more user friendly and available to a broader range of users. Since the release of the first publicly available version in 1996, subsequent versions of the IMPLAN software have continued to evolve and expand its flexibility for use in economic impact modeling. The current analysis utilized IMPLAN Professional™ Version 2.0.[‡]

The IMPLAN Version 2.0 modeling system is one of the most widely used and accepted regional economic analysis tools for predicting economic impacts in the United States. IMPLAN is currently used by over 2,000 public and private institutions, including government agencies, colleges and universities, nonprofit organizations, corporations, and business development and community planning organizations.[§] It is designed to perform economic impact analysis and assist in planning and policy decisions on a broad range of issues. Among others, these include natural

*For our purposes, emissions coefficients refer to ratios of CO_2 emissions per dollar of industry output.

[†]For a more comprehensive discussion of the IMPLAN model, see the IMPLAN discussion that follows in this appendix.

[‡]The most current version of the software is IMPLAN Version 3. It was released in November 2009, after the current analysis was complete. For additional information, see www.implan.com.

[§]For a current listing of registered IMPLAN users, see www.implan.com.

resource issues; plant openings, closings, and relocations; and economic related policy-driven scenarios.

IMPLAN is an "input-output" economic modeling tool. Input-output models, and the IMPLAN tool in particular, allow users to analyze how an economy responds to changes. Using inter-industry relationships (also known as supply linkages) within a particular region, input-output models show how an increase in demand for a product or service affects or causes changes in other industries. The increase in demand for a good or service affects the producer of the good or service and its employees and suppliers, as well as the supplier's employees and suppliers, among others. These linkages ultimately generate a total effect in the economy that is greater than the initial change in demand, commonly referred to as a multiplier effect.

In its most basic form, the IMPLAN system is composed of software and a database. The software provides a mechanism for data retrieval, model development, and the resulting impact analysis. The database consists of national and regional data in 528 separate sectors about employment, industry output, and institutional demand and transfers.* The sectors closely follow the accounting conventions used by the U.S. Bureau of Economic Analysis (BEA) and link to the standard industrial classifications (known as SIC codes). The database includes information derived from numerous published and unpublished sources, including surveys and reports from the U.S. Department of Agriculture, the U.S. Department of Commerce, the U.S. Department of Health and Human Services, and the U.S. Department of the Interior, among others.[†]

We started with the IMPLAN model by designating the entire United States as the study area and using the model to identify the total U.S. industry output (in dollars). According to IMPLAN, total industry output in 2006 was just under $27.8 trillion for all industry sectors. We then used

---

*Our analysis accounts for 509 separate industry sectors, as 19 sectors are not considered part of the traditional industry analysis. This includes sectors such as scrap, federal and state enterprises (that are part of other sectors), the U.S. Postal Service, domestic services, and used and secondhand goods.

†For a more comprehensive listing of data sources used to develop IMPLAN data files, see www.implan.com.

IMPLAN to identify total household expenditures (in dollars) by each industry sector. According to IMPLAN, total household demand in 2006 was just under $10.0 trillion,* with national household expenditures estimated for nine separate income classes using data from the BEA's Benchmark Input-Output Study and the Consumer Expenditure Survey (CES).†

IMPLAN reporting and analysis, similar to all input-output models, is based on producer prices and industry demand. To allocate consumer spending as accurately as possible, IMPLAN uses so-called margins. Margins represent the differences between producer and purchaser prices and are used to allocate consumer expenditures to the correct input-output sector. For example, when the IMPLAN model analyzes a consumer's purchase of a light fixture at a lighting store, it allocates a portion of the consumer's outlay to the retailer, a portion to the wholesaler, and a portion to the transportation and manufacturing sectors. Each sector, in other words, benefits to some extent from the consumer purchase. Household expenditures are thus allocated across the 509 industry sectors that we analyzed in IMPLAN.

Margins are applied only to retail purchases of manufactured goods that have markups. Purchases of services do not have margins applied because the service is produced at the same time it is purchased and has no markup by other sectors. Just as margins are used to allocate consumer purchases, IMPLAN also quantifies industry linkages for each producer sector. For example, when the portion of the purchase price for a light fixture is allocated to the manufacturing sector, the model in turn subtracts from the manufacturer a portion of that money it spent to purchase the raw materials, equipment, and services needed to manufacture the lamp.

By identifying the use of commodities by a given industry's production process, the model ultimately derives multipliers that are triggered

---

*Total household demand (consumer expenditures) in 2006 was actually just over $10 trillion; however, adjustments were made using margins to distribute wholesale, transportation, and retail, to avoid double counting.

†It should also be noted that IMPLAN is a so-called closed model of the U.S. economy; in other words, it assumes that expenditures from outside the United States have the same emissions profile as those within the United States.

by each \$1 of consumption for goods or services produced by a specific industry.*

With the emissions and economic data in hand, and the industry framework established, the modeling team then matched the emissions for each industry sector with the appropriate IMPLAN sectors. In this step of the analysis we were interested in determining how much CO_2e is emitted per dollar of industry output, both for the direct effects and for the indirect effects. In most instances, the emissions data provided breakouts by industry classifications that were easily matched to IMPLAN's sectors or to the North American Industry Classification System (NAICS) codes.[†] In those instances where the classification wasn't clear, we determined how to attribute the emissions on the basis of a variety of specific factors, such as fuel type or end-use category. This careful matching had two purposes: first, it provided a basis for identifying which sectors produce the most emissions; second, it allowed us to derive industry-specific intensities.

The next step in the process involved matching the total CO_2e emissions for each industry with the respective dollar outputs for each industry sector. By dividing each industry's total emissions by the total output, the team developed the CO_2e coefficients (metric tons CO_2e/\$1 output)— the key factor for completing the impact analysis.[‡]

To better understand how the analysis and modeling actually works to calculate CO_2e emissions impacts, we can look at a simplified example.

---

*For our purposes we utilize Type I multipliers, which incorporate direct and indirect impacts only. Our analysis does not include induced impacts, which are from increased household spending caused by the employment and income gains due to the direct and indirect impacts.

†NAICS replaced the Standard Industrial Classification (SIC) system used by the federal government for classifying industries by type.

‡To derive the direct emissions impacts, each dollar of consumer spending (margined) was matched directly with the emissions coefficient for each industry sector. To derive the indirect impacts, we again used the industry coefficients and the consumer expenditures (margined) but applied them to the Type I multipliers (noted earlier) developed with IMPLAN. Each dollar of consumer spending was multiplied by an industry-specific Type I multiplier to calculate the indirect output. This total was then multiplied by the emissions coefficient for each industry. The direct and indirect emissions impacts were summed to calculate a total impact for each expenditure.

Table C.1. CO_2e Emissions for a $100 Lamp

Industry Sector	Emissions Coefficients (Tons/$)			IMPLAN Margin
	Direct	Indirect	Total	
Furniture store	0.00009	0.00033	0.00042	0.465917
Truck transportation	0.00009	0.00010	0.00019	0.077677
Air transportation	0.00131	0.00024	0.00155	0.001592
Wholesaler	0.00152	0.00036	0.00188	0.030375
Lighting fixture manufacturer	0.00009	0.00010	0.00019	0.424439
Total	0.00310	0.00113	0.00423	1.000000

Industry Sector	Emissions (Tons)		
	Direct	Indirect	Total
Furniture store	0.0042	0.0155	0.0197
Truck transportation	0.0007	0.0008	0.0015
Air transportation	0.0002	0.0000	0.0002
Wholesaler	0.0046	0.0011	0.0057
Lighting fixture manufacturer	0.0039	0.0044	0.0083
Total	0.0136	0.0218	0.0354

Let's assume a consumer goes to a local furniture store and purchases a lamp for $100. Since the store is a retailer, it doesn't keep the whole $100, as we noted earlier. Based on the margins derived from IMPLAN, the $100 is actually split between the retailer, truck and air transportation, a wholesaler, and the lighting fixture manufacturer. In fact, as the table indicates, less than half of the cost of the lamp stays with the store. The remainder, approximately 53 percent, is funneled to other sectors to pay the suppliers and transportation costs. On the basis of the direct and indirect emissions coefficients for the industries noted, we see that the $100 expenditure for a lamp generates 0.03 metric ton of CO_2e emissions throughout the economy. The table offers a snapshot of how the model works in practice.

APPENDIX D

Research Results

Table D.1 U.S. Household Emissions by Category (Million Tons CO$_2$e)

Category	Production Emissions	Use Emissions	Disposal Emissions	Total GHG Emissions	% of Total GHG Emissions	Emissions Intensity for Production (lb./$)
Transportation						
Chapter total	**305.8**	**1,486.8**	**22.9**	**1,815.5**	**28.5%**	
Vehicles	115.3	1,486.8	17.6	1,619.7	25.4%	0.7
Transportation services	144.7	0.0	0.1	144.8	2.3%	2.7
Vehicle parts	45.9	0.0	5.2	51.0	0.8%	1.0
Heating and Cooling						
Chapter total	**1.4**	**1,089.7**	**0.1**	**1,091.2**	**17.1%**	
Heating and cooling appliances	1.4	1,089.7	0.1	1,091.2	17.1%	0.7
Household Energy Use						
Chapter total	**92.7**	**833.6**	**5.3**	**931.6**	**14.7%**	
Lighting fixtures	2.6	299.8	0.3	302.7	4.8%	0.7
Other electronics	33.0	109.3	2.0	144.3	2.3%	0.6
Refrigerators and freezers	4.3	111.7	0.2	116.2	1.8%	0.8
Washers and dryers	5.6	108.8	0.2	114.6	1.8%	0.8
Ranges and microwaves	4.6	83.2	0.2	88.0	1.4%	0.8
Other appliances	7.2	78.7	0.3	86.2	1.4%	0.7
Computers and peripherals	35.3	42.1	2.2	79.6	1.2%	0.6
Food						
Chapter total	**818.6**	**0.0**	**43.3**	**861.9**	**13.5%**	
Restaurants	190.9	0.0	15.2	206.1	3.2%	0.9
Red meat	130.5	0.0	3.2	133.8	2.1%	2.9
Fruit, nuts, and vegetables	109.5	0.0	3.9	113.4	1.8%	2.0
Dairy and eggs	97.9	0.0	2.4	100.4	1.6%	2.9
Beverages	78.2	0.0	6.7	84.9	1.3%	0.8
Grains, baked goods, and cereals	78.6	0.0	5.3	83.9	1.3%	1.1
Poultry	42.2	0.0	1.8	44.0	0.7%	1.7
Frozen food	23.9	0.0	1.4	25.3	0.4%	1.2
Condiments, oils, and sweeteners	19.8	0.0	0.9	20.6	0.3%	1.6
Other food	17.1	0.0	0.9	18.1	0.3%	1.4
Pet food	16.0	0.0	1.0	17.0	0.3%	1.2

Category	Production Emissions	Use Emissions	Disposal Emissions	Total GHG Emissions	% of Total GHG Emissions	Emissions Intensity for Production (lb./$)
Food (continued)						
Chapter total	**818.6**	**0.0**	**43.3**	**861.9**	**13.5%**	
Other animal products	9.5	0.0	0.1	9.6	0.2%	5.2
Seafood	4.4	0.0	0.4	4.8	0.1%	0.7
Stuff You Buy						
Chapter total	**1,587.0**	**0.0**	**81.9**	**1,668.8**	**26.2%**	
Healthcare services	269.6	0.0	6.4	276.0	4.3%	0.4
Residential construction and remodeling	255.0	0.0	14.2	269.2	4.2%	0.8
Water—sewage and other systems	142.6	0.0	0.0	142.6	2.2%	8.2
Other services	120.0	0.0	0.8	120.8	1.9%	0.4
Other	98.3	0.0	9.9	108.2	1.7%	0.1
Household supplies	88.8	0.0	9.9	98.7	1.5%	0.7
Legal, real estate, and insurance	95.8	0.0	0.9	96.7	1.5%	0.3
Clothing	76.8	0.0	12.0	88.9	1.4%	0.5
Medicines	83.8	0.0	1.3	85.1	1.3%	0.6
Furnishings	46.9	0.0	5.4	52.3	0.8%	0.6
Banks and financial services	47.9	0.0	0.7	48.6	0.8%	0.2
Education and day care	44.8	0.0	0.4	45.1	0.7%	0.4
Media	38.3	0.0	5.9	44.2	0.7%	0.5
Entertainment and media	39.4	0.0	0.4	39.8	0.6%	0.3
Car rental, repair, and wash	32.8	0.0	0.2	33.0	0.5%	0.5
Personal services	31.3	0.0	0.2	31.4	0.5%	0.6
Lawn and garden	28.5	0.0	1.0	29.5	0.5%	2.1
Office supplies	19.2	0.0	1.9	21.1	0.3%	0.7
Hotels and motels	16.5	0.0	0.1	16.6	0.3%	0.5
Waste management	0.0	0.0	9.9	9.9	0.2%	6.2
Nonresidential construction	8.1	0.0	0.4	8.5	0.1%	0.9
Building services	2.7	0.0	0.0	2.7	0.0%	0.5
Total emissions from household consumption	**2,805.5**	**3,410.0**	**153.5**	**6,369.0**	**100.0%**	

Table D.2 Average Emissions per Household by Category (Tons CO_2e)

Category	Production Emissions	Use Emissions	Disposal Emissions	Total GHG Emissions	% of Total GHG Emissions
Transportation					
Chapter total	2.74	13.32	0.21	16.27	28.5%
Vehicles	1.03	13.32	0.16	14.51	25.4%
Transportation services	1.30	0.00	0.00	1.30	2.3%
Vehicle parts	0.41	0.00	0.05	0.46	0.8%
Heating and Cooling					
Chapter total	0.01	9.76	0.00	9.78	17.1%
Heating and cooling appliances	0.01	9.76	0.00	9.78	17.1%
Household Energy Use					
Chapter total	0.83	7.47	0.05	8.34	14.7%
Lighting fixtures	0.02	2.69	0.00	2.71	4.8%
Other electronics	0.30	0.98	0.02	1.29	2.3%
Refrigerators and freezers	0.04	1.00	0.00	1.04	1.8%
Washers and dryers	0.05	0.97	0.00	1.03	1.8%
Ranges and microwaves	0.04	0.75	0.00	0.79	1.4%
Other appliances	0.06	0.70	0.00	0.77	1.4%
Computers and peripherals	0.32	0.38	0.02	0.71	1.2%
Food					
Chapter total	7.33	0.00	0.39	7.72	13.5%
Restaurants	1.71	0.00	0.14	1.85	3.2%
Red meat	1.17	0.00	0.03	1.20	2.1%
Fruit, nuts, and vegetables	0.98	0.00	0.04	1.02	1.8%
Dairy and eggs	0.88	0.00	0.02	0.90	1.6%
Beverages	0.70	0.00	0.06	0.76	1.3%
Grains, baked goods, and cereals	0.70	0.00	0.05	0.75	1.3%
Poultry	0.38	0.00	0.02	0.39	0.7%
Frozen food	0.21	0.00	0.01	0.23	0.4%
Condiments, oils, and sweeteners	0.18	0.00	0.01	0.18	0.3%
Other food	0.15	0.00	0.01	0.16	0.3%
Pet food	0.14	0.00	0.01	0.15	0.3%

Category	Production Emissions	Use Emissions	Disposal Emissions	Total GHG Emissions	% of Total GHG Emissions
Food (continued)					
Other animal products	0.08	0.00	0.00	0.09	0.2%
Seafood	0.04	0.00	0.00	0.04	0.1%
Stuff You Buy					
Chapter total	14.22	0.00	0.73	14.95	26.2%
Healthcare services	2.42	0.00	0.06	2.47	4.3%
Residential construction and remodeling	2.28	0.00	0.13	2.41	4.2%
Water- sewage and other systems	1.28	0.00	0.00	1.28	2.2%
Other services	1.08	0.00	0.01	1.08	1.9%
Other	0.88	0.00	0.09	0.97	1.7%
Household supplies	0.80	0.00	0.09	0.88	1.5%
Legal, real estate, insurance	0.86	0.00	0.01	0.87	1.5%
Clothing	0.69	0.00	0.11	0.80	1.4%
Medicines	0.75	0.00	0.01	0.76	1.3%
Furnishings	0.42	0.00	0.05	0.47	0.8%
Banks and financial services	0.43	0.00	0.01	0.44	0.8%
Education and day care	0.40	0.00	0.00	0.40	0.7%
Media	0.34	0.00	0.05	0.40	0.7%
Entertainment and media	0.35	0.00	0.00	0.36	0.6%
Car rental, repair and wash	0.29	0.00	0.00	0.30	0.5%
Personal services	0.28	0.00	0.00	0.28	0.5%
Lawn and garden	0.25	0.00	0.01	0.26	0.5%
Office supplies	0.17	0.00	0.02	0.19	0.3%
Hotels and motels	0.15	0.00	0.00	0.15	0.3%
Waste management	0.00	0.00	0.09	0.09	0.2%
Non-residential construction	0.07	0.00	0.00	0.08	0.1%
Building services	0.02	0.00	0.00	0.02	0.0%
Total emissions from household consumption	25.13	30.55	1.38	57.06	100.0%

Chapter 1

Page

3 **Swedish scientist named Svante Arrhenius:** S. Arrhenius, "On the Influence of Carbonic Acid in the Air upon the Temperature of the Ground," *Philosophical Magazine and Journal of Science* 41, no. 251 (Apr. 1896): 237–276. See www.globalwarmingart.com/images/1/18/Arrhenius.pdf.

4 **consider the "penny parable":** See www.commoncents.org.

5 **U.S. government's Energy Star program:** U.S. Environmental Protection Agency, Partnerships for Home Energy Efficiency, a joint program of the U.S. Environmental Protection Agency, U.S. Department of Energy, and U.S. Department of Housing and Urban Development (2006). See www.EnergyStar.gov/ia/home_improvement/PHEE_Report_final.pdf.

5 **people of Salina, Kansas:** See Leslie Kaufman, "In Kansas, Climate Skeptics Embrace Cleaner Energy," *New York Times*, Oct. 18, 2010.

6 **two-thirds of their energy as waste heat:** See www.ucsusa.org/clean_energy/coalvswind/c02d.html.

6 **less than 20 percent of the gasoline:** See, for instance, Dan Neil, "The Future of the Car," *Popular Science*, Sept. 2004, p. 66.

6 **technologies to recover energy from waste heat:** Owen Bailey and Ernst Worrell, "Clean Energy Technologies: A Preliminary Inventory of the Potential for Electricity Generation," LBNL-57451 (Berkeley, CA: Lawrence Berkeley National Laboratory, 2005).

6 **Canadian utility company drove home:** BC Hydro's 2010 "PowerSmart" campaign is available at www.youtube.com/user/BCHydroPowerSmart.

7 **21 tons of carbon dioxide:** Derived from UCS modeling. For more on the model, see appendix C, "An Explanation of Our Research and Analysis Methodology."

9 **ozone layer is on a path to recovery:** For up-to-date images of the ozone hole, see http://earthobservatory.nasa.gov/IOTD/view.php?id=49040.

9 **story of the Cuyahoga River:** For more information, see Ohio History Central, "Cuyahoga River Fire," at www.ohiohistorycentral.org. See also http://en.wikipedia.org/wiki/Cuyahoga_River.

10 **builder in Montana:** For more information on Steve Loken's work, see www.loken builders.com.

11 **8 percent of U.S. homes even had electricity:** U.S. Department of Energy, Energy Information Administration, "History of the U.S. Electric Power Industry, 1882–1991." Available at www.eia.doe.gov/cneaf/electricity/page/electric_kid/append_a.html.

11 **computer storage capacity of the *Apollo 11* spacecraft:** See, for instance, James Tomayko, *Computers in Spaceflight: The NASA Experience*, chap. 2, pt. 5, "The Apollo Guidance Computer: Hardware," NASA Contractor Report 182505 (1988). Available at www.hq.nasa.gov/office/pao/History/computers/Ch2-5.html.

11 **One survey of nearly 50 past forecasts:** Roger H. Bezdek and Robert M. Wendling, "A Half Century of Long-Range Energy Forecasts: Errors Made, Lessons Learned, and Implications for Forecasting," *Journal of Fusion Energy* 21, nos. 3 and 4 (Dec. 2002): 155–172.

12 **2002 *World Energy Outlook*:** International Energy Agency, *World Energy Outlook 2002* (Paris: Organisation for Economic Co-operation and Development and International Energy Agency, 2002). Available at www.worldenergyoutlook.com/docs/weo2002_part1.pdf.

12 **wind industry passed this mark:** Global Wind Energy Council and Greenpeace International, "Global Wind Energy Outlook 2008" (Brussels, 2008). Available at www.gwec.net/index.php?id=92.

12 **double the predicted capacity:** Global Wind Energy Council, "Global Wind Statistics 2010" (Brussels, 2011). Available at www.gwec.net/fileadmin/documents/Publications/GWEC_PRstats_02-02-2011_final.pdf.

12 **20-fold increase in installed wind capacity:** China Wind Power, "2009 China Wind Power Industry Review," p. 3. Available at www.chinawindpower.com.hk/English/Investor/Annual/09AnnualReportSummary.pdf.

Chapter 2

Page

13 **well over 1 billion tons:** This figure results from multiplying 308,745,538 Americans (see www.census.gov) by 21 tons each per year.

14 **200 of the nation's average-sized coal-fired plants:** As calculated using the U.S. Environmental Protection Agency's "Greenhouse Gas Equivalencies Calculator," available at www.epa.gov/cleanenergy/energy-resources/calculator.html.

14 **80 percent or more by the middle of this century:** See, for instance, A. L. Luers et al., "How to Avoid Dangerous Climate Change: A Target for U.S. Emissions Reductions (Cambridge, MA: Union of Concerned Scientists, 2007). The Intergovernmental Panel on Climate Change made a similar recommendation in *Climate Change 2007: Mitigation—Contribution of Working Group III to the Fourth Assessment Report of the Intergovernmental Panel on Climate Change*, ed. B. Metz et al. (Cambridge, UK: Cambridge University Press, 2007). Available at www.ipcc-wg3.org.

15 *Consumer's Guide*: Michael Brower and Warren Leon, *The Consumer's Guide to Effective Environmental Choices: Practical Advice from the Union of Concerned Scientists* (New York: Three Rivers Press, 1999).

16 **nearly the four tons:** This figure is based on 24 pounds of carbon emissions per gallon of gasoline and 12,000 miles of driving annually.

16 **Installing and using a programmable thermostat:** U.S. Department of Energy, Office of Energy Efficiency and Renewable Energy, "Energy Savers: Thermostats and Control Systems" (2011). Available at www.energysavers.gov.

17 **experience of Ann Luskey:** Elizabeth Festa, "A Green Dream in Suburbia: Bethesda Home Built to Leave Net-Zero Carbon Footprint," *Washington Post*, May 1, 2010.

17 **recent article in the *New York Times*:** Joanne Kaufman, "Completely Unplugged, Fully Green," *New York Times*, Oct. 19, 2008.

18 **2010 study:** S. Z. Attari et al., "Public Perceptions of Energy Consumption and Savings," *Proceedings of the National Academy of Sciences* 107, no. 37 (2010): 16054–16059.

20 **2002 psychological study:** L. T. McCalley and C. J. H. Midden, "Energy Conservation through Product-Integrated Feedback: The Roles of Goal-Setting and Social Orientation," *Journal of Economic Psychology* 23 (2002): 589–603.

24 **60 percent of all planned new electricity-generating projects:** Sindya N. Bhanoo, "Snapshot: Northeast Clean Energy Projects," *SNL Financial*, Oct. 29, 2009.

24 **two dozen average-sized coal-fired plants:** Based on an average midsized coal-fired power plant rated at 600 megawatts (MW) and operating at 80 percent capacity, producing roughly 4,204,800 megawatt-hours (MWh) of electricity per year. Comprehensive conversion information is available from the U.S. Environmental Protection Agency's "Greenhouse Gas Equivalencies Calculator" at www.epa.gov/cleanenergy/energy -resources/calculator.html.

24 **all of the 200 large buildings:** Keith Schneider, "Green Strategies Spur Rebirth of American Cities," *Yale Environment 360*, Oct. 13, 2008. Available at http://e360.yale.edu/ content/feature.msp?id=2072.

24 **Walmart recently pledged:** "Wal-Mart Vows Major Cuts in Carbon Emissions by 2015," *Yale Environment 360*, Feb. 26, 2010. Available at http://e360.yale.edu/content/digest .msp?id=2296.

24 **U.S. Secretary of the Navy Ray Mabus:** Office of Naval Research, Public Affairs Office, "Navy Secretary Announces Ambitious Energy Goals," press release, Oct. 16, 2009. See also Elizabeth Rosenthal, "U.S. Military Orders Less Dependence on Fossil Fuels," *New York Times*, Oct. 4, 2010.

24 **2007 report:** See Thomas Friedman, "The U.S.S. Prius," *New York Times*, Dec. 18, 2010. Available at www.nytimes.com/2010/12/19/opinion/19friedman.html.

25 **2008 was a watershed year globally:** United Nations Department of Economic and Social Affairs, Division for Sustainable Development, "Sustainable Development: Promotion of New and Renewable Sources of Energy" (Oct. 7, 2009). Available at www.un .org/esa/dsd/resources/res_pdfs/ga-64/briefings/EU_Brief.pdf.

25 **report by HSBC Global Research:** Nina Chestney, "World Climate Business Revenue $2 Trillion by 2020: HSBC," Reuters, Sept. 18, 2009.

Chapter 3

Page

27 **only one in every ten Americans:** A. Leiserowitz et al., *Climate Change in the American Mind: Americans' Global Warming Beliefs and Attitudes in May 2011* (New Haven, CT: Yale University and George Mason University, Yale Project on Climate Change Communication, 2011). Available at http://environment.yale.edu/climate/files/ClimateBeliefsMay 2011.pdf.

28 **People have been recording:** See, for instance, Thomas C. Peterson and Russell S. Vose, "An Overview of the Global Historical Climatology Network Temperature Database," *Bulletin of the American Meteorological Society* 78, no. 12 (Dec. 1997): 2837–2849.

29 **readings at thousands of locations:** D. S. Arndt, M. O. Baringer, and M. R. Johnson, eds., "State of the Climate in 2009," *Bulletin of the American Meteorological Society* 91, no. 6 (2010): S1–S224.

29 **Figure 3.1: Global Average Surface Temperature:** National Aeronautics and Space Administration, Goddard Institute for Space Studies, "Global Land-Ocean Temperature Index" (New York: National Aeronautics and Space Administration, Goddard Institute for Space Studies; and Columbia University, 2011). Available at http://data.giss.nasa .gov/gistemp/graphs/Fig.A2.gif.

30 **at the last ice age maximum:** See E. Jansen et al., "Palaeoclimate," in Intergovernmental Panel on Climate Change, *Climate Change 2007: The Physical Science Basis—Contribution of Working Group I to the Fourth Assessment Report of the Intergovernmental Panel on Climate Change*, ed. S. Solomon et al. (Cambridge, UK: Cambridge University Press, 2007).

30 **15 of the past 16 years:** The National Oceanic and Atmospheric Administration has detailed data on rankings of the warmest years. See, for instance, information available at www.ncdc.noaa.gov/paleo/globalwarming/paleolast.html.

31 **Carbon is a key building block:** Wallace S. Broecker, *How to Build a Habitable Planet* (Palisades, NY: Eldigio Press, 1985).

33 **highly accurate technique for measuring:** Information about the technique can be found at www.aip.org/history/climate/Kfunds.htm.

33 **Keeling Curve:** The graph is adapted from work first published by C. D. Keeling, "The Concentration and Isotopic Abundances of Carbon Dioxide in the Atmosphere," *Tellus* 12, no. 2 (May 1960). The Keeling Curve is updated by the University of California's Scripps Institute of Oceanography and by the National Oceanic and Atmospheric Administration.

35 **Box: Other Heat-Trapping Gases:** See chapter 2 of Intergovernmental Panel on Climate Change, *Contribution of Working Group I*, ed. Solomon et al., 2007.

36 **Cameron Wake:** K. Yalcin and C. P. Wake, "Anthropogenic Signals Recorded in an Ice Core from Eclipse Icefield, Yukon Territory, Canada," *Geophysical Research Letters* 28, no. 23 (Dec. 1, 2001). The quotes are from Seth Shulman, "Glacier Gumshoe Seeks Secrets of Climate Change in Ice," Union of Concerned Scientists Profile (2010). Available at www.ucsusa.org.

37 **for the 800,000 years:** See D. Lüthi et al., "High-Resolution Carbon Dioxide Concentration Record 650,000–800,000 Years before Present," *Nature* 453 (2008): 379–382.

38 **Benjamin Santer:** B. D. Santer et al., "A Search for Human Influences on the Thermal Structure of the Atmosphere," *Nature* 382 (July 4, 1996). See also W. D. Collins et al., "The Community Climate System Model Version 3 (CCSM3)," *Journal of Climate* 19 (June 1, 2006). Quotes are from Seth Shulman, "Climate Fingerprinter," Union of Concerned Scientists Profile (2010). Available at www.ucsusa.org.

40 **Julienne Stroeve:** See J. Stroeve et al., "Arctic Sea Ice Extent Plummets in 2007," *Eos, Transactions, American Geophysical Union* 89, no. 2 (2008): 13–20. Quotes are from Seth Shulman, "Measuring Fast-Melting Arctic Sea Ice," Union of Concerned Scientists Profile (2010). Available at www.ucsusa.org.

40 **Stroeve estimates, some 40 percent:** The extent of Arctic sea ice from 1978 to 2011 shows a drop from an average of 15.5 million square kilometers to around 14.5 million square kilometers, approximately a 6 percent loss in area. Available at http://nsidc.org/news/images/20081002_Figure4.jpg. See also http://nsidc.org/images/arcticseaice news/20110504_Figure3.png.

40 **Shrinking ice:** Source for the world average is available at www.ncdc.noaa.gov/bams-state-of-the-climate/2009-time-series/glacier.

41 **Greenland ice sheet lost roughly 385 cubic miles:** See I. Velicogna, "Increasing Rates of Ice Mass Loss from the Greenland and Antarctic Ice Sheets Revealed by GRACE," *Geophysical Research Letters* 36, L19503 (2009).

41 **two-thirds of the planet's freshwater:** U.S. Geological Survey. See http://ga.water.usgs .gov/edu/earthglacier.html.

41 **Chacaltaya Glacier:** B. Francou et al., "Tropical Climate Change Recorded by a Glacier in the Central Andes during the Last Decades of the Twentieth Century: Chacaltaya, Bolivia, 16° S," *Journal of Geophysical Research* 108 (2003). See also B. Francou et al., "Glacier Evolution in the Tropical Andes during the Last Decades of the 20th Century: Chacaltaya, Bolivia, and Antizana, Ecuador," *AMBIO: A Journal of the Human Environment* 29, no. 7 (2003): 416–422.

41 **6.7 inches over the past century:** See Intergovernmental Panel on Climate Change, *Contribution of Working Group I*, ed. Solomon et al., 2007.

42 **Figure 3.3: Global Average Absolute Sea Level:** Data are from Commonwealth Scientific and Industrial Research Organisation (CSIRO), *Sea Level* (Australia: CSIRO, 2011).

43 **oceans are already about 30 percent more acidic:** Royal Society, *Ocean Acidification Due to Increasing Atmospheric Carbon Dioxide* (London: Royal Society, 2005).

43 **threat to the ocean's phytoplankton:** See Daniel Boyce et al., "Global Phytoplankton Decline over the Past Century," *Nature* 466 (July 29, 2010). See also Ralph F. Keeling, Arne Körtzinger, and Nicolas Gruber, "Ocean Deoxygenation in a Warming World," *Annual Review of Marine Science* 2 (2010): 199–299. Available at www.annualreviews.org.

43 **John Guinotte:** John M. Guinotte and Victoria J. Fabry, "Ocean Acidification and Its Potential Effects on Marine Ecosystems," *Annals of the New York Academy of Sciences* 1134 (2008): 320–342; special issue, *The Year in Ecology and Conservation Biology*. See also John M. Guinotte et al., "Will Human-Induced Changes in Seawater Chemistry Alter the Distribution of Deep-Sea Scleractinian Corals?" *Frontiers in Ecology and the Environment* 4, no. 3 (2006): 141–146. Quote is from Seth Shulman, "Coral Doctor," Union of Concerned Scientists Profile (2010). Available at www.ucsusa.org.

44 **78 percent shifted their characteristic spring patterns:** National Research Council, Committee on Stabilization Targets for Atmospheric Greenhouse Gas Concentrations, *Climate Stabilization Targets: Emissions, Concentrations, and Impacts over Decades to Millennia* (Washington, DC: National Academies Press, 2010). Available at www.nap.edu/catalog/12877.html.

44 **Camille Parmesan:** Camille Parmesan, "Climate and Species' Range," *Nature* 382 (Aug. 29, 1996): 765–766. See also Camille Parmesan and Gary Yohe, "A Globally Coherent Fingerprint of Climate Change Impacts across Natural Systems," *Nature* 421 (Jan. 2, 2003). And see Seth Shulman, "Are Butterflies Silent Harbingers of Global Warming?" Union of Concerned Scientists Profile (2010). Available at www.ucsusa.org.

46 **ExxonMobil:** Union of Concerned Scientists, "Smoke, Mirrors, and Hot Air: How ExxonMobil Uses Big Tobacco's Tactics to Manufacture Uncertainty on Climate Science" (Cambridge, MA: Union of Concerned Scientists, 2010). Available at www.ucsusa.org/assets/documents/global_warming/exxon_report.pdf.

46 **emissions on track to increase by some 43 percent:** The U.S. Energy Information Administration projects that world emissions will rise from 29.7 billion metric tons in 2007 to 42.4 billion metric tons by 2035, a 43 percent increase over that period. See U.S. Department of Energy, Energy Information Administration, *International Energy Outlook 2010* (Washington, DC: U.S. Department of Energy, Energy Information Administration, July 2010). Available at www.eia.gov/forecasts/archive/ieo10/pdf/0484(2010).pdf.

47 **extreme weather events:** See T. Karl, J. Melillo, and T. Peterson, eds., *Global Climate Change Impacts in the United States*, report from the U.S. Global Change Research Program (Cambridge, UK: Cambridge University Press, 2009). Available at www.globalchange.gov.

47 **increased, on average, by 67 percent:** Ibid., p. 32.

47 **link between global warming and hurricanes:** See, for instance, M. A. Bender et al., "Modeled Impact of Anthropogenic Warming on the Frequency of Intense Atlantic Hurricanes," *Science* 327 (2010): 454–458. See also R. Pielke Jr. and C. W. Landseer, "Normalized Hurricane Damage in the United States: 1925–95," *Weather and Forecasting* 13 (1998): 621–631.

Chapter 4

Page

51 **one-quarter of your total carbon emissions:** UCS modeling.

51 **240 million cars:** U.S. Department of Transportation, Bureau of Transportation Statistics, "National Transportation Statistics" (2010), table 1-11. Available at www.bts.gov/publications/national_transportation_statistics.

51 **2.7 trillion miles annually:** Ibid., table 1-32.

51 **1.6 billion tons of carbon dioxide:** U.S. Department of Energy, *Transportation Energy Data Book*, 29th ed. (Oak Ridge, TN: Oak Ridge National Laboratory, 2010). Available at http://cta.ornl.gov/data.

52 **45 percent of the world's automotive carbon dioxide emissions:** John DeCicco and Freda Fung, *Global Warming on the Road: The Climate Impact of America's Automobiles*

(New York: Environmental Defense, 2006). Available at www.environmentaldefense
.org.

52 **nearly 25 pounds of carbon dioxide:** UCS modeling.

53 **more than 19 pounds per gallon:** Ibid.

54 **peak year of U.S. train ridership:** See, for instance, Mike Schafer et al., *The American Passenger Train* (St. Paul, MN: Motor Books International, 2001).

54 **As recently as 1950:** U.S. Department of Energy, *Transportation Energy Data Book*, chap. 8, "Household Vehicles and Characteristics," table 8.4.

54 **80 percent of the population:** Ibid.

54 **64 percent of Americans commuted:** N. McGuckin and N. Srinivasan, "Journey to Work Trends in the United States and Its Major Metropolitan Areas, 1960–2000," Publication no. FHWA-EP-03-058 (Washington, DC: U.S. Department of Transportation, Federal Highway Administration, Office of Planning, 2003).

55 **92 percent of Americans:** U.S. Department of Transportation, Bureau of Transportation Statistics, "National Transportation Statistics" (2011), table 1-38. Available at www.bts.gov/publications/national_transportation_statistics.

55 **more than three-quarters of all American workers drive:** See "Commuting," in *State of Metropolitan America, 2010* (Washington, DC: Brookings Institution, 2010).

55 **nearly double fuel economy by 2025:** See Union of Concerned Scientists and Natural Resources Defense Council, "The Technology to Reach 60 mpg by 2025: Putting Fuel-Saving Technology to Work to Save Oil and Cut Pollution" (Oct. 2010). Available at www.ucsusa.org.

55 **reduce U.S. global warming emissions:** See, for instance, Union of Concerned Scientists, "Model E: The UCS Family of Electric Cars; A Guide to the Present and Future of Electric Drive Technology" (2010). Available at www.ucsusa.org.

55 **Within just six years:** Ibid.

56 **16 million . . . cars and light trucks are replaced:** DeCicco and Fung, *Global Warming on the Road*.

58 **Box: But Aren't SUVs Safer?** See M. Anderson, "Safety for Whom? The Effects of Light Trucks on Traffic Fatalities," *Journal of Health Economics* 27, no. 4 (2008): 973–989.

60 **Box: Can the Auto Industry . . . ?** See A. Bandivadekar et al., *On the Road in 2035: Reducing Transportation's Petroleum Consumption and GHG Emissions*, Report no. LFEE 2008-05 RP (Cambridge, MA: MIT Laboratory for Energy and the Environment, 2008).

61 **higher resale value of more efficient vehicles:** See, for instance, Elisabeth Gilmore and Lester Lave, "Comparing Resale Prices and Total Cost of Ownership for Gasoline, Hybrid, and Diesel Passenger Cars and Trucks," working paper (Pittsburgh, PA: Carnegie Mellon University, Nov. 2010).

61 **Since 1950, our VMT has increased more than five-fold:** U.S. Department of Energy, *Transportation Energy Data Book*.

61 **more than 80 percent of all trips are taken by car:** Ralph Buehler and John Pucher, "Sustainable Transport in Freiburg: Lessons from Germany's Environmental Capital," *International Journal of Sustainable Transportation* 5, no. 1 (2011): 43–70.

62 **more than 60 percent . . . no more than six miles:** U.S. Department of Transportation, Federal Highway Administration, *2009 National Household Travel Survey*, Report no. FHW A-PL-ll-022 (Washington, DC: U.S. Department of Transportation, Federal Highway Administration, 2010). Available at http://nhts.ornl.gov.

62 **Suza Francina:** See "Carless in Carmaggedon" (editorial), *Ojai Valley News*, Apr. 22, 2008. Available at suzafrancina.com.

63 **Gina Diamond:** Warren Cornwall, "Simple Steps Reduce Carbon Footprints," *Seattle Times*, May 1, 2007.

63 **car-sharing companies such as Zipcar:** Information is available at www.zipcar.com.

63 **one recent study found:** See A. Millard-Ball et al., *Car-Sharing: Where and How It Succeeds* (Washington, DC: Transportation Research Board, 2005).

63 **Boulder's Driven to Drive Less program:** Information is available at www.drivento driveless.com.

64 **24 percent of the nation's workforce:** U.S. Department of Labor, Bureau of Labor Statistics, *American Time Use Survey Summary* (Washington, DC: U.S. Department of Labor, Bureau of Labor Statistics, 2010).

64 **eliminate 136 billion vehicle travel miles:** See W. Cox, *Improving Quality of Life through Telecommuting* (Washington, DC: Information Technology and Innovation Foundation, 2009).

65 **Journey to Work Survey:** U.S. Department of Transportation, Federal Highway Administration, *1995 Nationwide Personal Transportation Survey* (Washington, DC: U.S. Department of Transportation, Federal Highway Administration, 1997), and U.S. Department of Transportation, Federal Highway Administration, *2009 National Household Travel Survey*.

65 **average number of occupants:** 1980, 1990, and 2000 U.S. Census, U.S. Census Bureau, Population Division, Journey to Work and Migration Statistics Branch.

66 **nascent effort, called Avego:** For more on the Seattle pilot program, see http://go520 .avego.com.

66 **"slugging":** On slugging in San Francisco, see www.ridenow.org/carpool; on slugging in Washington, DC, including maps, see http://slug-lines.com.

67 **stressed-out driving:** Information is available at www.fueleconomy.gov.

67 **driving at 75 miles per hour:** U.S. Department of Energy, *Transportation Energy Data Book*.

67 **Driving Change program:** "Driving Change: City of Denver Case Study," produced in collaboration with Enviance Corp. Available at www.drivingchange.org.

67 **more than 100 million tons of carbon dioxide:** See, for instance, Amanda R. Carrico et al., "Costly Myths: An Analysis of Idling Beliefs and Behavior in Personal Motor Vehicles," *Energy Policy* 37, no. 8 (Aug. 2009): 2881–2888.

68 **low-rolling-resistance (LRR) tires:** More information is available at U.S. Department of Energy, Office of Energy Efficiency and Renewable Energy, Alternative Fuels and Advanced Vehicles Data Center. See www.afdc.energy.gov.

68 **roof rack can decrease:** Information is available at www.fueleconomy.gov.

68 **For every 100 pounds of extra weight:** Ibid.

69 **Box: Open the Windows or . . . ?** See Consumers Union, "Myth Busters: Air Conditioning vs. Opening Windows," in "Fuel Economy: Save Money on Gas" (2011). Available
at www.consumerreports.org. See also David Ellis, "Four Gas-Saving Myths" (2007),
http://CNNMoney.com.

70 **diesel will cause carbon emissions 10 to 15 percent higher:** For more information, see
www.hybridcenter.org, a project of the Union of Concerned Scientists.

70 **fuels are getting dirtier:** See, for instance, Michael T. Klare, *Rising Powers, Shrinking
Planet: The New Geopolitics of Energy* (New York: Metropolitan Books, 2008), p. 276. For
emissions information, see Alex D. Charpentier, Joule A. Bergerson, and Heather L.
MacLean, "Understanding the Canadian Oil Sands Industry's Greenhouse Gas Emissions," *Environmental Research Letters* 4, no. 1 (2009).

72 **entire U.S. corn crop:** See World Bank, "Biofuels: The Promise and the Risks," pp.
70–71 in *World Development Report 2008: Agriculture for Development* (Washington, DC:
World Bank, 2007). Available at http://siteresources.worldbank.org/INTWDR2008/
Resources/2795087-1192112387976/WDR08_05_Focus_B.pdf.

72 **cellulosic biofuel:** See Union of Concerned Scientists, "The Truth about Ethanol"
(2007). Available at www.ucsusa.org.

72 **electric-drive vehicles could be the start:** David Friedman, "The Evolution of a Revolution," *Catalyst* (Union of Concerned Scientists), Fall 2010. Available at www.ucsusa.org.

74 **Americans annually make some 2.6 billion trips:** U.S. Department of Transportation,
Bureau of Transportation Statistics, *Findings from the National Household Travel Survey:
Long Distance Transportation Patterns* (Washington, DC: U.S. Department of Transporta-
tion, Bureau of Transportation Statistics, 2009).

75 **single round-trip flight from Los Angeles:** See Union of Concerned Scientists, "Getting There Greener: The Guide to Your Lower-Carbon Vacation" (Cambridge, MA:
Union of Concerned Scientists, Spring 2008). Available at www.ucsusa.org.

75 **Flying a family of four in first class:** Scott Nathanson, "Getting There Greener,"
Catalyst (Union of Concerned Scientists), Spring 2009. Note that the calculation uses the
Oak Ridge National Laboratory's *Transportation Energy Data Book* figure that Americans'
daily work commute represents roughly 27 percent of their annual travel.

76 **Figure 4.4: CO_2 Emissions per 100 Passenger-Miles:** UCS modeling.

76 **as the "Getting There Greener" report found:** See Union of Concerned Scientists,
"Getting There Greener."

77 **Colin Beavan:** Colin Beavan, *No Impact Man: The Adventures of a Guilty Liberal Who
Attempts to Save the Planet, and the Discoveries He Makes about Himself and Our Way of Life
in the Process* (New York: Farrar, Strauss and Giroux, 2009).

77 **passenger air travel accounts for less than 3 percent:** M. Chambwera and B. Muller,
Fairer Flying: An International Air Travel Levy for Adaptation (London: International Institute for Environment and Development, 2008).

78 **405 million long-distance business trips:** U.S. Department of Transportation, Bureau
of Transportation Statistics, *U.S. Business Travel* (Washington, DC: U.S. Department of
Transportation, Bureau of Transportation Statistics, 2003).

78 **meeting 500 miles away can easily cost:** United Nations Environment Programme, *World Environment Day 2009: Twelve Steps to Unite to Combat Climate Change* (2009). Available at www.unep.org/wed/2009/english/content/steps12.asp.

79 **Freiburg, Germany:** Buehler and Pucher, "Sustainable Transport in Freiburg."

80 **Paris . . . bike-sharing program:** See, for instance, Steven Erlanger, "A New Fashion Catches On in Paris: Cheap Bicycle Rentals," *New York Times*, July 13, 2008.

80 **bike-sharing program in Hangzhou, China:** See, for instance, Elizabeth Press, "The Biggest, Baddest Bike-Share in the World: Hangzhou, China" (June 2011). Available at www.streetfilms.org.

81 **Capital Bikeshare:** See www.capitalbikeshare.com.

81 **New York City . . . bike-share program:** See Christine Haughney, "A Rider's Guide to the Public Bicycles," *New York Times*, Sept. 14, 2011.

Chapter 5

Page

83 **emit about 500 million tons:** U.S. Department of Energy, Energy Information Administration, *Emissions of Greenhouse Gases in the United States, 2007* (Washington, DC: U.S. Department of Energy, Energy Information Administration, 2008).

83 **energy costs of roughly $2,200:** See "Where Does My Money Go?" at www.energystar.gov, based on Lawrence Berkeley National Laboratory, "Typical House Memo" (2009).

83 **make up two-thirds:** Alex Wilson and John Morrill, *Consumer Guide to Home Energy Savings* (Washington, DC: American Council for an Energy-Efficient Economy, 1998), p. 53.

85 **Engineers at the Massachusetts Institute of Technology constructed:** A. L. Hesselschwerdt, "Performance of the M.I.T. Solar House," in *Space Heating with Solar Energy: Proceedings of a Course Symposium Held at the Massachusetts Institute of Technology, August 21–26, 1950,* ed. Richard Winfield Hamilton [TH7413 .M414 1950] (Cambridge: Massachusetts Institute of Technology, 1954), pp. 99–106. See also "M.I.T. Builds Solar-Heated Home," *Architectural Record* 105 (Apr. 1949): 135–138.

85 **70 passive solar homes:** For a discussion, see D. S. Parker, *Very Low Energy Homes in the United States: Perspectives on Performance from Measured Data* (Cocoa, FL: University of Central Florida, Florida Solar Energy Center, 2008).

85 **"superinsulated" home:** E. Leger, "Superinsulated Homes," *Environmental Science and Technology* 22 (1988): 1399–1400.

85 **"tale of two houses":** U.S. Department of Energy, Energy Information Administration, *Emissions of Greenhouse Gases.*

86 **consumption from the electric grid . . . 92 percent lower:** Ibid.

86 **1 billion tons of carbon dioxide:** R. Heede, *Cool Citizens: Everyday Solutions to Climate Change* (Snowmass, CO: Rocky Mountain Institute, 2002).

87 **Empire State Building:** Rocky Mountain Institute, "Retrofit Project Case Study: Empire State Building." Available at www.rmi.org/Retrofit. For more information, see the website of the Empire State Building: www.esbnyc.com/sustainability_energy_efficiency.asp.

See also M. Navarro, "The Empire State Building Plans a Growth Spurt, Environmentally," *New York Times*, Apr. 7, 2009.

89 **natural gas is the most commonly used fuel:** U.S. Department of Energy, Energy Information Administration, *Emissions of Greenhouse Gases*, table 1.

89 **electricity . . . in 44 percent of homes:** U.S. Department of Energy, Energy Information Administration, "South Atlantic Household Electricity Report" (2006). Available at www.eia.gov/emeu/reps/enduse/er01_so-atl.html.

89 **oil . . . used in some 36 percent of homes:** U.S. Department of Energy, Energy Information Administration, "Northeast Data Abstract" (2000). Available at www.eia.gov/emeu/reps/abstracts/northeast.html.

90 **Efficiency Vermont:** "Do It Yourself Audit Tools," available at http://efficiencyvermont.com/stella/filelib/HowEnergyEfficientIsYourHome_Final.pdf.

91 **one-third of the homes . . . have programmable thermostats:** U.S. Department of Energy, Energy Information Administration, "Residential Energy Consumption Survey" (Feb. 2011). Available at www.eia.gov.

92 **way to save 15 percent on home heating:** See, for instance, T. Peffer et al., "How People Use Thermostats in Homes: A Review," *Building and Environment* 46, no. 12 (2011): 2529–2541. See also U.S. Environmental Protection Agency, Energy Star program, "Summary of Research Findings from the Programmable Thermostat Market" (2001).

92 **A much-discussed study:** M. J. Nevius and S. Pigg, *Programmable Thermostats That Go Berserk? Taking a Social Perspective on Space Heating in Wisconsin* (Madison: Energy Center of Wisconsin and University of Wisconsin–Madison, Departments of Sociology and Rural Sociology, 1999).

92 **half of all American homes are empty:** U.S. Environmental Protection Agency, Energy Star program, "Summary of Research Findings."

93 **each degree Fahrenheit:** Information is from U.S. Department of Energy, Office of Energy Efficiency and Renewable Energy, "Energy Savers: Thermostats and Control Systems" (2011). Available at www.energysavers.gov.

93 **the EPA recommends:** Information is from U.S. Environmental Protection Agency and U.S. Department of Energy, Energy Star program, "Programmable Thermostats" (2011). Available at www.energystar.gov.

94 **Japan's per capita carbon dioxide emissions:** U.S. Department of Energy, Energy Information Administration, *International Energy Outlook 2010* (Washington, DC: U.S. Department of Energy, Energy Information Administration, July 2010). Available at www.eia.gov/forecasts/archive/ieo10/pdf/0484(2010).pdf.

95 **air leaks may account for 15 to 25 percent:** U.S. Environmental Protection Agency and U.S. Department of Energy, Energy Star program, "Methodology for Estimated Energy Savings from Cost-Effective Air Sealing and Insulating" (2011). Available at www.energystar.gov.

95 **unweatherized house . . . loses as much air:** Richard Heede et al., *Homemade Money: How to Save Energy and Dollars in Your Home* (Snowmass, CO: Rocky Mountain Institute, 1995).

95 **$13 billion worth of energy:** Information is from the American Council for an Energy-Efficient Economy. Available at www.aceee.org.

95 **air escapes through holes and cracks:** See www.energysavers.gov/tips/air_leaks.cfm.

97 **Box: Does My Fireplace Contribute . . . ?** Union of Concerned Scientists, "Your Heating Dollars—Up in Smoke," *Greentips*, Feb. 2009. Available at www.ucsusa.org.

97 **Box: 24,000 cubic feet of air per hour:** Information is from the U.S. Department of Energy, Office of Energy Efficiency and Renewable Energy (2006). Available at www .eere.energy.gov.

97 **Gary Reysa:** See his blog at www.builditsolar.com. See also Gary Reysa, "The Half Plan: Reducing Your Carbon Footprint, Part Three; Defeating Drafts and Improving Insulation," *Home Power* 120 (Aug.–Sept. 2007): 56–60.

98 **Insulating your home is one of the cheapest:** Union of Concerned Scientists, "Weatherizing Pays Dividends All Year," *Greentips*, Nov. 2005. Available at www.ucsusa.org.

99 **could save more than $1.8 billion:** See www.energystar.gov.

99 **turning your roof into a "cool roof":** A. Chen, "Cool Colors Project: Improved Materials for Cooler Roofs," *Lawrence Berkeley National Laboratory, Environmental Energy Technologies Division News* 5, no. 4 (Fall 2004): 1–3.

99 **studies at the Lawrence Berkeley National Laboratory:** A. Kimble-Evans, "White Roofs Bring Cool Savings," *Mother Earth News*, Feb.–Mar. 2010.

99 **U.S. Secretary of Energy Steven Chu:** See D. A. Gabel, "Transitioning to Green Roofs," *News Center*, July 21, 2010.

100 **double-paned windows and insulated frames:** D. Pimentel et al., "Energy Efficiency and Conservation for Individual Americans," *Environment, Development and Sustainability* 11, no. 3 (2007): 523–546.

100 **today's most efficient equipment:** U.S. Department of Energy, Office of Energy Efficiency and Renewable Energy, "Energy Savers: Furnaces and Boilers" (2011). Available at www.energysavers.gov.

100 **up to 50 percent more efficient:** U.S. Department of Energy, Office of Energy Efficiency and Renewable Energy, "Energy Savers: Air Conditioning" (2011). Available at www .energysavers.gov.

102 **AFUE (annual fuel utilization efficiency) rating:** Available at www.acee.org/ consumerguide/heating.htm.

102 **7 million tons of carbon dioxide:** U.S. Environmental Protection Agency and U.S. Department of Energy, Energy Star program, "Heating and Cooling" (Aug. 2008). Available at www.energystar.gov.

102 **Water heaters are responsible for about 15 percent:** U.S. Environmental Protection Agency and U.S. Department of Energy, Energy Star program, "High Efficiency Water Heaters Provide Hot Water for Less" (2006). Available at www.energystar.gov.

103 **An ideal temperature is 120 degrees:** For a discussion, see www.energysavers.gov/ your_home/water_heating/index.cfm.mytopic=13090.

103 **30 to 45 percent less energy:** P. J. Hughes, *Geothermal (Ground-Source) Heat Pumps: Market Status, Barriers to Adoption, and Actions to Overcome Barriers* (Oak Ridge, TN: Oak Ridge National Laboratory, 2008).

103 **100,000 systems installed:** See U.S. Department of Energy, Energy Information Administration, "Geothermal Heat Pump" (2010), table 4.1. Available at www.eia.gov.

104 **Box: the earth stays about 50 degrees:** U.S. Department of Energy, Office of Energy Efficiency and Renewable Energy, "Geothermal Technologies Program: Geothermal Basics" (2008). Available at www1.eere.energy.gov.

104 **30 percent tax credit:** For a discussion, see Hughes, *Geothermal (Ground-Source) Heat Pumps.*

104 **cogeneration:** See, for example, Amanda Chiu, "One Twelfth of Global Electricity Comes from Combined Heat and Power Systems," in *Vital Signs 2009: The Trends That Are Shaping Our Future* (Washington, DC: Worldwatch Institute, 2009).

106 **Cleveland Museum of Natural History . . . passive home:** Information is available at www.cmnh.org.

106 **as much electricity as two hair dryers:** See Renee Schoof, "Latest in Cutting-Edge Energy Efficiency: Furnace-Free Homes," McClatchy Newspapers, June 17, 2011.

107 **Viking Terrace:** For more information, see Rachel Cleetus, Steven Clemmer, and David Friedman, "Climate 2030: A National Blueprint for a Clean Energy Economy," chap. 4 (Cambridge, MA: Union of Concerned Scientists, 2009). Available at www.ucsusa.org.

107 **costs for green building:** For a discussion, see Greg Kats, *Greening Our Built World: Costs, Benefits, and Strategies* (Washington, DC: Island Press, 2009).

Chapter 6

Page

109 **residential electricity use has gone up:** U.S. Department of Energy, Energy Information Administration, *International Energy Outlook 2010* (Washington, DC: U.S. Department of Energy, Energy Information Administration, July 2010). Available at www.eia .gov/forecasts/archive/ieo10/pdf/0484(2010).pdf.

109 **projected to rise:** Ibid.

110 **Polls show that Americans:** See, for instance, S. Z. Attari et al., "Public Perceptions of Energy Consumption and Savings," *Proceedings of the National Academy of Sciences* 107, no. 37 (2010): 16054–16059.

112 **M-Power program:** Salt River Project, "SRP M-Power Price Plan" (2010).

114 **11,040 kilowatt-hours:** U.S. Department of Energy, Energy Information Administration, "Table 5. Residential Average Monthly Bill by Census Division, and State" (2009). Available at www.eia.doe.gov/cneaf/electricity/esr/table5.html.

115 **displayed at the 1939 New York World's Fair:** John H. Campbell, "The History and Technical Evolution of High Frequency Fluorescent Lighting" (Berkeley, CA: U.S. Department of Energy, Lawrence Berkeley National Laboratory, Energy and Environment Division, Dec. 1977).

116 **2007 federal energy bill:** Energy Independence and Security Act of 2007, 42 U.S.C. § 17001 (2007).

116 **about 4 milligrams of mercury:** Information is from the U.S. Environmental Protection Agency, available at www.epa.gov/cfl/cfl-hg.html.

117 **Box: Don't Compact Fluorescent Bulbs Contain Mercury?** U.S. Environmental Protection Agency and U.S. Department of Energy, Energy Star program, "Frequently Asked

Questions: Information on Compact Fluorescent Light Bulbs (CFLs) and Mercury" (Nov. 2010). Available at www.energystar.gov.

118 **LED lights offer:** Union of Concerned Scientists, "Let There Be LEDs," *Greentips*, Jan. 2010. Available at www.ucsusa.org.

118 **$190 annually on electricity for lighting:** Information on "electricity usage from residential lighting" is from the U.S. Department of Energy, Energy Information Agency, available at www.eia.gov. The figure reflects 15 percent of the annual household usage of 11,040 kWh of electricity at the current average electricity rate of 11.5 cents per kWh.

120 **Figure 6.4: Typical Annual Electricity Costs:** The numbers in this table were drawn from sources including www.eia.gov, www.energysavers.gov, and UCS modeling, and cross-checked against recent data compiled for consumers by local utility companies including Missouri Gas Energy and NV Energy.

120 **$123 per year to operate:** Information is from data at www.energysavers.gov on the average electric cost of running a single refrigerator, adjusting for the fact that 26 percent of American homes operate a second refrigerator as well—see U.S. Department of Energy, "Refrigerator Market Profile, 2009" (Dec. 2009). Available at http://apps1.eere.energy.gov/states/pdfs/ref_market_profile.pdf.

121 **an estimated 7 percent below:** U.S. Environmental Protection Agency, "Change the World, Start with Energy Star Campaign Overview" (2010). Available at www.energystar.gov.

121 **$700 million in annual energy costs:** Ibid.

121 **Six rounds of progressively stricter standards:** Information is from www.energystar.gov.

121 **new refrigerator was 60 percent cheaper:** Ibid.

121 **if it's avocado:** A. Tugend, "If Your Appliances Are Avocado, They Probably Aren't Green," *New York Times*, May 10, 2008.

122 **26 percent of all homes:** U.S. Department of Energy, "Refrigerator Market Profile, 2009."

123 **Washing in hot water uses:** Based on data from www.eia.gov and www.energysavers.gov.

123 **using 37 percent less energy:** See U.S. Environmental Protection Agency and U.S. Department of Energy, Energy Star program, "Clothes Washers" (2011). Available at www.energystar.gov.

124 **study at the University of Bonn:** R. Stamminger et al., "A European Comparison of Cleaning Dishes by Hand" (Jan. 2008), University of Bonn, Germany.

124 **boiling one cup of water:** Jennifer Mitchell-Jackson and Alan Meier, "Cooking with Less Gas," *Home Energy Magazine*, May–June 2001.

125 **up to 70 percent:** See, for instance, "Energy Efficient High Speed Cooking," at http://fastcooking.ca (an online distributor of pressure cookers.)

125 **some models consume more:** See Alan Meier, "Standby Power" (2010), Lawrence Berkeley National Laboratory. Available at http://standby.lbl.gov/standby.html.

126 **DVD on a gaming console:** Noah Horowitz, *Lowering the Cost of Play: Improving the Energy Efficiency of Video Game Consoles* (New York: Natural Resources Defense Council, Nov. 2008).

126 **power all the world's computers:** G. Boccaletti, M. Löffler, and J. M. Oppenheim, "How IT Can Cut Carbon Emissions," *McKinsey Quarterly*, Oct. 2008.

126 **cut its energy usage in half:** Information is available at www.energysaver.gov or at www.climatesaverscomputing.org.

127 **laptop . . . uses just one-quarter:** For data on specific models, see University of Pennsylvania, Information Systems and Computing, "Approximate Desktop, Notebook, and Netbook Power Usage" (2011). Available at www.upenn.edu/computing/provider/docs/hardware/powerusage.html.

128 **40 percent of American homes draw:** Google PowerMeter, "How Much Power Do You Use in the Middle of the Night?" (2010). Available at http://blog.google.org/2010/02/how-much-power-do-you-use-in-middle-of.html.

128 **investigation of phantom loads:** Meier, "Standby Power."

131 **carbon coefficient:** U.S. Department of Energy, Energy Information Administration, Office of Integrated Analysis and Forecasting, "Updated State-Level Greenhouse Gas Emission Coefficients for Electricity Generation, 1998–2000" (Apr. 2002). Available at ftp://ftp.eia.doe.gov/environment/e-supdoc-u.pdf.

133 **half of the nation's utility companies allow:** Lori Bird and Blair Swezey, "Conservation Update: Growth Spurt for Green Power" (2010), U.S. Department of Energy, Office of Energy Efficiency and Renewable Energy. Available at www1.eere.energy.gov/wip/update/2007-01_green_power.html.

133 **certification programs such as Green-e:** Ibid.

133 **figures from the DOE's National Renewable Energy Laboratory:** Lori Bird and Jenny Sumner, "Green Power Marketing in the United States: A Status Report (2009 Data)," Technical Report NREL/TP-6A20-49403 (Golden, CO: U.S. Department of Energy, Office of Energy Efficiency and Renewable Energy, National Renewable Energy Laboratory, Sept. 2010). Available at www.nrel.gov/docs/fy11osti/49403.pdf.

134 **dropped by nearly 90 percent:** U.S. Department of Energy, Office of Energy Efficiency and Renewable Energy, "Solar America Initiative" (2007).

134 **household photovoltaic system can cost:** See Union of Concerned Scientists, "Need Help Paying for Solar Power?" *Greentips*, Mar. 2011. Available at www.ucsusa.org.

134 **incentive programs:** Ibid.

134 **California Solar Initiative:** Information available at www.californiasolarstatistics.ca.gov.

134 **avoiding approximately 200 tons:** Assuming a 10-kilowatt turbine, a 20 percent annual capacity factor, and a national average emissions rate of 1.34 pounds of carbon dioxide per kilowatt hour. See also American Wind Energy Association, "Wind Power and Climate Change" (2009). Available at www.awea.org/learnabout/publications/upload/Climate_Change.pdf.

Chapter 7

Page

137 **diet can make a big difference:** See, for instance, L. Baroni et al., "Evaluating the Environmental Impact of Various Dietary Patterns Combined with Different Food Production Systems," *European Journal of Clinical Nutrition* 61, no. 2 (Feb. 2007): 279–286.

137 **account for about 14 percent:** UCS modeling.

138 **methane is 25 times more potent:** Intergovernmental Panel on Climate Change, *Climate Change 2007: Mitigation—Contribution of Working Group III to the Fourth Assessment Report of the Intergovernmental Panel on Climate Change*, ed. B. Metz et al. (Cambridge, UK: Cambridge University Press, 2007). Available at www.ipcc-wg3.org. For more on methane and beef, see Doug Gurian-Sherman, "Raising the Steaks: Global Warming and Pasture-Raised Beef Production in the United States" (Feb. 2011), Union of Concerned Scientists. Available at www.ucsusa.org.

138 **methane accounts for about 13 percent:** M. M. Kling and I. J. Hough, "The American Carbon Foodprint: Understanding Your Food's Impact on Climate Change" (2010), Brighter Planet. Note: this analysis employs a proprietary model for carbon accounting that is not available to the public.

141 **roughly 300 pounds of carbon dioxide:** See, for instance, U.S. Environmental Protection Agency, "Nitrous Oxide" (2010). Available at www.epa.gov/nitrousoxide/scientific.html.

141 **N$_2$O . . . responsible for about 15 percent:** Kling and Hough, "The American Carbon Foodprint."

141 **A number of research teams:** See, for instance, Brent Kim and Roni Neff, "Measurement and Communication of Greenhouse Gas Emissions from U.S. Food Consumption via Carbon Calculators," *Ecological Economics* 69 (2009): 186–196.

141 **study by the Union of Concerned Scientists:** Gurian-Sherman, "Raising the Steaks."

142 **One influential 2006 report:** H. Steinfield et al., *Livestock's Long Shadow: Environmental Issues and Options* (Rome: Food and Agriculture Organization of the United Nations, 2006). Available at www.fao.org.

142 **6 percent of total global carbon emissions:** Ibid.

142 **ten pounds of milk:** See, for instance, www.vermontdairy.com/cheese.

142 **a diet rich in grains:** See Baroni et al., "Environmental Impact of Various Dietary Patterns."

142 **seven pounds of grain:** R. Goodland, "Environmental Sustainability in Agriculture: Diet Matters," *Ecological Economics* 23 (1997): 189–200.

143 **Box: . . . Sustainable Palm Oil?** Union of Concerned Scientists, "Palm Oil and Tropical Deforestation: Is There a Sustainable Solution?" (Mar. 2011). Available at www.ucsusa .org.

144 **most cattle in the United States:** See N. Fiala, "The Greenhouse Hamburger," *Scientific American*, Feb. 4, 2009.

144 **manure cesspits used by CAFOs:** See, for instance, Doug Gurian-Sherman, "CAFOs Uncovered: The Untold Costs of Confined Animal Feeding Operations" (Cambridge, MA: Union of Concerned Scientists, 2008). Available at www.ucsusa.org.

144 **Farmers in the Netherlands:** See Arthur Max, "Energy from Pig Slurry Helps Fight Climate Change," Associated Press, June 3, 2009.

144 **several farms in California:** See for instance, Scott Anders, *Biogas Production and Use on California's Dairy Farms* (San Diego, CA: University of San Diego School of Law, Energy Policy Initiatives Center, 2007).

144 **270 pounds . . . per year:** Food and Agriculture Organization of the United Nations, *The State of Food and Agriculture* (Rome: Food and Agriculture Organization of the United Nations, 2009). Available at www.fao.org/docrep/012/i0680e/i0680e.pdf.

145 **three tons or more annually:** Derived from the FAO figures on consumption with the CO_2e numbers from UCS modeling.

146 **1.3 million tons' worth of plastic PET:** U.S. Government Accountability Office, *Bottled Water: FDA Safety and Consumer Protections Are Often Less Stringent Than Comparable EPA Protections for Tap Water* (Washington, DC: U.S. Government Accountability Office, June 2009).

146 **50 million barrels of oil:** Ibid.

146 **2.5 million tons of carbon dioxide:** Ibid.

146 **roughly 7 percent:** UCS modeling.

147 **Box: Is Bottled Water Safer . . . ?** U.S. Government Accountability Office, *Bottled Water.*

148 **wasted . . . 33 million tons:** U.S. Environmental Protection Agency, "Basic Information about Food Waste" (updated Mar. 24, 2011). Available at www.epa.gov/osw/conserve/materials/organics/food/fd-basic.htm.

148 **14 percent of all trash:** Ibid.

149 **saves close to a ton:** U.S. Environmental Protection Agency, *Solid Waste Management and Greenhouse Gases: A Life-Cycle Assessment of Emissions and Sinks* (2006). Available at www.epa.gov/climatechange/wycd/waste/downloads/fullreport.pdf.

151 **study comparing . . . dairy farms:** J. E. Olesen et al., "Modeling Greenhouse Gas Emissions from European Conventional and Organic Dairy Farms," *Agriculture, Ecosystems, and Environment* 112 (2006): 207–220.

152 **researchers at Carnegie Mellon University:** C. L. Weber and H. S. Matthews, "Food-Miles and the Relative Climate Impacts of Food Choices in the United States," *Environmental Science and Technology* 42, no. 10 (2008): 3508–3513.

153 **4 percent of total food emissions:** Ibid.

153 **Figure 7.4: Supply Chain Food Miles by Food Group:** Adapted from Kling and Hough, "American Carbon Foodprint."

154 **New Zealand researchers:** See Caroline Saunders, Andrew Barber, and Greg Taylor, *Food Miles—Comparative Energy/Emissions Performance of New Zealand's Agriculture Industry* (Canterbury, New Zealand: Lincoln University, Agribusiness and Economics Research Unit, 2006).

154 **50 times more than . . . ocean transport:** Weber and Matthews, "Food-Miles and Relative Climate Impacts."

154 **Michael Pollan has noted:** As quoted in Helen Wagenvoord, "Interview: Michael Pollan; The Cheapest Calories Make You the Fattest," *Sierra*, Sept.–Oct. 2004.

155 **Figure 7.5: Emissions by Mode of Transport:** Adapted from ibid.

155 **one in every five meals:** See National Restaurant Association, "Meal Consumption Behavior—2000" (2000), NPD Group Study. Information available at www.restaurant.org.

155 **Mercury Café:** Information available at www.mercurycafe.com.

156　**Green Restaurant Association:** Information available at www.dinegreen.com.

156　**the Grey Plume:** Information available at www.thegreyplume.com.

156　**Tesco . . . carbon-footprint labeling:** Available at www.tesco.com/greenerliving.

Chapter 8

Page

160　**about 10 percent:** UCS modeling.

161　**Scott and Béa Johnson:** T. J. Story, "The Zero-Waste Home," *Sunset*, 2010. Available at www.sunset.com/home/natural-home/zero-waste-home-0111-00418000069984.

162　**flurry of recent articles:** See, for instance, "Are E-Readers Greener Than Books?" *New York Times*, Aug. 31, 2009. Available at http://green.blogs.nytimes.com.

163　**20 to 40 books:** See Emma Ritch, "The Environmental Impact of Amazon's Kindle" (Mar. 2008), Cleantech Group LLC. See also Borealis Centre for Environment and Trade Research, "Environmental Trends and Climate Impacts: Findings from the U.S. Book Industry" (Mar. 2008), Book Industry Study Group and Green Press Initiative. Available at www.greenpressinitiative.org.

163　**five and one-half pounds of carbon emissions:** Ritch, "Environmental Impact of Amazon's Kindle"; Borealis Centre for Environment and Trade Research, "Environmental Trends and Climate Impacts."

163　**six miles round-trip:** Assuming 20 miles per gallon, driving six miles produces 5.7 pounds of CO_2 emissions.

164　**Box: Is Organic Cotton Really Greener?** N. L. Brooks, "Characteristics and Production Costs of U.S. Cotton Farms" (2001), U.S. Department of Agriculture, Economic Research Service. Available at www.ers.usda.gov/publications/sb974-2/sb974-2.pdf.

165　**Box: Does Wood Harvested Sustainably Really Make a Difference?** Information is from Doug Boucher et al., "The Root of the Problem: What's Driving Tropical Deforestation Today?" (Cambridge, MA: Union of Concerned Scientists, 2011). Available at www.ucsusa.org.

165　**Box: 15 percent of the world's total carbon emissions:** Ibid.

165　**Box: Forest Stewardship Council:** Information available at www.fscus.org.

165　**Box: 41 million acres of tropical forest:** Boucher et al., "Root of the Problem."

166　**2 percent of total U.S. carbon emissions:** UCS modeling.

166　**4.3 pounds of trash each day:** U.S. Environmental Protection Agency, *Municipal Solid Waste in the United States: 2009 Facts and Figures*, EPA530-R-10-012 (Dec. 2010). Available at www.epa.gov/wastes.

166　**Making a can from recycled aluminum:** See, for instance, "The Price of Virtue," *The Economist*, June 7, 2007.

166　**half of all the material recycled:** U.S. Environmental Protection Agency, *Municipal Solid Waste*.

167　**Figure 8.3: Pounds of CO_2e Emissions Saved:** U.S. Environmental Protection Agency, "Waste Reduction Model (WARM)" (2010). Available at www.epa.gov/warm.

167 **more than half of all the paper and cardboard:** Ibid.

167 **important benefit of paper recycling:** See U.S. Environmental Protection Agency, "Benefits of Paper Recycling" (2011). Available at www.epa.gov.

168 **25 times more potent:** See www.epa.gov/methane.

170 **8.2 pounds of carbon dioxide:** UCS modeling.

171 **19 percent of the state's electricity:** G. Klein et al., "California's Water-Energy Relationship" (2005), California Energy Commission. Available at www.energy.ca.gov.

171 **Box: one-third of the total electricity consumed:** R. Cohen, B. Nelson, and G. Wolff, *Energy Down the Drain: The Hidden Costs of California's Water Supply* (New York: Natural Resources Defense Council, 2004).

171 **Central Arizona Project:** CAPSmartEnergy, "About Us" (2011). Available at www.capsmartenergy.com/AboutUs.aspx.

172 **Box: 50 percent more carbon emissions:** J. R. Stokes and A. Horvath, "Energy and Air Emission Effects of Water Supply," *Environmental Science Technology* 43, no. 8 (2009): 2680–2687.

172 **Box: 13,000 desalination plants:** R. Matthews, "Are Desalination Technologies the Answer to the World Water Crisis?" (Mar. 24, 2011), Environmental News Network. Available at www.enn.com/business/article/42506.

172 **Box: 33 million tons of carbon dioxide per year:** Ibid.

173 **life cycle analysis of lawn and garden care:** J. Morris and J. Bagby, "Measuring Environmental Value for Natural Lawn and Garden Care Practices," *International Journal of Life Cycle Assessment* 13, no. 3 (2008): 226–234. Available at www.springerlink.com/content/0t03r5w260045272/fulltext.pdf.

175 **4.4 percent of the average American's:** UCS modeling.

175 **poorly insulated house of 1,500 square feet:** A. Wilson and J. Boehland, "Small Is Beautiful: U.S. House Size, Resource Use, and the Environment," *Journal of Industrial Ecology* 9, nos. 1 and 2 (2005): 277–287.

Chapter 9

Page

183 **one study in 2010:** Matthew Feinberg and Robb Willer, "Apocalypse Soon? Dire Messages Reduce Belief in Global Warming by Contradicting Just-World Beliefs," *Psychological Science* 22, no. 1 (2010): 34–38.

184 **many leading economists:** See, for instance, "U.S. Scientists and Economists' Call for Swift and Deep Cuts in Greenhouse Gas Emissions" (Mar. 2010), Union of Concerned Scientists. Available at www.ucsusa.org/assets/documents/global_warming/scientists-and-economists-1.pdf.

184 **Elinor Ostrom:** As quoted ibid.

184 **2006 Stern Report:** Nicholas Stern, *Stern Review on the Economics of Climate Change* (London: Her Majesty's Treasury, 2006).

185 **Businesses saved some $255 billion:** See Rachel Cleetus, Steven Clemmer, and David Friedman, "Climate 2030: A National Blueprint for a Clean Energy Economy" (Cambridge, MA: Union of Concerned Scientists, 2009). Available at www.ucsusa.org.

187 **A number of faith-based organizations:** See, for instance, Interfaith Power & Light (www.interfaithpowerandlight.org) or the National Religious Partnership for the Environment (www.nrpe.org).

188 **Erika Spanger-Siegfried:** See Erika Spanger-Siegfried, "Close to Home: Going Green with the Neighbors," *Earthwise* (Union of Concerned Scientists), Fall 2008. Available at www.ucsusa.org/publications/earthwise/going-green-with-the.html.

189 **Box: *Energy Smackdown:*** See the *Energy Smackdown* home page: www.energysmackdown.com. Also available from the Institute for Sustainable Communities at www.iscvt.org/clanetwork/case_studies.

190 **350.org organized global warming work parties:** Further details are available at www.350.org.

191 **ICLEI—Local Governments for Sustainability:** More information is available at www.icleiusa.org.

191 **more than 1,000 mayors:** For the complete list, see www.usmayors.org/climate protection/list.asp.

191 **Eighteen of the 20 largest U.S. cities:** Pew Center on Global Climate Change, "Climate Change 101: Local Action" (Jan. 2011). Available at www.pewclimate.org.

191 **Chicago:** See Dirk Johnson, "Chicago Unveils Multifaceted Plan to Curb Emissions of Heat-Trapping Gases," *New York Times*, Sept. 18, 2008.

192 **San Francisco has adopted energy efficiency measures:** Information is available from the San Francisco Planning Department at www.sf-planning.org.

192 **The city has especially excelled at reducing transportation emissions:** See, for instance, Matthew I. Slavin and Kent Snyder, "Strategic Climate Action Planning in Portland," chap. 2 in *Sustainability in America's Cities: Creating the Green Metropolis*, ed. Matthew I. Slavin (Washington, DC: Island Press, 2011).

192 **Greenburg, Kansas:** See the town's website: "Greensburg, KS: Rebuilding . . . Stronger, Better, Greener!" Available at www.greensburgks.org.

193 **solar panel arrays on capped landfills:** Jim Kinney, "Constellation Energy Solar Power Project Will Lower Rates for Holyoke Gas & Electric Commercial Customers, Officials Say," *Springfield Republican*, Apr. 13, 2011.

193 **Freshkills site:** See, for example, Sewell Chan, "Fresh Kills New York's Next Wind Farm?" *New York Times*, Aug. 22, 2008.

193 **Babcock Ranch, Florida:** See Kitson & Partners, "First Solar-Powered City to Fuel Clean Industry, Economic Recovery," press release, Apr. 9, 2009. Available at www.babcockranchflorida.com/press.asp.

193 **Fort Collins, Colorado:** See City of Fort Collins, "2008 Fort Collins Climate Action Plan: Interim Strategic Plan Towards 2020 Goal" (Dec. 2008). Available at www.fcgov.com/climateprotection/pdf/climate_action_plan.pdf.

194 **Box: a large majority—more than 80 percent:** See, for example, "Large Majorities in U.S. and Five Largest European Countries Favor More Wind Farms and Subsidies for

Bio-fuels, but Opinion Is Split on Nuclear Power," Harris Interactive, Oct. 13, 2010. Polling data are available at www.harrisinteractive.com.

194 **Box: American Wind Wildlife Institute:** More information is available at www.awwi .org.

195 **Holyoke, Massachusetts:** See "Constellation Energy Is Developing a 4.5 Megawatt Solar Installation with Holyoke Gas & Electric," press release, *Business Wire*, Apr. 13, 2011.

195 **San Diego, California:** Pew Center on Global Climate Change, "Climate Change 101: Local Action."

195 **Burlington, Vermont:** Ibid.

195 **Spirit Lake Elementary School:** Information is from Iowa Energy Center, Alternate Energy Revolving Loan Program. Available at www.energy.iastate.edu/AERLP/down loads/SpiritLake_07.pdf.

Chapter 10

Page

198 **DuPont . . . cut its worldwide heat-trapping emissions:** Rachel Cleetus, Steven Clemmer, and David Friedman, "Climate 2030: A National Blueprint for a Clean Energy Economy" (Cambridge, MA: Union of Concerned Scientists, 2009). Available at www .ucsusa.org. For further information, see DuPont, *Sustainability Progress Report*, 2008. Available at www2.dupont.com. See also A. J. Hoffman, *Getting Ahead of the Curve: Corporate Strategies That Address Climate Change* (Washington, DC: Pew Center on Global Climate Change, 2006), pp. 90–92.

198 **retail giant Walmart:** Information on Walmart's climate and energy policies is available at http://walmartstores.com/sustainability.

198 **3.5 million megawatt-hours:** Ibid.

198 *The Green Workplace:* Leigh Stringer, *The Green Workplace: Sustainable Strategies That Benefit Employees, the Environment, and the Bottom Line* (New York: Palgrave Macmillan, 2009).

199 **Tom Bowman:** Tom Bowman, "How One Small Business Cut Its Energy Use and Costs," *Yale Environment 360*, Oct. 7, 2010. Available at http://e360.yale.edu/content/ feature.msp?id=2326.

202 **software maker Adobe:** Stringer, *The Green Workplace*.

203 **One innovative website:** See www.carbonrally.com. See also Kyle Alspach, "Carbonrally Applies Gaming Concept to Cutting Carbon," *Mass High Tech: The Journal of New England Technology*, June 3, 2010.

204 **In 2010, Xerox lauded:** Xerox, "Xerox Earth Awards Drive Stronger Business Results," press release, July 15, 2009. See also "Xerox Employees Use Green Tactics to Boost Savings, Earn Earth Awards," press release, Nov. 11, 2010. Available at www.xerox.com.

204 **nearly 6,000 hospitals:** See, for instance, James B. Schultz, "Energy Efficiency Opportunities for Hospitals in the United States," SMG10x, Inc. (Oct. 2010). Available at www .smg10x.com/downloads/EnergyEfficiencyOpportunitiesHospitalsInUS.pdf.

204 **73 billion kilowatt-hours:** Ibid. See also U.S. Environmental Protection Agency and U.S. Department of Energy, Energy Star program, "Useful Facts and Figures" (June 2007), available at www.energystar.gov; and U.S. Department of Energy, Energy Information Administration, "Commercial Buildings Energy Consumption Survey (CBECS)" (2003) (most recent data available), available at www.eia.gov.

205 **16 percent of U.S. gross domestic product:** See, for instance, Congressional Budget Office, "The Long-Term Outlook for Health Care Spending" (2007). Available at www.cbo.gov/ftpdocs/87xx/doc8758/MainText.3.1.shtml.

205 **"seven elements of a climate-friendly hospital":** World Health Organization, "Healthy Hospitals, Healthy Planet, Healthy People: Addressing Climate Change in Health Care Settings," discussion draft, 2009. Available at www.who.int/globalchange/publications/climatefootprint_report.pdf.

205 **Cleveland Clinic:** "Cleveland Clinic Named an Energy Star Partner of the Year: Award from the U.S. EPA and Department of Energy Program Recognizes Leadership in Energy Management," press release, Mar. 14, 2011. Available at www.clevelandclinic.com.

206 **Box: *Green Guide for Health Care*:** Available at www.gghc.org.

206 **York Hospital:** Constellation New Energy, "York Hospital Is the First 100% Renewable Energy Customer of Constellation New Energy and Maine Power Options," press release, Mar. 6, 2003. Available at http://apps3.eere.energy.gov/greenpower/markets/pdfs/0303_york_pr.pdf.

206 **40 percent of all emissions:** Estimate from the U.S. Green Building Council, www.usgbc.org.

206 **widely recognized 2007 study:** Peter Morris and Lisa Fay Matthiessen, "Cost of Green Revisited: Reexamining the Feasibility and Cost Impact of Sustainable Design in the Light of Increased Market Adoption" (July 2007). Available at www.davislangdon.com.

206 **The EPA's Energy Star program:** Information is available at www.energystar.gov.

207 **Leadership in Energy and Environmental Design:** Information on the LEED program is available at the U.S. Green Building Council, www.usgbc.org.

207 **more than 21,000 buildings:** Ibid.

208 **LEED-certified buildings are selling for more:** See, for instance, John Goering, "Sustainable Real Estate Development: The Dynamics of Market Penetration," *Journal of Sustainable Real Estate* 1, no. 1 (2009): 167–201.

208 **Oberlin College:** See U.S. Department of Energy, National Renewable Energy Laboratory, "Highlighting High Performance: The Adam Joseph Lewis Center for Environmental Studies, Oberlin College, Oberlin, Ohio," fact sheet, Nov. 2002. Available at www.nrel.gov/docs/fy03osti/31516.pdf.

208 **678 colleges have signed:** For information and a list of signatories, see the American College and University Presidents' Climate Commitment (ACUPCC) at www.presidentsclimatecommitment.org.

208 **grocery store built by Whole Foods Market:** See, for instance, Paul Baier, "Whole Foods and the Greenest Grocery Store in the World," Reuters, Apr. 4, 2011.

209 **100 percent of the company's electricity needs:** Paige Brady, "Energy Credits Fund New Wind Farm" (Sept. 15, 2009). Available at http://blog.wholefoodsmarket.com.

209 **oil company BP:** James Ridgeway, "BP's Slick Greenwashing," *Mother Jones*, May 2010.

210 **Pure & Natural Huggies:** See, for instance, "The Top 25 Greenwashed Products in America," at www.businesspundit.com.

211 **"a truly *organic* experience":** See, for instance, Shireen Deen, "America's Ten Worst Greenwashers," *Valley Advocate*, Aug. 29, 2002. Available at www.greenwashing.net.

211 **Ceres, a nonprofit:** Information is available at www.ceres.org.

212 **Carbon Disclosure Project:** Carbon Disclosure Project, "Supply Chain Report 2011," compiled by A. T. Kearney. Available at www.cdproject.net.

212 **Climate Registry:** Information is available at www.theclimateregistry.org.

212 **more than 200 founding members:** Ibid.

213 **computer maker Dell:** See Carbon Disclosure Project, "Supply Chain Report 2011."

213 **Walmart asks suppliers:** Ibid.

214 **Patagonia:** Information on the Common Threads Initiative garment recycling program is available at www.patagonia.com.

214 **less than one-quarter of the energy:** Ibid.

214 **carpet manufacturer Interface:** Interface has set forth a "Mission Zero" campaign, pledging to eliminate any negative impacts on the environment by 2020. More information is available at www.interfaceglobal.com.

Chapter 11

Page

215 **study by the Environmental Law Institute:** Environmental Law Institute, "Estimating U.S. Government Subsidies to Energy Sources: 2002–2008" (Sept. 2009). Available at www.eli.org.

215 **twice the total of direct subsidies:** Ibid.

218 **analysis by the Union of Concerned Scientists:** Rachel Cleetus, Steven Clemmer, and David Friedman, "Climate 2030: A National Blueprint for a Clean Energy Economy" (Cambridge, MA: Union of Concerned Scientists, 2009). Available at www.ucsusa.org.

219 **saved some 1.3 percent:** S. Nadel et al., *Leading the Way: Continued Opportunities for New State Appliance and Equipment Efficiency Standards*, ACEEE report A061 (Washington, DC: American Council for an Energy-Efficient Economy, 2006).

219 **6.6 million households:** Ibid.

219 **Several states . . . have augmented:** For more information, see U.S. Environmental Protection Agency, *The Clean Energy Lead by Example Guide: Strategies, Resources, and Action Steps for State Programs* (Washington, DC: U.S. Environmental Protection Agency, June 2009). Available at www.epa.gov/statelocalclimate/resources/example.html. See also Barry G. Rabe, "Greenhouse and Statehouse: The Evolving State Government Role in Climate Change" (Nov. 2002), Pew Center on Global Climate Change. Available at www.pewclimate.org.

220 **2009 International Energy Conservation Code:** Available from the International Code Council at http://publicodes.citation.com/icod/iecc/2009/index.htm. More information is available from the U.S. Department of Energy at www.energycodes.gov.

220 **ASHRAE:** More information is available at www.ashrae.org.

220 **Energy Efficiency Resource Standards:** Cleetus, Clemmer, and Friedman, "Climate 2030."

221 **France, Italy, and the United Kingdom:** See Steven Nadel, *Energy Efficiency Resource Standards: Experience and Recommendations* (Washington, DC: American Council for an Energy-Efficient Economy, Mar. 2006). Available at www.aceee.org.

221 **Corporate Average Fuel Economy (CAFE) standards:** See Union of Concerned Scientists, "Fuel Economy Basics" (2007). Available at www.ucsusa.org.

221 **130 billion fewer gallons:** Union of Concerned Scientists, "The Costs of Delay: Fuel Efficiency and Auto Pollution Standards" (Mar. 2011). Available at www.ucsusa.org.

221 **1.65 billion tons:** Ibid. (Note: converted from 1.5 billion metric tons in the UCS analysis.)

222 **Analysis by the Union of Concerned Scientists:** Union of Concerned Scientists and Natural Resources Defense Council, "The Technology to Reach 60 mpg by 2025: Putting Fuel-Saving Technology to Work to Save Oil and Cut Pollution" (Oct. 2010). Available at www.ucsusa.org.

222 **nearly 4 million barrels per day:** Union of Concerned Scientists analysis. See, for instance, "UCS Applauds Obama Administration Agreement on Fuel Efficiency and Auto Pollution Standards," press release, July 29, 2011. More information available at www.ucsusa.org.

222 **770 million tons:** Ibid.

223 **More than two-thirds of the states:** Pew Center on Global Climate Change, "Climate Change 101: State Action" (Jan. 2009). Available at www.pewclimate.org.

223 **47 million typical homes:** Union of Concerned Scientists, "Renewable Electricity Standards at Work in the States" (2010). Available at www.ucsusa.org.

223 **30 million cars off the road:** Ibid.

225 **18 states require all their utilities:** Pew Center on Global Climate Change, "Climate Change 101: State Action."

226 **Germany and Spain become leaders:** See, for instance, Kate Galbraith, "Europe's Way of Encouraging Solar Power Arrives in the U.S.," *New York Times*, Mar. 12, 2009.

226 **Some 23 states have adopted:** Pew Center on Global Climate Change, "Climate Change 101: State Action."

226 **Oregon and Washington:** Ibid.

226 **generated more than $880 million:** Regional Greenhouse Gas Initiative, "Regional Clean Energy Economy Boosted with $25.5 Million in RGGI Auction Proceeds," press release, June 2011. Available at www.rggi.org/docs/Auction_12_Release_Report.pdf.

227 **U.S. Supreme Court confirmed:** *American Electric Power Company, Inc., et al., Petitioners v. Connecticut et al.* 564 U.S. ___ (2011).

228 **Climate Action Plans:** See www.epa.gov/statelocalclimate/state/state-examples/action-plans.html.

228 **more than half of all U.S. states:** Pew Center on Global Climate Change, "Climate Change 101: State Action."

234 **California won an important climate victory:** See Union of Concerned Scientists, "California Renewable Electricity Standard" (Apr. 2011). Available at www.ucsusa.org.

234 **one-quarter of the required renewable energy:** See Union of Concerned Scientists, "California Passes Renewable Energy Standard," press release, Apr. 14, 2011. Available at www.ucsusa.org.

Chapter 12

Page

237 **seven-story sign:** Carbon Counter, Deutsche Bank, DB Climate Change Advisors, New York. For more on the counter's methodology, see J. Huang et al., "A Semi-Empirical Representation of the Temporal Variation of Total Greenhouse Gas Levels Expressed as Equivalent Levels of Carbon Dioxide," Report no. 174 (June 2009), MIT Joint Program on the Science and Policy of Global Change. Available at http://globalchange.mit.edu/pubs/abstract.php?publication_id=1975.

238 **no matter what steps:** See, for example, T. Karl, J. Melillo, and T. Peterson, eds., *Global Climate Change Impacts in the United States*, report from the U.S. Global Change Research Program (Cambridge, UK: Cambridge University Press, 2009). Available at www.globalchange.gov.

238 **80 gigawatts . . . of renewable electricity capacity:** Information is from Renewable Energy Policy Network for the 21st Century (REN21), *Renewables 2010: Global Status Report* (Paris: REN21 Secretariat, 2010). Available at www.ren21.net.

238 **U.S. coal plants . . . 335 gigawatts:** U.S. Department of Energy, Energy Information Administration, "Electric Power Annual 2009," table 1.2, "Existing Capacity by Energy Source, 2009" (2010). Available at www.eia.gov.

238 **replace nearly one in every 10:** Even though the numbers would suggest that worldwide renewable capacity was equal to one-quarter the capacity of U.S. coal plants, the "one in every 10" figure takes into account the difference in capacity factors between coal-fired plants and renewable sources such as wind power and solar photovoltaics.

239 **produce just 3 percent:** REN21, *Renewables 2010*.

239 **roughly 60 percent per year:** Ibid.

239 **has risen 100-fold since 2000:** Ibid.

239 **cumulative capacity doubling:** Ibid.

240 **fifth-largest industry:** J. L. Coleman, "The American Whale Oil Industry: A Look Back to the Future of the American Petroleum Industry?" *Natural Resources Research* 4 (1995): 273–288.

240 **700 ships:** See L. E. Davis et al., "Technology, Productivity, and Profits: British-American Whaling Competition in the North Atlantic, 1816–1842," *Oxford Economic Papers*, new series, 39, no. 4 (Dec. 1987): 738–759.

240 **8,000 whales were slaughtered:** Peter Applebome, "They Used to Say Whale Oil Was Indispensable, Too," *New York Times*, Aug. 3, 2008.

242 **Denmark relied on oil:** Information is from Rachel Cleetus, Steven Clemmer, and David Friedman, "Climate 2030: A National Blueprint for a Clean Energy Economy,"

chap. 5 (Cambridge, MA: Union of Concerned Scientists, 2009). Available at www
.ucsusa.org.

242 **power plant serving Copenhagen:** Danish Ministry of Climate and Energy, "The
Danish Example: The Way to an Energy Efficient and Energy Friendly Economy"
(Copenhagen, 2009). Available at www.kemin.dk/en-us/facts/danishexample/sider/
thedanishexample.aspx.

242 **29 percent of Denmark's electricity:** Ibid.

242 **cut its carbon emissions in half:** Cleetus, Clemmer, and Friedman, "Climate 2030."

242 **roughly 20 percent of the country's electricity:** Danish Ministry of Climate and
Energy, "The Danish Example." See also Danish Wind Industry Association, "Denmark—Wind Power Hub," which claims that wind power now accounts for "nearly 25
percent" of Denmark's electricity supply. Available at www.windpower.org/en/news/
news.html#718.

242 **Sweden now gets some 56 percent:** REN21, *Renewables 2010.*

243 **18 percent of the planet's electricity:** Ibid.

243 **all the world's nuclear power plants:** According to the World Nuclear Association,
the planet's 440 commercial nuclear plants produce roughly 14 percent of the world's
electricity. Information is available at www.world-nuclear.org.

243 **300,000 people are currently employed:** Federal Ministry for the Environment, Nature
Conservation, and Nuclear Safety of Germany, "Development of Renewable Energy
Sources in Germany" (Berlin, Mar. 18, 2010).

243 **Germany's largest sector, the automotive industry:** Ibid.

243 **39 percent of all new electricity-generating capacity:** REN21, *Renewables 2010.*

243 **state of Iowa:** U.S. Department of Energy, Energy Information Administration, *Electric
Power Monthly* (Mar. 2011). Available at www.eia.gov. See also Iowa Utilities Board,
"Iowa's Electric Profile" (2011). Available at www.state.ia.us/government/com/util/
energy/electric_profile.html.

SETH SHULMAN

Seth Shulman is the senior staff writer at the Union of Concerned Scientists. He has worked for more than 25 years as a journalist and author focusing on issues in science, technology, and the environment and is the author of five books and hundreds of articles for magazines, including *The Atlantic, Discover, Nature, Parade, Rolling Stone, Smithsonian,* and *Time,* among many others. He also served as a columnist for *Technology Review* magazine, writing monthly about innovation. Among his accolades are a Guggenheim Fellowship (2011) and the first-ever Science Writing Fellowship at the Dibner Institute for the History of Science and Technology at the Massachusetts Institute of Technology (2004–2005). He has been a finalist for a National Magazine Award in the Public Interest category and received a research and writing grant from the John D. and Catherine T. MacArthur Foundation. His latest book, *The Telephone Gambit: Chasing Alexander Graham Bell's Secret,* was chosen as one of the best books of 2008 by the *Washington Post,* the *Christian Science Monitor,* and *Booklist,* the publication of the American Library Association. His other books are *Undermining Science: Suppression and Distortion in the Bush Administration; Unlocking the Sky: Glenn Hammond Curtiss and the Race to Invent the Airplane; Owning the Future;* and *The Threat at Home: Confronting the Toxic Legacy of the U.S. Military.*

JEFF DEYETTE

As a senior energy analyst for the Union of Concerned Scientists' Clean Energy Program, Jeff Deyette conducts analysis on the economic and environmental costs and benefits of renewable energy and energy efficiency policies. He has coauthored numerous reports, including "A Bright Future for the Heartland: Powering the Midwest Economy with Clean Energy"; "Burning Coal, Burning Cash: Ranking the States That Import the Most Coal"; "Plugging In Renewable Energy: Grading the States"; "Increasing the Texas Renewable Energy Standard: Economic and Employment Benefits"; "The Colorado Renewable Energy Standard Ballot Initiative: Impacts on Jobs and the Economy"; and "Renewing Where We Live: What a National Renewable Electricity Standard Means for You." He has also written articles for various publications in the renewable energy industry.

Prior to coming to the Union of Concerned Scientists, Deyette worked as an environmental protection specialist for the New England Division of the U.S. Army Corps of Engineers. He has a master's degree from Boston University in energy resource and environmental management and international relations and a bachelor's degree from St. Lawrence University in environmental science and government.

BRENDA EKWURZEL

Brenda Ekwurzel is a climate scientist with the Climate and Energy Program of the Union of Concerned Scientists. She leads the organization's climate science education work aimed at strengthening support for sound U.S. climate policies. Prior to joining the Union of Concerned Scientists, Ekwurzel was on the faculty of the University of Arizona's Department of Hydrology and Water Resources, with a joint appointment in the Department of Geosciences. She has published on topics that include climate variability and fire, isotopic dating of groundwater, Arctic Ocean tracer oceanography, paleohydrology, and coastal sediment erosion. Earlier in her career, Ekwurzel was a hydrologist with the Connecticut Department of Environmental Protection, working with communities to protect groundwater sources.

Ekwurzel holds a doctorate in isotope geochemistry from the Department of Earth Sciences at Columbia University's Lamont-Doherty Earth Observatory, and she conducted postdoctoral research at Lawrence Livermore National Laboratory in California.

DAVID FRIEDMAN

David Friedman is the deputy director of the Union of Concerned Scientists' Clean Vehicles Program and is the author or coauthor of more than 30 technical papers and reports on advancements in conventional, fuel cell, and hybrid electric vehicles, with an emphasis on clean and efficient technologies. His work includes "Climate 2030: A National Blueprint for a Clean Energy Economy"; "A New Road: The Technology and Potential of Hybrid Vehicles"; "Building a Better SUV: A Blueprint for Saving Lives, Money, and Gasoline"; and "Drilling in Detroit: Tapping Automaker Ingenuity to Build Safe and Efficient Automobiles." He is a member of the Committee on the Assessment of Technologies for Improving Light-Duty Vehicle Fuel Economy with the National Academies Board on Energy and Environmental Systems. In 2008, *Washingtonian* magazine profiled him as one of 30 people changing the environment in Washington.

Before joining the Union of Concerned Scientists, Friedman worked for the University of California, Davis, in the Fuel Cell Vehicle Modeling Program, developing simulation tools to evaluate fuel cell technology for automotive applications. He also worked on the UC Davis FutureCar Team to build a hybrid electric family car that doubled its fuel economy. He previously worked at the Arthur D. Little management consulting firm researching fuel cell, battery-electric, and hybrid electric vehicle technologies, as well as photovoltaics.

Friedman earned his bachelor's degree in mechanical engineering from Worcester Polytechnic Institute and is currently finishing his doctoral dissertation on transportation technology and policy at UC Davis.

MARGARET MELLON

Margaret Mellon is a senior scientist in the Food and Environment Program at the Union of Concerned Scientists. She is one of the nation's most respected experts on biotechnology and food safety. Mellon holds a doctorate in molecular biology and a law degree from the University of Virginia. She was formerly a research fellow in molecular virology at Purdue University and program director for the Environmental Law Institute.

Mellon has published widely on the potential environmental impacts of biotechnology applications. She is coauthor of "The Ecological Risks of Engineered Crops" and "Hogging It! Estimates of Antimicrobial Abuse in Livestock" and is coeditor of "Now or Never: Serious New Plans to Save a Natural Pest Control." She serves on the U.S. Department of Agriculture's Advisory Committee on Biotechnology and 21st Century Agriculture and teaches a course in biotechnology and the law at the Vermont Law School. In 1993, she received a Distinguished Alumni Award from Purdue University's School of Science.

JOHN ROGERS

John Rogers, a senior analyst with the Climate and Energy Program of the Union of Concerned Scientists, is an expert on renewable energy, energy efficiency, and the connection between energy generation and water consumption. He serves on the board of directors of the U.S. Offshore Wind Collaborative and of RENEW, an organization that promotes renewable energy in New England. He also serves on the advisory boards of several nonprofit organizations promoting U.S. renewable energy and global energy access.

Prior to joining the Union of Concerned Scientists, Rogers worked for 15 years on private and public clean energy initiatives, including as a cofounder of Soluz, a leading developer of clean energy solutions for rural markets, and as a Peace Corps volunteer in Honduras. He earned a bachelor's degree at Princeton University and a master's degree in mechanical engineering at the University of Michigan.

SUZANNE SHAW

Suzanne Shaw is director of communications at the Union of Concerned Scientists. For the past decade, she has helped scientists translate their research into easy-to-understand public presentations, print articles, and online materials. She has developed public education materials for major studies on the local impacts of climate change in the Northeast, California, and the Great Lakes region and a groundbreaking report on the pathway to a clean energy future, "Climate 2030: A National Blueprint for a Clean Energy Economy." Shaw co-led the Union of Concerned Scientists' effort to expose the abuse of science by the George W. Bush administration, which garnered coverage in media outlets throughout the nation and was named one of the top stories of 2004 by *Discover* magazine.

Prior to joining the Union of Concerned Scientists, Shaw ran the communications efforts at Project Bread, a nonprofit organization fighting hunger in Massachusetts, and in the private sector, marketing a range of technology products. She earned a bachelor's degree from the University of Connecticut and a master's degree in public relations and advertising at Emerson College. She serves on the advisory board for Climate Access, a learning network for local, regional, and national groups working on climate change.

INDEX

Figures/photos/illustrations are indicated by a " f " and tables by a " t ."

buying stuff, 22, 159–178; buying less,
161–163; buying smarter, 163–165; buying used or refurbished items, 164. *See
also* goods and services; *specific items*

CAFE. *See* Corporate Average Fuel
Economy
CAFOs (confined animal feeding operations), 139, 144
California: California Solar Initiative,
134; Cap-and-Trade Program, 227; low-
carbon fuel standards in, 225; renewable electricity standard in, 234–235;
targets and limits for carbon emissions
reduction in, 226–227; water supply in,
170–172. *See also specific cities*
Canadian commercial, 6–7
Cap-and-Trade Program, California, 227
cap-and-trade system, 229
Capital Bikeshare (Washington, DC), 81
carbon, 31; isotopes of, 38
carbon calculators, 19–20, 250
carbon cap, 229
carbon coefficient, 131
carbon counter, 237
carbon cycle, 31; oceans and, viii, 42–43;
overload of, 32
carbon dioxide (CO_2): creation process
for, 53; molecule fingerprint differences
and, 38; role of, 32, 35; weight of cars
compared to weight of, 53, 54. *See also*
carbon emissions
carbon dioxide equivalent (CO_2e), 7n, 139,
167f; emissions coefficients, 265, 265n,
268–269, 268n; emissions per dollar
spent, 169, 169f; research and analysis
on, 264, 264n, 268–269, 269t
carbon dioxide levels: evidence of excess,
27–28, 37; evidence of rising, 33–34, 34f,
36, 38; future of, 46–47; seasonal variation of, 34; temperatures and, vii–viii
Carbon Disclosure Project, 212
carbon emissions, 7n; from appliances and
equipment, 21, 110; from cars, 51–53, 59f;
from coal, 14, 30–32; consumer spend-

ing links with, 15, 22, 177–178; from
electronic devices, 21, 110–111; from
farms, 22, 71–72, 138–141; food-related,
137–141, 138f, 140f, 254; from goods and
services, 22, 159–161, 160f, 161f, 177;
from heating and cooling homes, 16–17,
21, 83–86, 84f; from lighting, 21; measurement of, 7n; from oil, 30–32; per 100
passenger miles, 76f; regulation of, 216,
229–230; sources of, 3, 15–17, 16f; standards, 227; from transportation, 15–16,
21, 51–81, 52f, 76f, 78f, 152–155, 155f;
U.S. compared to global average, 3, 8f, 9;
weight of gasoline compared to, 53. *See
also* household emissions
carbon emissions reduction: steps for,
13–25; targets and limits for, 226–227;
three-part strategy for, 244–245; 20 percent, 13–15, 81, 107, 123, 126, 134–135,
157, 177–178
carbon foodprint, 137–141, 147, 153
carbon footprint: calculating, 19–20; labeling for food, 156; reducing, 14, 17, 21,
24, 54, 257–262
carbon intensity, 169–170
carbon neutrality, 181, 208
carbon offsets, 77, 176–177, 253
carbon profile, 97, 174
carbon sequestration, 141, 150–151, 167–
168, 174
carbon tax, 229
Carbon Trust, 212
carbon-pricing approach, 229–230
Carbonrally.com, 203
Carnegie Mellon University, 152
carpooling, 55, 63, 65, 66
cars, 11; air conditioner in, 69; annual
miles driven in U.S., 51, 53, 56; battery-
electric, 55; carbon emissions from,
51–53, 59f; carpooling, 55, 63, 65, 66;
dependence on, 54, 61; driving habits
and techniques, 61–69; efficiency of,
16, 23, 24; electric-drive, 55; EPA on,
57, 60, 67; fuel economy impacted by
weight of, 68; fuel options for, 69–74;

Honda Civic, 57, 71
Honda Clarity, 73–74
hospitals, 205–206
household emissions, 13, 110–112, 110f;
    average emissions per household by
    category, 274t–275t; breakdown of, 16f,
    111f; by category, 272t–273t
HOV (high-occupancy vehicle) lanes, 66
human activity, 3, 7–8, 30–33, 38–40
hunters and anglers, 186
hurricanes, 47
hybrid cars, 55, 57, 71, 73, 250
hydrochlorofluorocarbons (HCFCs), 35
hydrogen, 73–74
hydropower, 131, 154, 206, 239, 242–243

ice, melting, 40–41
ice age, 30, 36
ice cores, vii–viii, 36–38
ICLEI—Local Governments for Sustain-
    ability, 191, 255
IEA. See International Energy Agency
IECC. See International Energy Conserva-
    tion Code
IMPLAN model, 265–269, 267n
incandescent lightbulbs, 115–116, 118–119,
    119f
incentives: federal renewable energy
    tax, 224; programs for appliances and
    equipment, 122, 219–220; workplace
    competition and, 203. See also Database
    of State Incentives for Renewables and
    Efficiency
incinerators, 148, 168
individual actions, impacts of, 3–12, 14–15,
    238; at work, 197, 200, 206; from electric-
    ity usage,112, 119, 120, 123; from food-
    related choices, 137, 144, 145–146; from
    getting involved in governmental poli-
    cies, 223-224, 234-235; from purchasing
    choices, 161–166, 171
Industrial Revolution, 30–32, 38, 43
insulation: in homes, 17, 85, 98–99, 106,
    175; behind radiators, 98; around water
    heaters, 103

Interface carpet manufacturer, 214
Interfaith Power & Light, 187, 255
inter-industry relationships, 265–269, 266n
International Energy Agency (IEA), 11–12
International Energy Conservation Code
    (IECC), 220
International Energy Outlook 2010 (DOE),
    109
International Geophysical Year, 33
isotopes of carbon, 38

Japan, 94, 105, 214, 238
Johnson, Béa, 161–162
Johnson, Scott, 161–162
Journey to Work Survey, Census Bureau's,
    65

Kansas, 5–6, 192–193
Keeling, Charles David, 33–34, 36
Keeling Curve, 33–34, 34f
Keller, Helen, 215
Kelley, Donald, 189
Kennedy, Aaron, 64
kilowatt-hours, 114–115
kilowatts, 114

land: changes in use of, 143; trouble on,
    43–45
landfills: methane in, 148–149, 168, 195;
    solar panel arrays on capped, 193; waste
    in, 147, 148–149, 168
Lappé, Frances Moore, 137
laptops, 127
Larson, Doug, 51
laundry, 123–124
lawn and garden care, 173–174
lawnmowers, 173, 263
Lawrence Berkeley National Laboratory,
    20, 90, 99, 128, 250
lead, 37
LED (light-emitting diode) lighting,
    117–118, 119f
LEED (Leadership in Energy and Environ-
    mental Design), 207–209, 209f, 220
Leger, Eugene, 85

About Island Press

Since 1984, the nonprofit Island Press has been stimulating, shaping, and communicating the ideas that are essential for solving environmental problems worldwide. With more than 800 titles in print and some 40 new releases each year, we are the nation's leading publisher on environmental issues. We identify innovative thinkers and emerging trends in the environmental field. We work with world-renowned experts and authors to develop cross-disciplinary solutions to environmental challenges.

Island Press designs and implements coordinated book publication campaigns in order to communicate our critical messages in print, in person, and online using the latest technologies, programs, and the media. Our goal: to reach targeted audiences—scientists, policymakers, environmental advocates, the media, and concerned citizens—who can and will take action to protect the plants and animals that enrich our world, the ecosystems we need to survive, the water we drink, and the air we breathe.

Island Press gratefully acknowledges the support of its work by the Agua Fund, Inc., The Margaret A. Cargill Foundation, Betsy and Jesse Fink Foundation, The William and Flora Hewlett Foundation, The Kresge Foundation, The Forrest and Frances Lattner Foundation, The Andrew W. Mellon Foundation, The Curtis and Edith Munson Foundation, The Overbrook Foundation, The David and Lucile Packard Foundation, The Summit Foundation, Trust for Architectural Easements, The Winslow Foundation, and other generous donors.

The opinions expressed in this book are those of the author(s) and do not necessarily reflect the views of our donors.